Law of International Trade

EDITED BY

Robert M. MacLean LLB, DipLP, LLM

HLT Publications

HLT PUBLICATIONS
200 Greyhound Road, London W14 9RY

ISBN 1 0 7510 0454 5

British Library Cataloguing-in-Publication.

A CIP Catalogue record for this book is available from the British Library.

Printed and bound in Great Britain.

CONTENTS

ACKNOWLEDGEMENTS

The Author and the Publisher wish to thank the University of London for their kind permission to reproduce and publish problems from past LLB (External) examination papers.

Caveat

The answers given are not approved or sanctioned by the University of London and are entirely our responsibility. They are not intended to be model answers but rather suggested solutions.

The solutions themselves are designed to perform two fundamental purposes, namely:

a) to provide detailed examples of suggested solutions to examination questions; and

b) to assist students with research into the subject of the law of international trade and to further their understanding and appreciation of the subject.

Note

Please note that the solutions to this WorkBook incorporate the law as it stood at April 1994. It has not been possible to include legislation or cases after this date.

INTRODUCTION

This Revision WorkBook has been designed specifically for the use of students studying international trade law at the undergraduate level, although it is acknowledged that this topic is normally an advanced subject in studying for a law degree. Each individual chapter deals with a particular subject matter found in the curricula of most courses dealing with the law of international trade. At the same time, coverage has not been restricted to any one particular syllabus, but has been designed to embrace all the principal topics which are normally found in university and college examinations on this subject. The text is best used as a supplement to the recommended reading suggested by course organisers of individual programmes.

Each chapter contains an introduction which explains the scope and general contents of the topic covered. This is followed by detailed key points which provide guidance to students on the minimum content of materials with which they must be familiar to fully understand the topic. Recent cases and relevant materials are included where appropriate.

The most valuable feature of the Revision WorkBook remains the examination questions themselves and the solutions written to them. In general, questions have been selected in order to cover the most popular issues raised during examinations. Each question has a general comment and a skeleton solution followed by a suggested solution. Although students are not expected to produce a skeleton solution in examinations, it is a useful examination technique which assists ensure a well structured, balanced and logical answer.

This Revision WorkBook has been prepared by a university lecturer and solicitor experienced in both the teaching and practice of international trade law. The solutions are intended to be illustrations of full answers and it is recognised that, under examination conditions, similarly full and detailed answers may be impossible in the light of time constraints.

The opportunity has also been taken, where appropriate, to develop themes, to suggest alternatives and to set out additional material. This has been done to permit the examination candidate access to a full answer from which he or she might select the most relevant points, while at the same time benefiting from the variety of the questions. It is believed that, in reading full opinions to each question, the student can further his or her understanding of the law of international trade.

Once again, it must be reiterated that the solutions are not Model Answers for at this level there is almost certainly more than one solution to each problem. At the same time, where alternative options are possible, these have been highlighted, where appropriate, in the text of the solution.

HOW TO STUDY
LAW OF INTERNATIONAL TRADE

The Law of International Trade is undoubtedly a difficult subject and one which requires knowledge of other aspects of law such as the law of contract. There are few situations where the applicable law is straightforward, particularly with hypothetical factual problems. Hence, it is essential to thoroughly review the key points in each chapter before proceeding to consider the problems presented.

In this WorkBook an attempt has been made to present the various chapters in a constructive order, yet often the dictates of a particular question require the examination of issues which have not yet been fully elaborated. This is inevitable because problems in this area of law are generally not focused on any single legal issue but usually involve a combination of elements. For example, questions involving international sales may also raise issues relating to methods of payment, bills of exchange or marine insurance. This is an unavoidable consequence of the nature of this subject.

The place to begin the study of the law of international trade is by reading one of the main textbooks on the subject. This will allow familiarisation with the leading cases and the most important statutes. All courses recommend at least one leading textbook and this should be referred to in order to ensure that all the areas covered by the syllabus of a particular course have been encompassed. Becoming familiar with the recommended text also has the advantage of allowing a candidate to identify those areas of the law which might arise in the final examination paper.

Once the contents of such a textbook has been digested, a good point at which to start this Revision WorkBook will have been reached. The purpose of the WorkBook is to refresh minds as to the pertinent points of the law of international trade. If study of the recommended textbook has been adequately achieved, the task of going through this Revision WorkBook will be made that more simple. An overall general knowledge of each individual topic in this area of law, combined with revision through the exercises in this WorkBook, should ensure an extensive and detailed knowledge of the complete subject.

In international trade law, legal authority is derived primarily through statutes, judicial decisions and international conventions. Although the common law is becoming progressively less and less significant in international trade law there are still important judicial decisions which play a critical role in properly answering questions. Successful candidates are always aware of how the law is applied by courts to factual situations.

However, the growing importance of statutes and international conventions can be gleaned from the fact that since 1990 there have been substantial revisions made to the INCOTERMS and the Uniform Customs and Practice for Documentary Credits, as well as the innovations brought to the law on bills of lading by the Carriage of Goods by Sea Act 1992 and to choice of law in commercial contracts by the Contracts (Applicable Law) Act 1990. These changes to the law illustrate the dynamic nature of this subject.

Authority for a proposition should be cited whenever possible and a basic knowledge of the leading cases, important statutes and conventions is absolutely essential to any answer. Vagueness should be avoided whenever possible; accuracy must be the keyword and accuracy comes from a thorough knowledge of authority.

Once a thorough knowledge of the law has been acquired and an appropriate methodology adopted to approaching problems involving legal issues of international trade, the task of identifying and applying the relevant legal principles to an issue becomes increasingly simplified. These skills may be polished through a study and appreciation of the techniques involved in answering examination questions. The primary objective of this WorkBook is therefore not to provide students with pro forma answers to questions but to teach them the skills involved in approaching questions in the area of the law of international trade.

REVISION AND EXAMINATION TECHNIQUE

It is not the purpose of this Revision WorkBook to serve as a substitute for attending lectures when possible, studying the recommended reading or attempting take-home essay questions. Engaging in such practices would not only be dangerous because individual lecturers stress different areas of the syllabus, but also can never lead to a proper appreciation of the subject. A failure to spend time learning the law will inevitably be exposed. Acquiring legal qualifications is only the beginning of a legal career. In a competitive legal environment, those not thoroughly familiar with the law will be less likely to succeed.

Engaging in such practices also has other limitations. They deprive the student of opportunities to clarify points of difficulty and to expand upon difficult matters during the course of the programme. An exchange of ideas is essential for a complete appreciation of the complexities involved in the application of international trade law, and may provide an insight into difficulties which might arise in final examinations. This WorkBook is designed to supplement diligence and effort, the combination which most often leads to success.

An individual syllabus should therefore be supplemented by reference to the various relevant chapters in this WorkBook. Familiarity with the principal issues and the type of question which might arise allows a student an opportunity to formulate appropriate responses to possible questions arising during the term. In turn, this should encourage the expansion of ideas and alternative proposals for answering questions at the end of the course.

A number of points are expressly relevant to the study and revision of the law of international trade. A proportional relationship may be established between relevancy and final score. Students should therefore avoid commentary and deviation from the terms of the question. As many relevant points as possible should be included in an answer. Vagueness can be avoided by becoming acquainted with the main concepts and principles in each individual area of the syllabus. For this purpose, the WorkBook emphasises the most important basic issues in the key points' section at the beginning of each chapter.

Further, in law, relevancy is almost invariably related to authority. The sounder the legal authority adduced in support of a proposition, the greater the cogency of the argument. Frequently, although a student has correctly answered the question, the answer will not score highly. This may often be attributed to the lack of authority cited to support the arguments. Problems are posed not only for the purpose of testing common sense but also in order to ascertain a candidate's knowledge of the law.

At the same time, methodology is important. This is the style adopted by a candidate for reaching a particular conclusion to a question. Although methodology is often related to organisation, it is also acquired through practice. While this WorkBook is designed to facilitate the acquisition of an appropriate methodology by proposing suggested solutions, there is no substitute for trial and error prior to the examination.

In the law of international trade, questions fall into two main categories. On the one hand, an examiner may pose an 'essay-type' question which will specify a particular topic for discussion. Although at first it might appear that such questions allow an almost infinite discretion for answering, in fact the examiner will undoubtedly have a number of basic points in mind which must be covered in a successful answer. Consequently, essay-type questions are best attempted on subjects in which the student has acquired a familiarity with the basic concepts.

On the other hand, an examiner may set a 'problem type' question. In such cases, the student is presented with a set of hypothetical facts and instructed to apply the law. Unless suggested to the contrary, the stated facts require no proof and the student should proceed on the basis that these facts are supported by sufficient evidence. The student should refrain from deducing the existence of facts to the contrary unless such an inference is unavoidable.

Obviously, in order to remain relevant, the student must be able to distinguish between relevant and irrelevant facts and must be able to apply the law to the relevant facts. Again an examiner will require that a number of basic points are covered to score a reasonable mark. In order to attempt such questions, read the facts carefully, ascertain the most important matters and sketch out the applicable law prior to attempting the problem itself. Organisation will also ultimately result in a higher score and more often than not less time will be spent answering the question.

Where the law on a certain matter is unsettled the examiner will be attempting to solicit comment on the nature of the controversies which have created this state of affairs. In addition, the examiner may be looking for an outline of the opposing view. The candidate need not support one or other opinion but should refer to which side of the argument is legally most plausible.

Questions may also be divided into a number of parts. Most frequently, all the sections will relate to the same topic, if not the same principles behind a specific area of the law of international trade. The problem may be phrased in such a way that the only plausible answer to another part of the question is to answer the first in a certain manner. If a discrepancy does arise between the answer to the first part and the answer suggested by the language of the second part, most often this will not be fatal if a cogent, reasoned legal argument has been advanced in the answer to the first part. A student may propose alternative solutions to the later part of the question, although most likely this process will be time consuming.

Finally, there is no substitute for proper preparation before entering the examination room. If a student has to ascertain distinctions and differentiations under examination conditions, not only will the answer be confused but it will also most likely be insufficient. An appreciation of the major concepts, principles and rules in international trade law is best acquired before endeavours are made in the examination room.

TABLE OF CASES

TABLE OF STATUTES

1 THE CONTRACT FOR THE SALE OF GOODS

1.1	Introduction
1.2	Key points
1.3	Recent cases and statutes
1.4	Relevant materials
1.5	Analysis of questions
1.6	Questions

1.1   Introduction

International sales contracts are simply agreements between buyers and sellers situated in different countries, but it is this transnational or cross-border element which complicates the transaction. The parties will be located in different legal jurisdictions which will therefore require the selection of an appropriate law to regulate the transaction. Similarly, the remedies available to the buyer and seller in the event that all does not go according to plan will have to be enforced by the courts of one or other jurisdiction.

Where the parties decide that English law is applicable to the sales contract, then the relevant provisions of common law together with statutes such as the Sale of Goods Act 1979 and the Supply of Goods and Services Act 1982 will apply. In some cases mandatory provisions of English law will be applied if a contractual dispute is brought before the English courts, regardless of whether the applicable law is English law or a foreign law.

For the formation of the contract, the relevant rules remain primarily of a common law nature. As regards the obligations of buyers and sellers under a contract of sale the law implies certain statutory rights and duties to regulate issues such as the buyer's warranty for title, description of the goods, quality and fitness for purpose.

1.2   Key points

a) *Formation of the contract*

   i)   Offer and acceptance

       A sales contract is constituted by the acceptance of an offer. The offer may be to buy or sell the goods. In any event, the acceptance of the offer must be unqualified and unconditional.

Invitations to treat, advertising materials, price lists, tenders and approaches subject to contract are not deemed to be offers and it is the response to these overtures from the buyer that is considered to be the offer which requires acceptance from the seller.

To be valid, an acceptance must not only be unconditional but also made within the requisite time and certain in its terms.

Once agreement between the parties is reached a valid contract is constituted subject to the rules for avoiding the agreement on the grounds of mistake, misrepresentation, error and duress.

ii) Incorporation of the applicable law

International contracts almost invariably contain a provision which refers to the legal system which is to be applied in the interpretation, application and enforcement of the contract. In the absence of such a term, the courts will impute an intention to select a legal system to the parties in order to choose the proper law of the contract; this matter is now regulated to a large extent by the Contracts (Applicable Law) Act 1990.

The parties must select English law as the applicable law of the contract in order to avail themselves of the rights and duties of buyer and seller under English statute and common law. Unless stated otherwise, throughout this WorkBook the presumption is that the parties have opted for English law as the applicable law of the contract.

iii) Contractual terms contrary to mandatory provisions of English law

Where a contractual term is inconsistent with mandatory provisions of English law, such as those contained in the Unfair Contract Terms Act 1977, the English courts will not give effect to the term. Similarly, where the performance of a contract is illegal under English law, the courts will not enforce its terms: see *United City Merchants (Investments) Limited v Royal Bank of Canada* [1982] 2 WLR 1039.

b) *The application of the Sale of Goods Act 1979 to international sales contracts*

Whenever there is a contract for the sale of goods governed by English law, the Sale of Goods Act 1979 (SGA 1979) applies. A contract for the sale of goods is defined in s2(1) of the SGA 1979 as:

'a contract by which the seller transfers or agrees to transfer the property in the goods to the buyer for a money consideration, called the price.'

For the buyer, the legal objective of the contract of sale is to obtain ownership of the goods and for the seller the objective is to receive the price.

There are six key concepts in this definition which require further elaboration:

i) Contract of sale – since the object of the contract of sale is for the transfer of property, contracts for the supply of services are excluded.

ii) Seller – the person who agrees to sell the goods.

iii) Buyer – the person who agrees to purchase the goods.

iv) Property – the general property in the goods in total: s61(1) SGA 1979.

v) Goods – all personal chattels other than chose in action and money.

vi) Money consideration – an amount as a price must be exchanged and contracts of exchange or barter fall outside the scope of the Act.

c) *The distinction between conditions and warranties*

The law of contract classifies the respective rights and duties of the parties as conditions or warranties. The difference is simply that major terms of the contract, breaches of which are considered to go to the root of the contract, are conditions and entitle the innocent party to treat the contract as discharged in the event of breach. A warranty is a minor term considered collateral to the main purpose of the contract and breach of such a term merely entitles the innocent party to claim damages; in such an event both parties continue to remain bound to honour their contractual obligations.

To determine whether a particular term is a condition or a warranty, s11(3) of the SGA 1979 provides:

'Whether a stipulation in a contract is a condition, the breach of which may give rise to a right to treat the contract as repudiated, or a warranty, the breach of which may give rise to a claim for damages but not a right to reject the goods and treat the contract as repudiated, depends in each case on the construction of the contract; and a stipulation may be a condition, though called a warranty in the contract.'

It should be noted at this stage that rescission, repudiation and rejection are three different concepts:

i) Rescission is when the contact is so vitiated as to never have had any legal effect.

ii) Repudiation is the legal effect of a breach of a condition of the contract; if the innocent party accepts the repudiation the contract is terminated as at the time of the breach of the condition.

iii) Rejection occurs when the innocent party refuses to accept the modified performance of the contract by the party in breach of a condition of the contract.

d) *Principal provisions of the Sale of Goods Act 1979*

There are four main terms of the SGA 1979 which are implied into every contract of sale regulated by the Act.

i) Right to sell

In a contract of sale there is an implied condition on the part of the seller that he or she has the right to sell the goods, or in the case of an agreement to sell at a future date that he or she will have such a right at the time property is to pass: s12(1).

Since this is a condition of the contact, breach on the part of the seller will entitle the buyer to repudiate the contract and to reject the seller's performance for total failure of consideration: see *Rowland* v *Divall* [1923] 2 KB 500.

In addition, there are two further implied warranties connected to this obligation, namely:

- that the goods are free from any encumbrance or charge known by or disclosed to the buyer before the contract is made; and

- the buyer will enjoy quiet possession of the goods: s12(2).

These implied warranties, if breached, only allow the buyer to raise an action for damages.

ii) The goods correspond to the description

Where there is a contract for the sale of goods by description, there is an implied condition that the goods will correspond to that description: s13(1). The courts have construed this duty to allow the buyer to rely on this obligation to reject the goods even in the case of minor discrepancies unless purely microscopic: *Re Moore & Co and Landauer & Co* [1921] 2 KB 519.

If the contract specifies shipment of the goods on a particular vessel, this term will form a part of the contractual description. The time of shipment is also a term of description and therefore a condition of the contract as is the place of shipment: see *J Aron & Co* v *Comptoir Wegimont* [1921] 3 KB 435.

iii) Merchantable quality

It is an implied condition of the contract of sale that the goods will be of merchantable quality: s14. The concept of merchantable quality means that the goods will be of the appropriate level of quality expected from goods of the type sold and at the price agreed. The structure of the section is nevertheless unusual.

Section 14(1) provides that, except as stipulated in the section, there is no implied condition or warranty about the quality of goods supplied under a contract of sale. The next subsection, 14(2), then goes on to provide:

'Where the seller sells goods in the course of a business, there is an implied condition that the goods supplied under the contract are of merchantable quality, except that there is no such condition:

a) as regards defects specifically drawn to the buyer's attention before the contract is made; or

b) if the buyer examines the goods before the contract is made, as regards defects which that examination ought to reveal.'

Merchantable quality is defined in s14(6) in the following terms:

'Goods of any kind are of merchantable quality within the meaning of subsection (2) if they are fit for the purpose or purposes for which goods of that kind are commonly bought as it is reasonable to expect having regard to any description applied to them, the price (if relevant) and all the other relevant circumstances.'

iv) Fitness for purpose

Where the seller sells the goods in the course of a business and the buyer expressly, or by implication, makes known to the seller that the goods are for a particular purpose, there is an implied condition that the goods supplied under the contract are reasonably fit for their normal purpose whether or not that is the purpose for which the goods are commonly supplied: s14(3).

This duty is subject to the proviso that there must be actual and reasonable reliance by the buyer on the seller's skill or judgment.

e) *The passing of property*

The question of when property passes is important as this determines which of the parties will have liability for loss or damage to the goods. As a general principle, s17(1) of the SGA 1979 provides:

'Where there is a contract for sale of specific or ascertained goods, the property in them is transferred to the buyer at such time as the parties intend it to be transferred.'

Thus, by way of illustration, in cif contracts the intention of the parties is that property will only pass when all the relevant documents are transferred: see *Enichem* v *Ampelos Shipping* [1988] 2 Lloyd's Rep 599. In fob contracts, property passes on shipment, the moment the goods cross the ship's rail.

There are two important exceptions to this rule:

i) section 18, r2 provides that if something needs to be done to goods to put them in a deliverable state, property will not pass until this is done.

ii) section 18, r3 states that where goods need to be weighed or measured to calculate the price, property will only pass after the weighing or measuring.

This general rule, and these two exceptions, apply where the goods have been ascertained. Where the goods remain unascertained, s16 of the SGA 1979 provides that property can only pass when the goods become ascertained. Section 16 itself is silent as to what might constitute ascertainment but s18, r5 states that if the goods are unconditionally appropriated to the contract this will be sufficient for property to pass.

The simplest form of appropriation is the delivery of the goods to the carrier for shipment. However, delivery must be unconditional and mere labelling or crating of the goods is not sufficient; there must be an unequivocal act or sign of appropriation.

All the rules in the SGA 1979 as to the passing of property are subject to the overriding right of the parties to agree to allow property to pass at some point other than that provided for in the statute.

f) *Romalpa clauses*

A Romalpa clause is a particular means whereby a seller indicates that he does not wish property in the goods to pass in the manner and at the time provided for in the SGA 1979: see *Aluminium Industrie Vaassen BV* v *Romalpa Aluminium Ltd* [1976] 1 WLR 676. Instead he is reserving his proprietary rights in the contract goods usually until payment in full is made.

Where such a clause is put into a contract, whether or not it is effective to retain the seller's title as security for the purchase price will depend on the circumstances of each case.

Where goods in which the title is retained are sold to a third party buying in good faith and without notice of the reservation of property, from a party in possession of the goods, a Romalpa clause may not be adequate to prevent that third party from acquiring a valid title under s25 of the SGA 1979.

g) *Delivery of the goods*

Unless otherwise agreed, it is the duty of the seller to deliver the goods and the buyer to accept and pay for them in accordance with the terms of the contract: s27 SGA 1979. A delivery of the goods which is not in conformity with the contract of sale will not necessarily be ineffective; a breach may not entitle the buyer to reject the goods or, where the buyer is entitled to reject the goods, he or she may elect not to do so.

Section 6(1) defines 'delivery' as the 'voluntary transfer of possession from one person to another'. As a concept, it is divorced from those of transfer of property or risk in the goods.

Delivery may be either actual or constructive. Actual delivery is self-explanatory. Constructive delivery is a common form of delivery in international sales contracts and may take one of the following forms:

   i)   by the transfer of documents of title;

   ii) by the delivery of an object giving physical control such as the key to the warehouse where the goods are stored; or

   iii) by attornment which is when one party in possession lawfully acknowledges that goods which are previously held by himself are in fact held for the buyer; or

   iv) by delivery to a carrier in pursuance of the contract of sale.

The place of delivery and whether the buyer is to collect the goods or not depends in all cases on the terms of the contract: s29(1) SGA 1979.

6

h) *Exception clauses*

The Unfair Contract Terms Act 1977 applies to contracts where one of the parties is a consumer within the definition of that statute. However, the Act is specifically stated not to apply to international supply contracts.

Therefore, if an exclusion clause is incorporated into a sales contract, whether or not it will be effective will be largely a question of construction.

i) *Buyer's remedies for breach by the seller*

In the event that the buyer does not accept the goods because they do not conform to the contract, his or her remedies depend on:

i) whether the disconformity amounts to a breach of a condition or a warranty of the contract; or

ii) if there is such a breach, whether he or she elects to treat the breach as repudiatory or a breach of warranty; or

iii) whether the seller's conduct estops him or her from asserting the rights available under the SGA 1979 or the common law.

The principal remedy for a breach of a condition is to reject the goods and to sue the seller for non-delivery. This right is subject to the ability of the seller to re-tender conforming goods which he or she is entitled to do if time is not of the essence of the contract or the goods are unascertained.

The measure of the buyer's damages for non-delivery is assessed under ss51 and 54 of the SGA 1979.

The measure of damages for the breach of warranty is found in s53(3) of the Act which states that if a breach is one of quality the loss is prima facie the difference between the value of the goods at the time of delivery to the buyer and the value they would have had if the seller fulfilled the warranty.

j) *Seller's remedies for breach by the buyer*

Sections 38 and 39 of the SGA 1979 cover the rights of the unpaid seller in the event of breach of contract by the buyer. In particular, the unpaid seller is entitled to exercise a lien over goods, to stop the goods in transit and even, in certain circumstances, to re-sell the goods.

1.3 Recent cases and statutes

Kaines (UK) v *Osterreichische Warrenhandelsgesellshaft mbH* [1993] 2 Lloyd's Rep 1: where the seller repudiated the terms of a sales contract and the repudiation was accepted by the buyer, damages for breach were calculated from the date on which the buyer should have mitigated its loss by purchasing substitute goods.

Nissho Iwai Petroleum Co v *Cargill International SA* [1993] 1 Lloyd's Rep 80: it is an implied term of a sales contract that the buyer will not obstruct or prevent the seller from performing the contract.

1.4   Relevant materials

Charlesworth, *Business Law* (15th edition, 1991).

D Campbell, *Remedies for International Sellers of Goods* (1994).

J Crabtree, *International Sale of Goods* (1991), pp1–60.

Benjamin's Sale of Goods (4th edition, 1992).

M P Furmston, *Sale and Supply of Goods* (1993).

1.5   Analysis of questions

The application of the Sale of Goods Act 1979 and associated legislation to export sales is a topic which has cropped up on many occasions in University of London (External) LLB past papers which is why all the following questions have been selected from that reservoir of exam papers.

Typically, questions on the sale of goods are combined with questions concerning the rights and duties of the parties in cif and fob contracts. These problems might include defects in the contract goods, risk, passing of property, acceptance, repudiation, damages, etc. Therefore, the questions sampled in this chapter overlap to a certain extent with those in the following two chapters.

1.6   Questions

Question 1

'The implied terms in the Sale of Goods Act 1979 are simply a method – though an incomplete and imperfect one – of endeavouring to ensure that the buyer of goods gets what he pays for. They serve a useful function, albeit no doubt they could be improved upon.'

Do the current implied terms work well? Could they be made better?

University of London LLB Examination
(for External Students) Commercial Law June 1990 Q3

General comment

A relatively straightforward essay for the well prepared candidate. From the phrasing of the question it appears that a broad brush approach is required in relation to the detail of the implied terms themselves; and that the examiner wishes the candidate to concentrate on the business efficacy of the terms.

Skeleton solution

Terms, conditions and warranties – 'inalienable rights'.

The 1979 Sale of Goods Act implied terms in context.

Particular advantages and disadvantages of present implied terms.

Recent developments and proposals for the future.

Suggested solution

It is generally accepted there are three major categories of contractual terms; namely conditions, warranties and innominate terms (sometimes referred to as intermediate stipulations).

To describe these briefly in the same order as above, conditions are vital or major terms which go to the 'root of the contract', breach of which entitles the innocent party to treat the contract as ended and to claim damages. Warranties are subsidiary or minor terms, breach of which entitles the innocent party to damages only. Section 61 of the Sale of Goods Act 1979 defines a warranty as being 'collateral to the main purpose' of the contract.

The third category referred to above – 'innominate' or intermediate terms, originated in their present form from the decision in the *Hongkong Fir* case (1962) and were affirmed as such in *Bunge Corporation* v *Tradax Export SA* (1981) by Lord Scarman. An innominate term is one, the effect of non-performance of which the parties expressly (or as is more usual) impliedly agree will depend on the nature and consequences of the breach. Prior to these decisions it was widely thought that terms in a contract could only be conditions or warranties. In *Cehave NV* v *Bremer Handelsgesellschaft, The Hansa Nord* (1976) the doctrine of innominate terms was extended to contracts for the sale of goods where an express term that goods were to be 'shipped in good condition' were in effect an intermediate stipulation.

The proposition herein is that the implied terms of the Sale of Goods Act 1979 are an 'incomplete and imperfect' method of 'endeavouring to ensure that the buyer of goods gets what he pays for'. In essence this sums up the rationale behind both the 1893 and 1979 Sale of Goods statutes, but it represents an over-simplification of the complex legal draftsmanship and motivation behind these sections. The proposition continues that 'no doubt they could be improved upon'; this belies the longevity (albeit with some slight amendment) of the sections since their introduction in 1893 and the fact that they are substantially the same now as then.

Some reference, without undue attention to detail, is necessary to the actual provisions of ss12–15 SOGA 1979 in order to consider the proposition that they merely ensure the consumer gets what he pays for and to consider if improvement is possible.

Section 12 SOGA 1979 contains an implied condition on the part of the seller that, in the case of a sale, he has a right to sell the goods, and in the case of an agreement to sell he will have such a right at the time the property is to pass. The section also contains implied warranties of freedom from undisclosed encumbrances and the right (s12(2)) to quiet possession of the goods. This applies to all contracts. Section 13 SOGA 1979 contains an implied condition in a contract for the sale of goods by description, there is an implied condition that the goods will correspond with the description; and in a contract for the sale of goods by sample as well as description, a condition that the goods must correspond with both (s13(1)). Section 13 applies to all contracts as does s12 and not just to sales made by traders to consumers.

9

Section 14 SOGA 1979 applies to sales 'made in the course of a business' by the seller and contains an implied condition that 'goods supplied under such a contract are of merchantable quality' (with the exception of defects specifically drawn to the buyer's attention and defects which examination by the buyer before purchase ought to reveal)'. Additionally, 'where the seller sells goods in the course of a business and the buyer expressly or by implication makes known to the seller any particular purpose for which the goods are being bought, there is an implied condition that goods supplied under the contract are reasonably fit for the purpose ... except ... where the buyer does not rely on the skill or judgement of the seller.' (s14(3) SOGA 1979).

Finally s15, SOGA 1979 covers sales by sample where there are implied conditions that the bulk shall correspond with the sample in quality and that the buyer shall have reasonable opportunity of checking this; and that the goods shall be free from any defect rendering them unmerchantable which would not be apparent on reasonable examination of the sample.

Taking all these implied terms together it is apparent that a comprehensive protection is afforded to the consumer and that with other related legislation, in particular the UCTA 1977, these rights cannot be overridden or contracted out of. It cannot therefore be realistic to describe the terms as 'incomplete and imperfect'. The parties are free to make the bargain they choose in the way they choose, doctrines such as 'caveat emptor' still apply; as, for example, where examination takes place and defects should be discovered (s14) but the consumer is protected from unscrupulous dealing by the seller and from the ambiguities that inevitably arise in commercial consumer sales.

The implied terms have not remained static since the 1893 statute; in particular two important modifications have improved them to the advantage of the consumer. The 1973 Supply of Goods (Implied Terms) Act reworded and rearranged the original 1893 s14 and these amendments were incorporated into the 1979 SOGA s14. Section 14(1) begins with the statement of the general principle of caveat emptor, then follows the worded implied condition that goods are of merchantable quality s14(2), and finally the reworded condition that goods are fit for their purpose, s14(3).

In particular, s14(3) represents an improved and simplified provision when compared with the old s14(2) because it is no longer limited to sales by description but covers all 'sales in the course of a business' (the latter being defined to include a 'profession the activities of any government department... or local or public authority') and s14(3) applies even if the seller has not previously dealt in goods of a similar kind or does not normally deal in such goods.

Recently the Law Commission published a report on the sale and supply of goods (Law Comm No 160, Cmnd 137) which proposed certain developments and proposals; chief amongst these being to replace the statutory definition of 'merchantable quality' by one of 'acceptable quality'. The definition of acceptable quality was to consist of two elements; a basic principle that goods sold or supplied under a contract should be such as would be 'acceptable' to a reasonable person and that there should be a list of aspects of 'quality' any of which could be important in a particular case (eg appearance, finish, fitness of goods for all their common purposes, safety, durability and freedom from minor defects). The Law Commission also proposed that a consumer should not lose the right to reject goods merely because he has signed an 'acceptance note'.

The draft Bill that has resulted from these reports and developments may introduce some more balance between the 'fitness for purposes' and what Atiyah describes as 'non functional aspects of merchantability' – but the same author is of the opinion that 'in general it does not seem likely that the changes proposed by the draft Bill will make much difference to the law ... the concept of 'acceptable quality' ... has even less genuine meaning than the concept of 'merchantable quality' and must be fleshed out by the case law in the various circumstances." (p168 *Sale of Goods* – P S Atiyah).

In conclusion then, despite their great age, and the fact that they have remained relatively unchanged, the implied conditions of the SOGA 1979 do not appear to be either 'incomplete or imperfect'. Of course their function of ensuring the buyer gets what he pays for is a useful one; the conditions ensure this in a comprehensive fashion by the way they inter-relate with one another and with other supporting statutes. The Law Commission and learned writers appear to concur that they work well in practice and are hard-pushed to improve them.

Question 2

Explain the meaning of, and the relationship between, the terms 'property', 'risk' and 'title' in the Sale of Goods Act 1979.

University of London LLB Examination
(for External Students) Commercial Law June 1987 Q2

General comment

Many candidates would have found this question difficult because it touches on a subject which is not clearly dealt with in any of the standard text books. The relationship between the three concepts mentioned in the question is made all the more difficult to discuss by the absence of explanation in the Act itself. Nevertheless, like so many essay questions, if the effect of the sections of the Act dealing with each concept are remembered then it should not be impossible to say something about their meanings and relationship.

Skeleton solution

The absence of adequate definitions of these terms in the SGA 1979.

The rules of the Act relating to the passing of ownership.

Definition of risk and the rules for the transfer of risk.

The relationship between title and ownership.

Suggested solution

'Property', 'risk' and 'title' are not fully defined in the Sale of Goods Act (SGA) 1979, indeed the only definition to be found is of property and even that does not pretend to be exhaustive (s61(1) SGA 1979). Within the Act the three concepts all arise in Part III which is entitled 'Effects of the Contract' and, generally, deals with three different matters:

a) when the buyer becomes the owner of the goods;

b) whether the buyer becomes the owner in cases where the seller was not the owner; and

c) the undefined concept of 'risk'.

The term 'property' is reserved for describing the passing of ownership from the seller to the buyer. Section 2 recognises that contracts of sale of goods can provide for ownership to pass immediately or at a future date or on the happening of some condition. If ownership is to pass immediately then the contract is one of sale, if it is to pass at a later date or on the happening of some condition then the contract is an agreement to sell. But in all cases, whether or not the seller is the owner, the parties will agree that ownership should pass at some time. In general the Act states that the parties' agreement on the time of passing of ownership will be respected (s17 SGA 1979), but it recognises that in many (if not most) sales the parties will not say when ownership passes. Therefore certain rules are laid down in s18 which will be applicable in the absence of express or implied agreement to the contrary. The rules differ according to the other terms of the contract and the nature of the goods: (a) there are rules for specific goods and others for unascertained goods, (b) there are rules where the parties provide that something must be done to the goods by one or other party and others where nothing has to be done to the goods prior to delivery.

The definition of property in s61(1) as meaning the general property in goods rather than any special property, shows that it is the global aspect of ownership rather than some equitable interest in the goods which is covered by the s18 rules.

Furthermore, it is noticeable that the rules in s18 have two effects: firstly they identify who is the owner at any time in order to see who, prima facie, should bear any loss caused by damage that is done to the goods; and secondly they determine the remedies open to the parties.

The first of those matters is what is meant by risk. The risk in goods is the duty of one party to bear the cost of their loss or damage. The prima facie rule, both at common law and under the 1979 Act, is that the owner of goods must bear such costs (s20(1) SGA 1979). But the parties may always agree that ownership shall pass to the buyer on a particular date or on the happening of a particular event and the risk on another, be it before or after he becomes the owner. For example, in Romalpa cases the contract invariably provides that property will only pass on full payment, whereas risk passes to the buyer immediately.

In fact risk is used to describe concepts other than the costs of loss or damage. It can be used in cases where the seller is unsure of his rights of ownership to describe the position of a buyer who buys and takes a chance – he bears the risk of the seller not being the owner and, accordingly, must pay for the goods whether or not he becomes owner. This idea of risk is not one covered by the Act, but arises at common law. The Act is concerned, when talking of risk, with loss or damage only.

The incidence of property also dictates the remedies open to the parties to a limited extent. The buyer cannot be sued for the price unless property has passed to him (s49 SGA 1979), even if it is his fault that it has not passed (*Colley* v *Overseas Exporters Ltd* (1921)). The seller will therefore be obliged to sue for damages for non-acceptance rather than for the price. In relation to third parties who damage the goods, an action will not lie in negligence unless the plaintiff had property rights at the time they were damaged (*The Aliakmon* (1986)). Cases can, therefore, arise where the parties agree that the buyer has to bear the risk of the goods being damaged, but he cannot sue the third party because he did not have property at the time the damage was done.

'Title' also involves concepts of ownership, but is concerned with the question *whether* the buyer has become owner not *when* he became owner. In ss21 to 25 there are rules allowing a buyer to obtain good title even though the person from whom he bought was not the true owner. The buyer's title does not derive from the seller but vests in him by operation of law. In effect, therefore, ownership passes from the true owner to the buyer and the seller is never owner himself.

The rule nemo dat quod non habet prevails unless the buyer can prove that one of the statutory exceptions applies. Where a seller (S) owns goods and sells them to a buyer (B), B will be able to pass ownership by a sale to a third party (T) if he has obtained ownership himself. Conversely if B is not the owner at the time he sells to T then T can only become the owner if one of the nemo dat exceptions applies. Accordingly it is important to know whether property has passed to B in order to be able to appreciate the effect of his sale to T.

Although the Act refers to property and title as apparently different concepts, they are both concerned with ownership. When the seller of goods is their owner the rules on property determine when the buyer becomes owner, and when the seller does not own them the rules on title allow ownership to be vested in the buyer regardless.

Question 3

Slimbo buys from Adolf a quantity of corn pellets which Adolf has for a number of years imported from Germany and which he supplies to Slimbo on the basis that 'ownership in the goods remains in the supplier until all outstanding liabilities are discharged to the supplier, who is under no liability for the suitability of the goods for any of the purposes to which they may be put.'

Slimbo also buys from Bismak a quantity of Algerian Skanoil which Bismak has imported on Slimbo's instructions. The Skanoil is delivered to Bismak in sealed drums which Bismak delivers to Slimbo unopened. The small print of the accompanying invoice, which Bismak does not read or pass on to Slimbo, states that, once Skanoil is exposed to air, it must be used within five days to avoid deterioration.

Over a period of several months, Slimbo immerses the corn pellets in the Skanoil to produce Kornskam, a product which he retails as animal feedstuff. He sells some of this to Gorby 'on the terms as in my agreement with Adolf'. Gorby feeds some of the Kornskam to his cattle, which develop an allergic reaction to it and go mad, rampaging across and destroying the wheatfield of his neighbour Boris.

Advise Slimbo and Gorby.

University of London LLB Examination
(for External Students) Commercial Law June 1991 Q6

General comment

This a straightforward, if lengthy, question primarily concerned with implied terms under s14 of Sale of Goods Act, with some peripheral matters, most notably exclusion clauses. Provided the student has the persistence and stamina to follow each alternative through to a logical conclusion, the only difficulty it should present to a well prepared student is how to get all the necessary information down on paper in the time available.

Skeleton solution

Slimbo – Adolf

Implied terms under ss13–15 SGA, esp s14.

Purported exclusion clause and the effect of UCTA.

Reservation of title; Romalpa clauses.

Slimbo – Bismak

Implied terms under s14 SGA.

Goods defective – or packaging?

Consumer Protection Act 1987.

Slimbo – Gorby

Implied terms under s14 SGA.

Slimbo and Gorby dealing business-consumer.

Effect of UCTA.

Suggested solution

This is a question best answered by dealing with the main problems separately.

Slimbo's purchase of corn pellets from Adolf

Sections 13–15 of Sale of Goods Act (SGA) 1979 now imply into virtually all contracts for the sale of goods a series of provisions as to quality of the subject matter. It is not clear from the wording of the question whether this is a sale by description, or by sample. Indeed it is not clear whether the corn pellets are in any way faulty either before or after the combination with Skanoil. Finally it is not apparent whether or not Adolf is aware of the intended use to which Slimbo is going to put the pellets. So what, from this somewhat vague scenario, can we advise Slimbo?

Firstly, if the goods were sold by description then s13 SGA will apply. Most authorities are of the opinion that virtually all sales will be by description (save where the goods are unique in some way and sought out by the buyer). Thus if Slimbo contacts Adolf and asks for 'some more of those corn pellets' or 'corn pellets suitable for combining with other substances' or whatever, then this will be a sale by description. Section 13 requires that the goods in bulk comply with description. The same rules by virtue of s15 apply to sale by sample, though we do not know if

Slimbo bought on the basis of a sample. *Ashington Piggeries Ltd* v *Christopher Hill Ltd* (1972) makes it clear that if the description is so crucial to the contract that if the goods sold do not tally with the description it becomes a different contract, then the description becomes in effect a term of the contract, not merely a representation.

The first thing we need to know therefore is if Slimbo gave Adolf a description of the goods he wanted, or if Adolf described the goods in such a way as to convince Slimbo that these goods were suitable for his purpose. We need to know much the same thing for another purpose too: s14(3) SGA provides: 'Where a seller sells goods in the course of a business, and the buyer expressly or impliedly makes known to the seller ... any particular purpose for which the goods are being bought, there is an implied condition that the goods will be fit for that purpose.' Obviously, whether or not Slimbo mentioned his intention of combining the corn pellets with Skanoil is of crucial importance. Section 14(3) only applies to sales in the course of a business and will not apply if it can be shown that the buyer does not rely on the seller's guidance. Similarly s14(2), which overlaps considerably, requires goods to be of merchantable quality ie fit for the purpose or purposes for which such goods are commonly bought. Again the question arises: is it usual to combine different substances to make cattle food ... is this 'a purpose for which such goods are commonly bought'?

We are told that Adolf supplies the goods on a particular basis: 'that ownership in the goods remains in the supplier until all outstanding liabilities are discharged to the supplier, who is under no liability for the suitability of the goods for any of the purposes to which they may be put.' The first part of this clause is clearly an attempt on Adolf's part to reserve title in the goods until such time as he is paid. Normally property (and consequently risk) passes as and when the goods are delivered regardless of time of payment. Such clauses amending the usual rule are often called 'Romalpa clauses' (*Aluminium Industrie Vaassen BV* v *Romalpa Aluminium Ltd* (1976)). Unfortunately what we do not know is whether Slimbo has paid Adolf in full and whether property (and consequently, risk) has now passed from Adolf to Slimbo. The second part of the conditional requirement, the exclusion clause, needs to be looked at carefully. Nowhere in the question does it say whether this is a written clause or an oral one.

The question of incorporation of exclusion clauses is such that a number of possibilities spring to mind. Incorporation by signature is possible, but we do not know if Slimbo has signed any documentation. Previous dealings, if they have consistently been on the same terms, are enough to incorporate a clause: we are told that Adolf has 'for a number of years' imported the corn pellets, but have his contracts always been with Slimbo and always on the same terms? It seems most likely that incorporation, if it has occurred at all, is on the basis that it is conspicuously displayed on documents that are clearly contractual (*McCutcheon* v *MacBrayne* (1964)). The actual time and method of making the contract is also important (*Levison* v *Patent Steam Carpet Cleaning Co* (1978)).

But even if the exclusion clause has been incorporated, is it in any case, valid? We must look first at the Unfair Contract Terms Act 1977 (UCTA). Firstly, it is worth noting that s26 exempts international supply contracts. We are told the goods are imported from Germany, but not whether Adolf is actually in Germany and whether the goods form the basis of such an international contract. If this is the case, of course, it does not necessarily mean that the exclusion clause will have no effect, simply that it will not be governed by UCTA. The Act is stated in s1(3) to apply to business contracts and there have been a number of cases defining 'business' (*Davies* v *Sumner* (1984); *R & B Customs Brokers Co* v *United Dominions Trust* (1988)). It is not entirely clear whether Slimbo is in fact 'in business' on a full time basis. Nevertheless he will for convenience be presumed so to be, as will Adolf. The position would in any event be similar (even if not exactly the same) if he were dealing as a consumer. Only where two individuals deal together will UCTA not apply at all. Section 6(2) provides that exclusion of implied terms as to description, quality, fitness for purpose and correspondence with sample (ss13–15 SGA) is ineffective where one of the parties deals as a consumer. As stated above it will be assumed that Slimbo and Adolf are dealing on an equal business footing. In such cases an exclusion clause may be acceptable if the 'reasonableness' test applies. That test, as set down in s11 and Sched 2 of UCTA, provides similar guidelines to those used in common law prior to the Act's introduction. Such criteria include the relative status of the parties, the availability of the goods, whether other suppliers may use similar exclusion clauses, whether the goods could be insured and so on. Superficially at any rate there seems no glaring reason why the clause should not satisfy the reasonableness test, but there is one point to ponder. The clause reads ... 'no liability' ... and is thus extremely wide.

Finally, despite the foregoing there is no evidence in the question that the corn pellets are in any way faulty; all the pointers indicate that the Skanoil is to blame. It is to this aspect of the question that we shall next proceed.

Slimbo's purchase of Skanoil from Bismak

The same sort of imponderable factors tend to apply as much to this transaction as to the first. Since the question says that Bismak imports the oil 'on Slimbo's instructions' it does not sound as though the contract is an international sale contract. The main problem here appears to be that while the goods are not in themselves faulty, the instructions that go with them are very precise, but, unfortunately, not well communicated. Bismak delivers the drums of oil unopened, but he fails to pass on the accompanying invoice which has on it a warning about exposing Skanoil to air.

It has long been settled that the implied conditions in SGA under s14 as to fitness for purpose and merchantability relate not only to the goods, but also to the container or packaging in which the goods are supplied (*Geddling* v *Marsh* (1920); *Wormell* v *RHM Agricultural (East) Ltd* (1986)). But is a phrase or two incorporated into the small print of the invoice part of the packaging? Certainly there would appear to be nothing on the drums themselves. Any sort of preliminary examination of the oil drums by Slimbo would presumably not reveal this problem; it is not apparent from the drums and Bismak has not drawn it to Slimbo's attention. In disregarding the invoice and throwing it away unread, Bismak may, of course, by the ordinary rules of negligence be liable in tort to Slimbo and possibly also Gorby.

The main test as to merchantable quality is that quoted in *Henry Kendall & Sons* v *William Lillico & Sons* (1969) in which Lloyd LJ stated:

'To bring s14(2) into operation, a buyer had to show that the goods had been bought by description from a seller dealing with goods of that description. If so ... the goods were required to be of merchantable quality ... the goods did not have to be suitable for every purpose within a range of purposes for which goods were normally bought under that description. It was sufficient that ... they were commercially saleable under that description'.

We do not know what information Slimbo gave to Bismak, only that the oil was imported from Algeria 'on Slimbo's instructions'. Nor do we know what quantity of oil is involved. Obviously oil which cannot be exposed to air for more than five days is not of merchantable quality, especially if it is normally used in fairly small quantities. But a great deal will depend on just what information Slimbo gave Bismak, and also on whether normal usage is to use Skanoil quickly and in large quantities.

Note incidentally that under the Consumer Protection Act 1987 s2(2)(c) that those who import into the EC (the oil is from Algeria) defective products will be liable in tort. The term 'importers' will cover both Bismak and Slimbo.

But is the oil, or more likely its packaging with the lack of any warning label, defective? Or is it the combination of corn pellets and Skanoil that constitutes the problem?

Slimbo's sale of Kornskam to Gorby

Whatever the background of its constituent parts it seems clear that as an animal foodstuff Kornskam is defective. It fails to comply with the implied conditions of s14 as to merchantability or fitness for purpose. We are not told just how Gorby purchases the goods, whether by description or sample or whatever; it seems unlikely that the defect which causes the cattle to go. mad would be apparent on any inspection that Gorby might or might not make. The *Ashington Piggeries* case (above) establishes that this is almost certainly a sale by description.

Slimbo deals by way of business with Gorby as a consumer and since his contract is on the same terms as that with Adolf the UCTA will presumably apply. Liability as to death and personal injury cannot be excluded (s2(1) UCTA as noted above). The only difference between the two contracts is that Adolf and Slimbo deal on an equal (presumably) business footing; whereas Slimbo and Gorby are on a business-consumer customer footing. In the latter case, since Gorby is dealing as a consumer, or seems to be, exclusion or purported exclusion of, inter alia, s14 as to fitness and merchantability under SGA will be ineffective.

Slimbo's attempt to exclude liability for the defective Kornskam as against Gorby will therefore be ineffective. This is of course provided Gorby is not dealing as another business as sometimes happens where large companies manage a farm. If Slimbo and Gorby are on an equal business footing then the 'reasonableness' test, as already mentioned, will be applicable to the clause excluding liability.

Finally note the effect of the case of *H Parsons (Livestock) Ltd* v *Uttley Ingham & Co* (1978) on likely damages which may be awarded to Gorby.

Question 4

Robinson Ltd, an exporter and importer of toys, entered into the following transactions:

i)   A sale of 2,000 boxes of 'toy soldiers in French uniform' to Northern Supplies Ltd cif New York 'cash against documents'.

ii) A purchase of 4,000 'toy pistols' from Advanced Products Ltd fob Singapore for delivery at London.

iii) Sales of 2,500 Christmas tree lights to members of the public at £3 each through Robinson Ltd's mail order department.

Each contract excluded liability 'for (a) a breach of any implied terms as to fitness or merchantable quality; (b) negligence of the supplier; or (c) death or personal injury suffered by customers using the goods'.

Robinson Ltd consult you and state:

i)   As to the toy soldiers

We tendered to the buyers a certificate of insurance, an invoice and a bill of lading. The buyers accepted them and paid us the price. They sold 1,000 cases of the goods to Palace Developments Ltd, who rejected them on the ground that the cases contained soldiers in German uniform. We are told that 500 other cases were damaged by fire while at sea. Northern Supplies Ltd are claiming back the whole of the purchase price from us.

ii) As to the toy pistols

We heard that the goods might have been damaged by rain at Singapore before they were loaded, but the sellers refused to allow us to inspect them until the vessel, which we had nominated to carry the goods, reached London. We did not insure the goods as we expected the sellers to do so. Forty five of the pistols were lost at sea in a storm. When the rest arrived, we discovered that 500 pistols were made of metal, and they could not be sold in this country because of various safety regulations.

iii) As to the Christmas tree lights

The electrical circuits on the tree were faulty. The lights bought by Mrs Smith caught fire, and her dining room furniture was destroyed. Another set was bought by Mrs Jones, and she died as a result of burns when they exploded. Mrs Jones' executor and Mrs Smith have made claims against us.

Advise Robinson Ltd.

University of London LLB Examination
(for External Students) Commercial Law June 1983 Q4

General comment

This is a factually complex case with three separate and distinct situations. The best approach is to take the three situations individually because different law applies to each. In fact, there is little overlap between the three aspects of the question making the solution rather lengthy.

Skeleton solution

i) Cif, cash against documents sale.

Property in goods passes when – who bears risk of damages in transit?

Breach of condition?

Exclusion clause – UCTA – reasonableness.

Right of rejection.

ii) Fob contract, risk until shipment on seller – s32 does it alter position?

Frustration.

Right of rejection.

iii) Section 14(2), 14(3) as to quality of goods – action in tort.

Measure of damages.

UCTA, s6 – does Mrs Smith deal as a consumer?

Suggested solution

i) On this cif, cash against documents sale, two issues arise – firstly whether property in the goods has passed so that Northern Supplies bear the risk of damages in transit, and secondly, whether Northern Supplies are prevented from rejecting the goods, thus losing their right to claim the price, if indeed they have such a right.

The sellers have fulfilled their obligations to the buyer in relation to the tender of the appropriate documents – invoice, certificate of insurance and the bill of lading, which is the document title to the goods. The prima facie presumption in the cif sale is that the buyer bears the risk from the passing of the goods over the rail but, of course, he is protected via insurance. But this depends usually on the price of the goods being paid when the documents are tendered, so that the right of the buyer to reject, at least the documents, is lost when they were taken up on exchange for payment. That coincides with an unconditional appropriation of the goods to the contract. The transfer of the bill of lading is prima facie evidence of an intention to pass property.

However, where the contract is cash against documents, the inference is that no property passes until the price has been paid – *Ginzberg* v *Barrow Haematite Steel Co Ltd* (1966). That has occurred, so when the buyers accepted the documents and paid the price, property in the goods passed and it is an inference that the buyers bore the risk – s20(1) 1979 Act. As Lord Parker said in *Comptoir D'Achat et de*

Vente du Boerenbond Belge SA v *Luis de Ridder Lda, The Julia* (1949) in a cif sale, property generally passes on shipment. So, Northern Supplies have no cause of action against the sellers for damage by fire at sea.

To claim the price, the buyers must terminate the contract. To do this, they must show either a repudiatory breach on the part of the sellers or a breach of condition. That will enable the buyers to reject (s11(4) allowing) and thereby treat the contract as discharged. In that event, the buyers have two options, either they can recover the price on the basis of total failure of consideration, or, instead of pursuing their restitutionary remedy, they may claim damages for non-delivery under s51(1). However, that is dependent upon either:

a)   the buyers rejecting *all* the goods; or

b)   the buyers rejecting part and keeping part, if the contract is severable.

In that instance they may claim part of the price related to what they reject.

Now there is not evidence that the contract is anything other than an entire contract with an individual delivery obligation, as in *J Rosenthal & Sons Ltd* v *Esmail* (1965), so possibility (b) can be discounted. The right of the buyers to claim the price will depend on their ability to reject the 2,000 boxes.

Is there a breach of condition? There is a purported exclusion of liability under the statutorily implied conditions in s14(2) and s14(3). That there is a breach of s13, would seem to be difficult to argue. What is delivered to the buyers were still toy soldiers so that the descriptive words used to identify the goods would not seem to cover the uniform description. Such is not necessary to identify the goods (*Ashington Piggeries* (1972)) . There cannot be a breach of s14(2) – the defect, if any, is a descriptional defect, (possibly rendering the goods unfit for their normal purpose if that is considered to be resale) and is *not* a quality defect. Clearly the goods were merchantable within s14(6). Re s14(3), it could be argued that there was a breach. The sub-buyers did, after all reject, and it is almost certain that Northern would know that the buyer's purpose for which the goods had to be reasonably fit, was *resale*. If that is the case, then following Lord Guest in *Ashington Piggeries* (1972) actual communication need not be proved, provided Northern *knew*.

On the assumption that there was a sufficient breach of condition, the purported exclusion must be reasonable within Sch 2 of the 1977 UCTA s6. The term itself must be reasonable, to be tested in the light of the circumstances prevailing at the date of contracting. This applies even though the parties were not consumers because s6 has a wider operation than the rest of the Act – s6(3).

If there is a right to reject, it may well have been lost, under the doctrine of acceptance. If it is lost, then the condition sinks to the level of a warranty, and the only remedy the buyer can pursue is damages for breach of warranty under s53(1) – which, in this case, will be substantially less than damages under s51(1) because, in hypothesis, there will be no right to claim under s51(1) unless all the goods have been successfully rejected – damages under s53(1) will only be awarded in relation to half the boxes.

The question is whether the buyer has done an act inconsistent with the ownership of the seller, within s35. For the purposes of the mechanics of rejection, we must assume that for the purposes of s26, the buyers, actually *can return the goods*, when they come to give notice of rejection. Of course, if they cannot, then the rule in *J Lyons & Co v May & Baker* (1923) bars rejection. This part of s35 is subjected to s34(1). Now these sections were drafted on the basis that it is the goods themselves which the buyer must have had a reasonable opportunity of examining so they sit uneasily with cif contracts – where acceptance of the documents and acceptance of the goods are separate acts. If the defects in the goods were apparent on the fact of the documents, then the right to reject will be lost – if the buyer accepted the documents when they indicated that some boxes contained soldiers in different uniforms, s35 would bar rejection. The buyer would have had a reasonable opportunity to examine for the purposes of s34(1) and *Hardy & Co v Hillerns & Fowler* (1923) says that a resale is an act inconsistent with the ownership of the seller. On the other hand, if as is much more likely, the defect was not apparent on the fact of the documents, then the rule in *Hardy* cannot apply unless there is examination first, so the buyers would be able to reject and claim the price back.

ii) In an fob sale apart from the provisions of s32, risk, until shipment will be on the seller, and will pass to the buyer on shipment. If that applies then Robinson Ltd will have no remedy for the pistols lost at sea. Generally this will mean that in an fob contract, provided the seller fulfils his obligations, it will be the buyer's duty to insure. All that the seller has to do is to ensure that conforming goods are put over the rail of a ship nominated by the buyer in Singapore for delivery to London and to provide the buyer with documents enabling him to obtain possession. Insurance is the business of the buyer, because property in general, will pass as soon as the goods are placed on board (s18 r5(2)). Even if a contrary intention could be inferred, through the seller retaining a bill of lading, risk will pass to the buyer on shipment.

While this is the general position, it could be that s32(3) alters the obligation on Robinson Ltd. Although there is not enough information in the problem to reach a definite conclusion, under s32(3), the seller must give such notice to the buyer to enable him to insure (*Wimble Sons & Co v Rosenberg & Sons* (1913)) held that that applied to fob contracts, as a risk-deeming provision). However, the practical effect of that is limited by the fact that the Court of Appeal in *Wimble* held that the 'notice' requirement under s32(3) was satisfied if the buyer already had sufficient information at his disposal to insure. Considering that it is the buyer who nominates the ship, that will generally be complied with.

a) Frustration

If the safety regulations were imposed after the contract was concluded it could amount to a frustrating event, on account of supervening illegality for the effects of which cf the 1943 Act.

b) Rejection

The buyer has the right to reject goods if there is a breach of contract by the seller. The most likely possibility is comprised in s14(3). To establish a breach, the buyer would have to show that the particular purpose – resale – was communicated to the seller, although the observations of Lord Guest in *Ashington Piggeries* (1972) raise a presumption of communication if the sellers can be shown to have known of the purpose. However, generally, the suitability of goods for resale is up to the buyers – as the Court of Appeal made clear in *Teheran-Europe Co v S T Belton (Tractors)* (1968). If metal pistols could not be sold, on that basis, there would be no breach of s14(3). It will be difficult for the buyers to show that they relied on the skill and judgment of the seller with respect to the fitness of the goods for resale. However, the onus under s14(3) is on the seller to prove that there was no reliance by the buyer and as Lord Denning MR in Teheran-Europe said, reliance can be assumed until the contrary is proved.

As before, the purported existence of liability under s14(3) must be subjected to the requirement of reasonableness in Sch 2, even though the parties were not dealing as consumers.

iii) Mrs Smith can proceed against Robinson under s14(2) of the 1979 Act, s14(3) or sue in tort. Her contractual action will be aimed to recover damages for breach of warranty. The first limb of the rule in *Hadley* v *Baxendale* (1854) (in s53(2)) will present no difficulty – damage to her furniture as the result of defective electrical equipment, is, most probably, a direct and natural consequence.

This was the rule adopted by the trial judge in *H Parsons (Livestock) Ltd* v *Uttley Ingham & Co* (1978) and, to a certain extent, it conflicts with the formulation of the majority of the Court of Appeal, although, in this instance, there is unlikely to be any practical difference. The Court of Appeal were attempting to formulate a rule covering the recovery of consequential loss arising, after defective goods have been accepted, and stated that it sufficed that the sellers should appreciate the 'serious possibility' of physical damage, even if the severity of the loss could not reasonably have been envisaged. The trial judge had eschewed that technical approach and applied s53(2) – the first limb of the rule in *Hadley* – on the basis that the *exact* physical damage was the direct and natural consequence of the breach.

Now, assuming a breach and that the loss is not too remote, s6 of the 1977 UCTA renders any purported exclusion of ss13–15 void as against a consumer. The three requirements of 'dealing as a consumer' would have to be made out here – and Robinson Ltd would seem to be selling in the course of business, Mrs Smith was not buying in the course of business and the goods are probably those ordinarily supplied for private use. A void exclusion clause attracts penal consequences.

Alternatively, Mrs Smith could sue in tort although little would be gained by that step.

Mrs Jones' executor has exactly the same claim on the same basis and in a consumer contract, s2(1) of the 1977 Act ensures that any attempt to exclude liability for death or personal injury is *void*.

Question 5

In 1900, the Noreuropean Post Office issued a commemorative set of stamps, most of which are generally on the market except the Danish Pink and the Norwegian Blue. Scando, a dealer in rare stamps, obtains a Danish Pink and two Norwegian Blues. He agrees to sell the Danish Pink and a Norwegian Blue to Balt and the other Norwegian Blue to Perot. The contracts provide for free insurance to destination, a returnable ten per cent deposit and any outstanding sums to be paid on delivery. By mistake, Scando places the two Norwegian Blues in the envelope addressed to Balt and the Danish Pink in the envelope addressed to Perot. He hands the envelopes to Easyrider for delivery. On his way, Easyrider swerves into a canal. The envelope addressed to Perot is lost and one of the stamps in the envelope addressed to Balt is damaged by canal water.

Advise Scando, Balt and Perot.

University of London LLB Examination
(for External Students) Commercial Law June 1993 Q5

General comment

Delivery has often cropped up in past questions but usually only as a small part of an answer. It is therefore unusual to find a whole question devoted to the topic.

While this question is a gift to those students who 'just happen' to be familiar with the buyer's duty to deliver, it is a fairly specialised area. Many students might be hard put to rake together sufficiently detailed information to answer this question in the depth and at the length needed in such a way as to score high marks.

Skeleton solution

Delivery and place of delivery.

Passing of property.

Risk in transit.

Buyer's right to sue for non-delivery.

Delivery of faulty goods; buyer's right to reject, rights under s53 SGA.

Suggested solution

The duty of the seller in a contract for sale of goods includes the duty to deliver. The term 'deliver' is defined in s61(1) Sale of Goods Act 1979 (SGA) as 'a voluntary transfer of possession from one party to another'. Delivery may be actual eg physically handing over the goods, or constructive eg by handing over a document of title. Which applies here? Scando (S) obviously intends to send the stamps to Balt (B) and Perot (P) by courier; which would amount to physical delivery. At the same time however, the question mentions contract documents providing for free insurance, a

10 per cent deposit and outstanding sums to be paid on delivery. Can these contracts then be said to amount to constructive delivery? This is very doubtful, partly because the deposit is said to be returnable, and partly because cash is to be paid apparently on the actual delivery of the stamps rather than, for example, a bill of exchange or a bill of lading.

So, what, if any, is the significance of the contracts referred to? It is suggested that it may have some relevance in determining the place of delivery. Section 29(2) provides that unless the parties indicate otherwise, the place of delivery will be the seller's normal place of business. *But* s29(2) only comes into operation if the parties make no provision to the contrary. It should be noted also that cases such as *Wiskin* v *Terdich Bros* (1928) make clear that place of delivery will be inferred from such phrases as 'please send us ...'. Thus the question refers to contracts stipulating payment on delivery, thereby implying the parties' intention that place of delivery be elsewhere than the seller's place of business. Place of delivery may be important for a number of reasons, not least because it will indicate whether the seller has properly delivered the goods.

When goods are sent from seller to buyer the question often arises as to who must bear the liability if goods are lost (as with P's stamp) or deteriorate (as with B's) in transit. The seller may be in breach of s14(2) as to implied conditions on merchantability and fitness for purpose if the goods fail to withstand a normal journey. Also s32(2) of SGA makes it clear that if the damage, loss or deterioration is because the seller has failed to make adequate arrangements for carriage he will be responsible. Cases like *Thomas Young & Sons* v *Hobson & Partners* (1949) demonstrate that negligent arrangements for carriage will render the seller responsible for any loss. Is S responsible for choosing Easyrider (E) who hardly seems the most capable of despatch riders? Unless S is aware of some problem with E then usually he is not negligent. Obviously if E's rates were very cheap, or S knew he regularly lost goods entrusted to him, or kept crashing, then the situation might be different.

So, if place of delivery is to be at P's and B's homes or offices (the question merely talks of addresses without specifically saying which) then the first thing to note is that delivery is never effected at all to P. His remedies will thus differ from those of B who receives the goods, but in a damaged condition.

To look at P's situation first. By virtue of s51 SGA P has the right to sue for non-delivery of the goods. The measure of damages is the estimated loss directly and naturally resulting in the ordinary course of events, from the seller's breach of contract. The stamps are, we are told, rare. How can the value of them be estimated? The concept of 'available market' is a useful one here, (see cases such as *Esteve Trading Corporation* v *Agropec International, The Golden Rio* (1990) and *Williams* v *Agius Ltd* (1914) for more details on assessing contract prices and available market).

Does it make a difference that in packing up the stamps S sends not goods that P has ordered, but other goods which he has not? Effectively not, because property never passed anyway; it is still non-delivery. But it may make a difference to B who receives goods not only damaged, but in part, not what he ordered. B has ordered a Pink and a

Blue stamp. What he gets is two Blues, one damaged. It is not clear whether all stamps have the same value, but they are all said to be rare. Delivery of the wrong goods is covered by s30(4) which states that when goods which were contracted to be sold and delivered mixed with other goods the buyer may accept the goods which are in accordance with the contract and reject the rest. However when goods are delivered mixed with other goods of defective quality, as opposed to goods of a different description; then s30(4) will apply. What B wanted was a Blue and a Pink stamp. What he has are two Blues, one damaged. Can he accept the undamaged Blue, arguing that the Blue and the Pink are quite different goods and that by sending a pair of Blues these are quite different from a Blue and a Pink? Or will they be considered to be all generically just 'stamps' in which case s30(4) will not apply?

In practical terms it may not be all that important. If s30(4) does apply B will be able to keep the perfect Blue and reject the other as being different from the Pink he ordered. If it does not he will be able to sue for damages, only instead of damages for non-delivery like P, B will be suing under s53 SGA for breach of condition or warranty. If B seeks to reject which is presumably the case, he must make no move which might be construed as acceptance. Obviously if no delivery is effected at all, as in P's case, no rejection is necessary. But B does receive stamps and must decide as already discussed whether according to s30(4) to reject both or only the imperfect Blue. Section 53 permits the buyer to sue for breach of warranty as to merchantability and fitness. The measure of damages will be, prima facie, the difference between the value of the goods at the time of delivery and the value they would have had had they fulfilled the warranty. It should not be forgotten that S imposed a 10 per cent deposit which is, of course, recoverable.

One final point to remember is that in the case of unusual items like paintings or, in this case rare stamps, merchantability may be a difficult concept to establish (*Harlingdon & Leinster Enterprises Ltd* v *Christopher Hull Fine Art* (1990)). A painting for example might be said to be merchantable even if it is not by an attributed artist. But in this case the non-compliance with s14(3) does not consist in a quibble about the value of a rare stamp, but involves water-damage. No stamp, rare or otherwise, could be said to be merchantable following immersion in a canal.

2 INTERNATIONAL SALES CONTRACTS

2.1 Introduction

International sales naturally involve the transport and shipment of goods between different countries. Over the years, international traders have evolved highly specialised forms of contracts which reflect the fact that most of their business is transacted at great distance. The terminology, which is very specific, denotes the obligations which mercantile law implies into such contracts.

Thus, for example, fob (meaning free on board) signifies that the seller places the goods on the agreed ship and bears the expenses of getting them onto the ship; thereafter the buyer takes responsibility for the additional expenses incurred in importing them into his own country. Similarly, the term ex works means that the buyer must take possession of the goods at the seller's warehouse and pay the expenses incurred in the transport of the goods to his own premises.

These descriptions also determine the point at which property and risk in the goods passes from the seller to the buyer.

In the following key points the main types of international sales contracts will be considered and contrasted against each other. Detailed consideration of the two most popular types of contracts – fob and cif – will be reserved until the next chapter but will be briefly considered at this stage in order to place them into their proper context.

2.2 Key points

a) *The elements involved in an international sales contract*

Unlike a sales contract between a buyer and a seller in the same country, an international sales contract involves incurring expenses in addition to the price. The apportionment of liability for such charges is resolved according to the type of international sales contract selected by the parties.

Typically there are four separate charges involved in an international sales transaction:

    i)   payment of the price for the goods;

    ii) the cost of the contract of carriage for transportation of the goods from the seller to the buyer whether by land, sea, air or a combination of each of these;

   iii) a charge made for the insurance of the goods during transportation;

   iv) charges imposed by national authorities for the importation and exportation of goods including customs duties, taxes and the costs of obtaining import and export licences.

Liability for these charges is translated into rights and duties on the part of the buyer and the seller respectively. Which party will bear responsibility for these costs will depend on the terms of the sales contract.

The form of contract selected also decides the rights and duties of the parties vis-à-vis other considerations other than those which are purely financial. For example, passing of property, risk in the goods and delivery each vary according to the type of contract.

b) *The use of trade terms*

Trade terms have been developed through usage to facilitate and simplify international sales transactions. When these terms are used, the parties are deemed to have fixed their respective rights and duties in law and cannot evade these responsibilities in the absence of an express exclusion.

Countries have developed different terms for this purpose but the influence of English law in this respect has been significant. Many of the terms used in other jurisdictions have been adopted from the English legal terminology.

The International Chamber of Commerce has successfully introduced a codification of these terms as a widely accepted uniform system which allows the buyer and seller to establish their rights and duties by reference to standard terms. These standard contract forms are known as INCOTERMS. The latest set of INCOTERMS is the 1990 revision which entered into force on 1 July 1990.

Where reference is made in a sales agreement to the application of these terms, this body of rules is adopted into the contract. But, in the absence of an express incorporation, the contract will be interpreted according to the law of the legal system which applies to the contractual relationship. INCOTERMS are not automatically imported into a contract by English law and it is important to note that in some cases, especially cif contracts, there are differences in the obligations of the parties under the INCOTERMS in contrast to the common law.

c) *Ex works, ex factory or ex warehouse contracts*

When the contract is ex works, ex factory or ex warehouse, the foreign purchaser, or his agent, is required to collect the goods at the location at whichever of these locations the seller makes the goods available.

According to the INCOTERMS, the seller is required to perform the following duties:

- i) to supply goods in conformity with the contract of sale;
- ii) to place the goods at the disposal of the buyer at point of delivery named by the buyer and for the loading of the goods onto the choice of vehicle provided by the buyer;
- iii) to provide, at his own expense, any packaging necessary to enable the buyer to take delivery of the goods;
- iv) to give the buyer reasonable notice of when the goods will be available;
- v) to bear all risks and expenses in the goods until they have been placed at the disposal of the buyer as provided in the contract;
- vi) to render the buyer every assistance in obtaining any documents which are issued in the country of delivery or origin and which the buyer may require for the purposes of exportation and/or importation.

In turn the buyer is obliged to do the following:

- i) to take delivery of the goods as soon as they are placed at his disposal by the buyer at the place and the time provided for in the contract;
- ii) to bear all charges and risks in the goods from the time they have been placed at his disposal;
- iii) to pay all customs duties and taxes which are levied on the goods by reason of their exportation;
- iv) pay all costs and charges incurred in obtaining the necessary exportation and importation documentation involved in the transportation of the goods.

The purchase price is due on delivery of the goods unless the parties have made alternative arrangements for payment.

It is obvious that this type of contract is the most onerous arrangement for the buyer and least onerous for the seller. As we move through the remaining terms, the burdens will gradually grow on the part of the seller and gradually decrease as far as the buyer is concerned.

d) *Free alongside ship (fas) contracts*

Where the goods are to be delivered 'free alongside ship', the seller's responsibilities under the contract are discharged when he or she delivers the goods at the side of the ship where they can be loaded on board the vessel. Usually, the buyer nominates the port of shipment where the goods are to be loaded. Hence the contract specification is usually described as fas (named port of shipment).

Given this is the point of delivery, the seller's obligations are as follows:

- i) to supply goods in conformity with the contract of sale;

ii) to deliver the goods alongside the ship at the port named by the buyer at the date or within the period stipulated and to notify the buyer that the goods have been delivered alongside the vessel;

iii) to render the buyer every assistance in obtaining any documents which are issued in the country of delivery or origin and which the buyer may require for the purposes of exportation and/or importation;

iv) to bear all risks and expenses of the goods until they have been effectively delivered alongside the vessel at the named port of shipment;

v) to provide, at his own expense, any packaging necessary to enable the goods to be shipped;

vi) to obtain at his own expense the customary clean document of proof of delivery of the goods alongside the vessel;

vii) to supply the buyer, at his request and expense, with a certificate of origin for the goods;

viii) to render the buyer, at his request, risk and expense, every assistance in obtaining any documents required to export the goods.

The buyer takes over responsibility for the goods at the port of shipment and therefore his duties are as follows:

i) to give the seller due notice of the named port, loading berth and delivery dates;

ii) to bear all the charges and risks of the goods from the time when they have been effectively delivered alongside the vessel at the named port of shipment and pay the price as provided in the contract;

iii) to pay any additional costs incurred because the vessel named by him has failed to arrive on time, or is unable to take the goods on board, and to bear all the risks in the goods from the time when the seller has placed the goods at his or her disposal;

iv) in the event that the buyer fails to name the vessel in time or give detailed instructions to the seller, he or she must bear any additional costs incurred due to such failure;

v) to pay all costs and charges incurred in obtaining the necessary exportation and importation documentation involved in the transportation of the goods.

As an additional point, the buyer has the duty to nominate a suitable ship for the transport of the goods unless the parties have expressly agreed other arrangements.

e) *Free on board (fob) contracts*

With an fob contract, the seller assumes even greater responsibilities for the transportation of the goods such as the obligation to place them on board a ship that has been notified to him or her by the buyer. The respective liabilities of the parties under such a contract differ slightly under the INCOTERMS in contrast to the common law position, but for the present we shall continue to examine the rights and duties under the INCOTERMS in order to remain consistent. The points of departure between the two regimes will be considered in more detail in the next chapter.

The INCOTERMS identify the following duties of the seller in an fob contract:

i) to supply goods in conformity with the contract of sale;

ii) to deliver the goods on board a vessel named by the buyer at the port named by the buyer at the date or within the period stipulated and to notify the buyer that the goods have been delivered aboard the vessel;

iii) to obtain any export licences or other governmental approvals required for the exportation of the goods;

iv) to bear all risks and expenses of the goods until they have been effectively delivered over the ship's rail at the named port of shipment;

v) to provide, at his own expense, any packaging necessary to enable the goods to be shipped;

vi) to obtain at his own expense the customary clean document of proof of delivery of the goods on board the named vessel;

vii) to supply the buyer, at his request and expense, with a certificate of origin for the goods;

viii) to render the buyer, at his request, risk and expense, every assistance in obtaining a bill of lading and any other documents necessary for the importation of the goods into the country of destination.

In turn, the buyer is required to fulfil the following duties:

i) at his or her own expense to charter a vessel or reserve the necessary space on board a vessel and give the seller due notice of the name of the vessel and the delivery dates;

ii) to bear all the costs and risks of the goods from the time when they have effectively passed the ship's rail at the named port of shipment and pay the price as provided in the contract;

iii) to pay any additional costs incurred because the vessel named by him has failed to arrive on the stipulated date or is unable to take the goods on board, and to bear all the risks in the goods from the time when the seller has placed the goods at his or her disposal;

iv) in the event that the buyer fails to name the vessel in time or give detailed instructions to the seller, he or she must bear any additional costs incurred due to such failure;

v) to pay any costs and charges for obtaining a bill of lading if required;

vi) to pay all costs and charges incurred in obtaining the necessary exportation and importation documentation involved in the transportation of the goods.

Note carefully the nature of these rights and duties at this point since these will be elaborated on in the following chapter.

f) *Cost, insurance and freight (cif) contracts*

As Lord Wright has observed, cif sales contracts are 'a type of contract which is more widely and more frequently in use than any other contract used for the purposes of seaborne commerce': *T D Bailey, Son & Co* v *Ross T Smyth & Co Ltd* (1940) 56 TLR 825.

In general, in a cif contract the port of destination is expressly specified. Hence, the normal form of the contract will be cif (named port of destination). The named port of destination will normally be a port in the buyer's country.

Under a cif contract, the obligations of the seller are onerous. He or she must perform the following functions:

i) to supply the goods in conformity with the contract of sale;

ii) to procure a contract of carriage by sea under which the goods will be delivered at the destination specified in the contract;

iii) to arrange for an insurance contract in terms current in the trade which will be made available for the benefit of the purchaser;

iv) to obtain any export licences or other governmental approvals required for the exportation of the goods;

v) to bear all risks and expenses of the goods until they have been effectively delivered over the ship's rail at the named port of destination;

vi) to provide, at his own expense, any packaging necessary to enable the goods to be shipped;

vii) to obtain at his own expense the customary clean document of proof of delivery of the goods on board the named vessel;

viii) to supply the buyer, at his request and expense, with a certificate of origin for the goods;

ix) to render the buyer, at his request, risk and expense, every assistance in obtaining a bill of lading and any other documents necessary for the importation of the goods into the country of destination.

The buyer's obligations are generally restricted to the following duties:

i) to pay the price specified in the contract;

ii) to obtain any necessary import licences and to carry out all customs formalities required for the importation of the goods;

iii) to take delivery of the goods at the port of destination;

iv) to bear the risks of loss or damage to the goods from the time they have passed over the ship's rail at the port of shipment.

g) *Delivered ex quay (duty paid) (deq) contracts*

International sales contracts on deq terms are infrequently used for exports from the United Kingdom because normally the seller will not wish to bear responsibility for the processing of the goods at the port of destination. This is the major additional responsibility of the seller in addition to those in the cif contract, namely to accept responsibility for the import duties and unloading charges payable at the port of destination.

h) *Delivered duty paid (ddp) contracts*

Ddp contracts are the most favourable available to the buyer. It means that the seller bears all costs, expenses and risks in getting the goods to the place specified by the seller, usually his or her place of business in the country of importation.

2.3 Relevant materials

International Chamber of Commerce, INCOTERMS 1990.

D Campbell, *Remedies for International Sellers of Goods* (1993).

Hoyle, *Cases and Materials on the Law of International Trade* (1989), pp23–48.

J F Wilson, *Carriage of Goods by Sea* (1993).

Benjamin's Sale of Goods (4th edition, 1992), pp1310–1374.

2.4 Analysis of questions

Questions on international sales contracts other than fob or cif have been relatively rare in University of London examinations, yet to omit to consider the other variants of sales contract in a work of this nature would be a serious omission which would render the work incomplete. Hence, the majority of questions in this section have been prepared by the author.

It is rare for a question to arise on this subject without reference to other topics such as, for example, the issue of financing of the transaction or defects in the goods. Hence, answers to such questions tend to be relatively long. Nevertheless, it is a worthwhile exercise to consider the following questions in detail in order to verify how the rights and duties of the buyers and sellers in these contracts vary from those in fob and cif contracts.

2.5 Questions

Question 1

Outline the problems presented by sales transactions conducted by parties in different countries. How, in practice, are these problems overcome by the techniques adopted in international commercial transactions?

Question prepared by the Editor
April 1994

General comment

A simple, straightforward essay-type question to start this section. The question is not really legal in the sense that it asks about the practical difficulties of conducting international sales. Yet, it is a good place to start because it is necessary to think about the real problems for which certain commercial practices have been adopted.

Skeleton solution

Distance and mutual distrust as factors which must be overcome.

The use of standard trade terms, ie INCOTERMS.

The choice of law in the contract.

Alternative methods of payment – direct payment and open account.

Documentary credits and letters of credit as means of ensuring against non-payment and non-delivery.

Suggested solution

In an international sales contract, the buyer and seller are, by definition, located in different countries. It may easily be the case that they have never dealt with each other before and are therefore unaware of each other's commercial practices, creditworthiness or viability. In other words, distance engenders a certain degree of mutual distrust which may or may not be justified in reality. This is particularly the case when companies are importing or exporting to a new market for the first time.

Consider for a moment the practical difficulties raised by the very fact of physical distance. The parties will not generally meet and negotiations are conducted by correspondence or telephone. Hence, international sales contracts are rarely formal documents produced as a result of intensive negotiations; there is simply not the opportunity to conduct business in this manner. Although standardised forms of contract are extensively used in some types of transactions, generally a more simplified method is required otherwise international trade would suffer from thrombosis.

The fact that there is rarely as formal contract does not mean that there is no binding contract between the buyer and seller. Generally the buyer or seller makes an offer using certain trade terms which is accepted by the other party, or a qualified acceptance is made which itself constitutes an offer requiring acceptance. It is the use of these trade terms that simplifies the process and yet allows the parties to determine their respective rights and duties to a sufficient degree.

Trade terms are simply standard terms accepted in international trade as meaning a particular type of contract. The most commonly used trade terms are the INCOTERMS, which are a set of standard contracts which can be imported into the contract by the parties. The INCOTERMS have been prepared by the International Chamber of Commerce but do not apply unless they are expressly incorporated into the contract. They have no binding force of law. Other trade terms may be adopted by the parties but no other set of terms are as widely recognised as INCOTERMS.

The fact that the buyer and seller are in different countries means that both will be subject to different legal systems and that the law which applies to the contract will be one of these, or the law of a third country if both parties agree. Which legal system applies depends to a large degree on the relative negotiating strengths of the parties. In any event, an applicable law must be included in the contract; failure to do so will create legal uncertainty in the interpretation and application of the contract.

As the goods must be transported from one country to another, additional expense will be incurred than would otherwise be the case if the contract was purely domestic. As a general rule, in an international trade transaction the difference in the price quoted for the goods in a domestic sale and that in the international sale will be due to these additional costs. In terms of transport costs, it will be necessary to pay for inland transport for delivery of the goods to the port of shipment, dock dues, freight forwarding charges and the cost of ocean transport.

In addition to pure transport costs, there will also be charges for customs duties (import and export), the costs for obtaining export or export licences, and charges for customs procedures. Again, due to the risks involved in sea and ocean transportation, insurance cover may be required to cover the risk of destruction or damage during the voyage. Once the goods arrive at the port of destination, costs will be incurred to carry the goods from the vessel to the buyer's warehouse or place of business.

It is essential that both parties are aware of their respective responsibilities and liabilities for these charges when the sales contract is entered into. Obviously, where the seller undertakes to pay for some or all of these expenses, the amount which will eventually be charged on the invoice will be greater than if the goods were simply picked up at the seller's warehouse. Nevertheless, the liabilities of the parties for these expenses must be determined at the outset of the contract in order that responsibility for breach of one of these duties can be apportioned. For example, if under the contract it is the seller's responsibility to insure the goods in transit, then failure to do so will render the seller liable in the event that the goods are not delivered in accordance with the contractual description.

Responsibility for delivery of the goods is only one side of the sales contract; the other side is the obligation to make payment. Here, the seller may be reluctant to pay in advance in case the buyer is not creditworthy or will find fault with the goods for no valid reason and refuse to pay. Conversely, the buyer may not wish to part with the money for the goods unless he or she is sure that goods of the contractual description will be delivered. Hence, payment in advance is only made in the situation where the level of trust between the parties is extremely high. Similarly, open account trade, where sales are credited to an account, are normally only used in three situations:

a) where the buyer and seller have been dealing with each other over a prolonged period and have developed a relationship of absolute trust;

b) where the buyer and seller are located in geographically proximate countries which allow domestic type payment to be made; and

c) where the buyer and seller are members of the same international organisation.

The alternative is to use documentary credits to make payment. The most common type of credit is a letter of credit which is simply an undertaking made by a bank, on behalf of the purchaser, to the seller that payment will be made on presentation of the necessary documents. So, a seller can present documents of title, such as an invoice, a bill of lading and an insurance document, to a bank in his country to obtain payment. The bank in the seller's country remits the documents of title to the corresponding bank in the buyer's country, which passes them on to the buyer in exchange for the sum paid and a commission. The buyer uses the documents to collect the goods once they arrive in the port of destination.

By this means, the exposure of both the buyer and seller to non-delivery of the goods or non-payment of the price is minimised. The bank will not pay the seller unless the documents of title confirm that the goods conform to those of the contractual description and that the expenses attributable to the seller have been paid. Similarly, the seller can be assured of payment for the goods before they come under the control of the buyer. In practice, this is considered to be a reasonable apportionment of risks for non-payment and non-delivery.

As we can see from the above, it is the element of distance that causes much of the inconvenience in international sales transactions. However, commerce has developed sufficient mechanisms to overcome this inconvenience. Further, there is even a certain degree of flexibility built into many of these mechanisms to cater for the interests of both the buyer and seller.

Question 2

Explain the significance of INCOTERMS in the conduct of international transactions. To what extent are these rules a codification of the law of international sale of goods?

Question prepared by the Editor
April 1994

General comment

Another essay-type question requiring a narrative answer. The question does not, however, require full elaboration of the different terms, but instead the focus of the question is on the role of these particular terms in international commerce.

Skeleton solution

The origins of the INCOTERMS and the role of the ICC.

Incorporation of INCOTERMS into the law of some countries; the position in English law.

The eight major terms used in practice.

The example of fas and ddp contracts as illustrations of the buyer's and seller's respective rights and liabilities.

Suggested solution

In practice, the use of INCOTERMS in international trade is extremely common. They provide a useful and practical body of rules which allow buyers and sellers to fix their respective rights and duties in any international sales transactions. In other words, by referring to a particular INCOTERMS a Germany company, for example, can sell goods to a UK company with both parties being certain of their responsibilities and liabilities in the transaction.

The terms themselves are published by the International Chamber of Commerce (ICC) which, although not a public international organisation, has consultative status with the United Nations. The ICC is a private body constituted by national chambers of commerce with the object of facilitating international business.

In addition to the INCOTERMS, the ICC has also published codes on other aspects of international business, including the Uniform Customs and Practice for Documentary Credits (UCP 500) which is the primary source of law for documentary credits. It has also adopted uniform rules for combined transport documents, commercial agency as well as uniform rules for contract guarantees.

The latest edition of the INCOTERMS was published in 1990 and came into effect in July 1990. The present edition updates the previous edition mainly by tackling the problems brought about by modern communications. Nevertheless, most of the actual terms themselves remain fundamentally unchanged.

In some countries such as Spain, the terms have statutory effect. In other countries, including France and West Germany, the terms are regarded as international custom and are applied unless the parties indicate an intention to the contrary. In the United States, businessmen are recommended by the Department of Commerce to use the terms to regulate their transactions.

The United Kingdom is different in this respect. The terms do not have statutory effect and do not apply to a commercial transaction unless the parties expressly or impliedly agree that the rules are incorporated into their contract. However, in practice, this is frequently the case. Since referring to the terms is one of the most simple ways of ascertaining the rights and duties of the parties, contracts of sale are often constituted by using these terms. In the absence of incorporation, the common law rules regulating agreements such as fob and cif contracts will apply. The distinction is important because the English common law rules for such arrangements differ slightly from the corresponding terms of the INCOTERMS.

There are essentially eight major INCOTERMS. These are as follows:

Exw	–	Ex works
Fas	–	Free alongside ship
Fob	–	Free on board
Cfr	–	Cost and freight
Cif	–	Cost, insurance and freight
Cpt	–	Carriage paid to
Des	–	Delivered ex ship
Ddp	–	Delivered duty paid

As one moves down this list, the liabilities of the seller for the costs of carriage, insurance, etc increase and the corresponding duties of the buyer decrease. For example, if the contract is fas, the seller must bear all the expenses incurred in delivering the goods to the port where the ship is waiting to load them. However, where the contract is ddp, the seller must bear all costs up to the point where the goods are delivered to the buyer's nominated place of business in his own country.

By selecting a particular term, responsibilities for these costs can be allocated between the parties. It is this prospect which is one of the most attractive aspects of using the terms.

Question 3

Selim contracts to sell the following goods:

a) To Barbara, 500 tons Western White Wheat cfr Liverpool; the wheat is shipped from New York on 1 June; on 5 June, the carrying vessel sinks; on 6 June, Selim tenders the shipping documents to Barbara.

b) To Betty, 1,000 gallons Australian perfume des *Mangel* at Liverpool; Betty fails to pay Selim for a previous cargo (of cork hats, which she has been unable to resell), so Selim orders the master of the *Mangel* to deliver the perfume to Thurstan, a friend of Selim's to whom Selim wishes to make a present of the perfume.

c) To Billy, 60 chainsaws. Billy contracts to resell them to Tom, and instructs Selim to deliver them to Tom. Six weeks after delivery of the chainsaws, two of Tom's customers complain to Tom that they have been injured because of defects in the chainsaws. Tom recalls all the chainsaws which he has sold, reimburses his customers for their losses and returns the whole consignment to Billy, from whom he claims repayment.

Advise Barbara, Betty and Billy.

University of London LLB Examination
(for External Students) Commercial Law June 1990 Q6

General comment

This is a problem in three parts, but in fact each part must be treated separately as there is little overlap. The third part of the question is not strictly a matter of international trade law but has been retained in order to provide a full specimen of an actual exam question.

Skeleton solution

a) Definition of cfr, effects thereof, documents of title in relation thereto, frustration of contract by natural disaster.

b) Des contracts – definitions thereof, implications of such contract, rights and duties of parties to cfr contract.

c) Defects in products. Consumer Protection Act – SGA 1979 s14(2) and (3).

37

Suggested solution

a) In this contract we are told that the wheat has been shipped from New York on 1st June and that four days later the ship sinks; two days subsequent to the sinking the seller (Selim) tenders the shipping documents to the buyer (Barbara). The contract has been made 'cfr'. This stands for 'cost and freight'; the basis of the agreement is that the seller has to arrange the carriage of the goods to the named foreign port of destination at his (ie the seller's) expense but not at his risk (which latter ceases when he places the goods on board ship at the place of shipment). In one aspect the 'cfr' contract differs from the cif contract (namely the seller does not have to arrange marine insurance, but if he does then this must be paid for at his expense). In all other respects it is the same.

The essential element that is missing then in the contract is that of insurance. Sometimes a 'cfr' contract will contain words such as 'insurance to be effected by the buyer' and it has been held that these words are not merely declaratory but amount to a contractual obligation on the part of the buyer to take out the usual insurance policy (see *Reinhart Co* v *Joshua Hoyle & Sons Ltd* (1961)). So we are presented with a situation where the goods are placed on the ship and ostensibly where the seller has discharged his responsibilities. In the absence of express agreement to the matter of insurance it must be decided who bears the loss of the wheat and also whether or not the seller is lawfully entitled to tender documents of title after the loss of the goods in ocean transit and thus claim the purchase price of the goods.

It has been held that even though goods are lost in a cif contract the seller still has the lawful right to tender the documents of title and to claim the purchase price - even in one case where the seller 'knew' the goods were lost when he offered the documents (*Manbre Saccharine Co* v *Corn Products Co* (1919)). As already stated, the same principles apply in cif and cfr contracts and thus the tender of documents to claim the price is lawful. The buyer's usual remedy is a claim against the carrier either on the basis of the latter's negligence or because the buyer is an assignee of the bill of lading. There is one (albeit small) possibility of a claim by Barbara against Selim here and that is that if, contrary to the terms of s32(3) of Sale of Goods Act 1979 the seller has failed to give adequate notice of the shipment of the goods to enable the buyer sufficient time to insure the goods, then the goods would travel, exceptionally at the seller's and not the buyer's risk - but this does not appear to be the case as Barbara's claim will be against the carriers.

b) This contract is expressed to be 'des' Mangel and is for 1,000 gallons of perfume. There appears to be some dispute about a previous contract for shipment by Selim to Betty of cork mats, and in respect of these Selim appears to be an 'unpaid seller'; Betty's excuse for not paying being related directly to her inability to resell goods delivered to her under a contract of sale.

The Judicial Committee of the Privy Council examined and defined the meaning of an 'ex-ship' contract, which was the term which preceded des, as denoting 'that the seller has to cause delivery to be made to the buyer from a ship which has arrived at the port of delivery and has reached a place in which is usual for the delivery of goods of the kind in question.'

The clause is also contained and defined in the INCOTERMS that regulate such international shipping contracts. The nature of the obligations under the term des are that the seller has to pay the freight and the buyer is only bound to pay the purchase price if actual delivery of the goods is made at the stipulated port of delivery. Thus if for example, the goods are lost in transit the buyer is not obliged to pay the price upon tender of the documents and can in certain cases claim the price he paid in advance.

Thus the property in the goods will only pass (unless otherwise agreed) when the goods are handed over to the buyer after arrival of the ship at the agreed port of destination.

The seller herein appears to have exercised his right of 'stoppage in transit in accordance with s45 Sale of Goods Act 1979'; under this section three conditions must be present before the right to stop in transit arises. Namely

1) The goods must be in transit and the goods are in transit when they have passed out of possession of the seller into possession of an independent carrier.

2) The seller must be an unpaid seller.

3) The buyer must be insolvent.

All three of these conditions appear to have been satisfied in particular the third one as under s61(4) SGA 1979 a person is 'deemed to be insolvent with the meaning of the Act if he has either ceased to pay his debts in the ordinary course of business or he cannot pay his debts as they become due ...'. The goods are in transit according to section 45(1) 'goods are deemed to be in transit from the time when they are delivered to a carrier ... for the purpose of transmission to the buyer ... until the buyer or his agent in that behalf, takes delivery of them from the carrier.

As delivery has not taken place this appears to be the valid exercise of the remedy of stoppage in transit by Selim which Betty will have no defence against.

c) Selim has contracted to sell 60 chainsaws to Billy who in turn has re-sold them to Tom; it appears that the goods have not been delivered to Billy who has instructed Selim to act on his behalf and deliver them on to Tom. When, six weeks later Tom's customers are injured by defects in the saws, Tom takes the prudent step of re-calling them and he also reimburses his customers and returns the goods to Billy from whom he bought them. We are concerned therefore with the duties of the seller and the retailer and possibly also the manufacturer (we do not know if Selim has manufactured the goods).

There are statutory duties imposed upon sellers under s14(2) and (3) Sale of Goods 1979 which are 'inalienable'; the seller is liable in this respect for 'merchantable quality' and 'fitness for purpose' without proof of lack of care on his part, in other words liability is strict. A common law expedient available to a seller who receives defective goods from a manufacturer and sells them on to the buyer is that of breach of implied warranty. If the buyer sues the seller fro breach of warranty of fitness for purpose then the seller may sue his manufacturer and in turn claim an indemnity (eg *Dodd* v *Wilson* (1946)).

Product liability is now covered by the Consumer Protection Act 1987 and the basic principles of protection for consumers are contained therein. These are that any person who suffers damage which is caused by a defective product, is entitled to sue the producer without being required to prove fault. Section 5(1) of the CPA defines damage as 'death or personal injury or any loss of damage to any property (including land)'.

It appears therefore, that Tom can return the goods to Bill and claim damages under SGA 1979 s14(2) and (3). Additionally, the two injured customers can claim against the manufacturer under CPA 1987 if they can prove their injuries resulted from the defects in the product. Billy will be entitled to recover the price paid for the products from the manufacturer and damages for loss of profit.

3 FOB AND CIF SALES CONTRACTS

3.1 Introduction

3.2 Key points

3.3 Recent cases and statutes

3.4 Relevant materials

3.5 Analysis of questions

3.6 Questions

3.1 Introduction

Since fob and cif international sales contracts are the most commonly used means of effecting sales transactions across frontiers, this is an important topic of study in the subject of international trade. This is reflected in the frequency of questions which arise in examinations and the reason that a whole chapter has been dedicated in this WorkBook to these two types of contracts.

In this chapter, we shall examine the obligations of the parties under fob and cif contracts separately and in sufficient detail to allow for the proper tackling of questions. It should be noted that the rights and duties of buyers and sellers differ significantly between these two different contracts and attention should be paid in order not to confuse the different legal regimes which apply.

3.2 Key points

Free on board (fob)

a) *Definition*

The fob international sales contract is a flexible instrument but, in its most basic form, requires the seller to place the goods on board a vessel nominated by the buyer within the stipulated contractual period.

The three most common variants of fob contracts have been distinguished by the Court of Appeal in *The El Amria and El Minia* [1982] 2 Lloyd's Rep 28, in the following terms:

'In *Pyrene & Co* v *Scindia Steam Navigation Co* Mr Justice Devlin instanced three types of fob contract. In the first, or classic type, the buyer nominates the ship and the seller puts the goods on board for account of the buyer, procuring a bill of lading. The seller is then a party to the contract of carriage and if he has taken the bill of lading to his order, the only contract of carriage to which the buyer can become a party is that contained in the bill of lading which is endorsed to him by the seller. The second is a variant of the first, in that the seller arranges for the ship to come on the berth, but the legal incidents are the same. The third is where the seller puts the goods on board, takes a mate's receipt and gives this to the buyer or his agent who then takes a bill of lading. In this latter type the buyer is a party to the contract of carriage *ab initio*.'

Notwithstanding these variants, the basic concepts such as delivery, property and risk remain common to each.

b) *The obligations of the parties under an fob contract*

Since the fob contract is inherently flexible the respective rights and duties of the parties cannot be separated in the same way as they can in a cif contract. The most convenient method of describing the rights and duties of the parties is to consider these obligations under a strict fob contract and then to describe the deviations for the other variants later.

i) Identification of the port of shipment

The due delivery point is the port of shipment, usually designated by the buyer in the contract of sale. Failure on the part of the buyer to nominate the port of shipment when specified in the contract, or alternatively failure to notify the seller of the nomination by an agreed date, may amount to a breach of condition precedent: see *Gill & Duffus* v *Société Pour l'Exportation des Sucres SA* [1985] 1 Lloyd's Rep 621.

ii) Date of shipment

In an fob contract a date or period of shipment for the goods will normally be specified. Until the buyer has made an effective nomination of the date of shipment, the seller's obligation to have the goods ready to load at the port does not arise: see *Cunningham* v *Munro* (1922) 28 Com Cas 42.

Unless the contract provides that the buyer's nomination is final, he or she is not confined to the single nomination and may substitute an earlier nomination with a subsequent one provided that the substitute nomination is made in time: see *Cargill UK Ltd* v *Continental Can* [1989] 2 Lloyd's Rep 290. However, the parties may also expressly or impliedly preclude substitution.

If the buyer substitutes one nomination for another one, the seller's expenses incurred by reason of the substitution are his own loss in the absence of an express or implied contractual stipulation to the contrary. In order to protect the seller from such an eventuality, three terms may be used:

- a clause is incorporated which restricts the parties' ability to substitute nominations to a specific period;

- a clause may be included to extend the shipping period in the event of a substituted nomination; or

- a prohibition on substituted nomination may be added to the contract.

iii) Nomination of the vessel

The buyer also is required to nominate a particular vessel. The nomination must be made and communicated to the seller within a reasonable period to allow the seller sufficient time to complete the loading by the end of the shipping period: see *Bunge & Co v Tradax England* [1975] 2 Lloyd's Rep 235.

Again in the absence of a contractual stipulation to the contrary, in a strict fob contract, it is the buyer's duty to procure shipping space on the nominated vessel.

iv) The seller's duty to load the goods

The seller is required to place the goods aboard the ship nominated or designated by the buyer and the goods must comply with the contractual description, quality and quantity and must be sufficiently packed to withstand the rigours of the voyage.

The duty to load is generally considered to have been discharged when the goods have passed over the ship's rail, even if the goods were in mid-air when they were lost: *Pyrene & Co v Scindia Navigation Co* [1954] 2 QB 402.

The method of loading specified in the contract is a strict obligation and the seller is not entitled to load by any other means.

v) The duty to procure an export licence

Again the seller is required to procure any export licences which are required even though he or she may not be the actual shipper. The standard of duty is to use his or her best endeavours and failure to do so will operate to frustrate the contract: *Pagnan SpA v Tradax Ocean Transportation SA* [1987] 2 Lloyd's Rep 342.

vi) Delivery of the documents

Unless otherwise agreed, the seller must furnish the buyer with the documents necessary to allow the buyer to obtain possession of the goods from the carrier at the port of destination. This need not be a bill of lading and usually is another form of documentation such as a mate's receipt which enables the buyer to exchange the receipt for a bill of lading.

If any export or other licences are procured by the seller, these too must be transferred to the buyer.

The seller must furnish the required documents within a reasonable period of completing the loading of the goods onto the vessel.

In the absence of agreement to the contrary, the seller can demand payment in exchange for the documents since the delivery obligation in s28 of the SGA 1979 is deemed to be satisfied by the furnishing of the documents.

vii) Buyer's obligations for expenses and payment of the price

The buyer must pay all expenses connected with the contract of carriage after shipment, including the charges for insurance, freight and import licences.

The buyer must also fulfil any arrangements made for the method of payment and failure to do so is a repudiatory breach: see *Warde* v *Feedex International Inc* [1985] 2 Lloyd's Rep 289. For example, failure by the buyer to set up a letter of credit facility in favour of the seller when required under the contract amounts to such a breach: *Transpetrol Ltd* v *Transol Olieprodukten Nederland BV* [1989] 1 Lloyd's Rep 309.

c) *Variations under a classic fob contract*

The main characteristics of the classic fob contract are that the seller will make the contract of carriage either as principal or as the buyer's agent by taking out a bill of lading and will then transfer the bill of lading to the buyer.

The buyer remains obliged to nominate the ship and the duties relating to the identification of the port of shipment, the date of loading, loading itself and the procurement of export licences will apply in like manner as under a strict fob contract.

In addition, the seller must also make the contract of carriage in accordance with the contract of sale which must satisfy the following requirements:

i) the contract must be for carriage with the agreed, nominated or designated ship;

ii) the goods must be stowed in a manner in accordance with any stipulations in the contract or, in the absence of an express term, in a manner customary to the transport of the type of goods;

iii) the contract of carriage must specify that the ship will sail within the agreed shipping period;

iv) the transit must comply with the stipulations as to route in the contract of sale;

v) unless deviation is permitted by the terms of the contract, the contract of carriage must be for direct transit to the port of destination.

Again the buyer must pay for the goods on receipt of conforming documents in the manner specified in the contract of sale.

d) *Variations under an extended fob contract*

In an extended fob the seller is the principal to the contract of carriage and has the duty to nominate the ship and the time of shipment. Any one or more of the other duties on the buyer in the strict and classic fob contract will be excluded by the express terms of the contract.

Cost, insurance, freight (cif)

a) *Definition*

When goods are purchased under a cif contract, the obligations of the seller end only when he ships the goods to the port of shipment specified in the contract, at his own expense, and insures the goods under a policy of marine insurance for the sea voyage in terms usual for the type of goods and voyage involved.

The letters 'cif' indicate the three separate types of contracts involved: cost (the sale contract), insurance (the contract of insurance) and freight (the contract of carriage). It should be noted that not all these contracts are negotiated directly between the buyer and the seller. Thus, for example, the seller contracts with an insurer to procure the insurance policy even though the buyer will normally be the beneficiary under the policy.

Since the contract involves the use of documents, the cif contract has been described as 'a contract for the sale of goods to be performed by the delivery of documents': *Arnold Karlberg* v *Blythe* [1916] 1 KB 495. The documents which must be delivered to the buyer are usually the following:

i) a shipped bill of lading covering the contract goods and no others or some other document specified by the buyer;

ii) a commercial invoice representing the goods;

iii) a policy of insurance for the goods for the duration of the sea voyage or a certificate of insurance if permitted by the terms of the contract.

In addition, the following documents may also be required:

i) a certificate of inspection from a competent inspectorate;

ii) a certificate of quality from a designated authority.

The seller completes performance of the contract by delivering to the buyer or his authorised agent (often his bank) all the documents required under a cif contract. If the seller presents the buyer or his authorised agent with the conforming documents the buyer is required to pay the price even if at the time the documents are tendered the goods have been lost: see *Gill & Duffus* v *Berger* [1984] AC 382.

b) *Identifying a contract as a cif contract*

Although the parties often state that the contract is to be on cif terms, the true nature of a contract may only be ascertained by an examination of all its terms; on occasion such an analysis reveals that the contract in question is not truly cif. The contract may take on a different form depending on how the parties exercise any options they might have under its terms.

In deciding whether a contract is cif, the description as cif adopted by the parties is important but not decisive. As Lord Porter observed:

'The true effect of all [the contract's] terms must be taken into account, though of course, the description cif must not be ignored entirely': *Comptoir D'Achat et de Vente du Boerebond Belge SA* v *Louis de Ridder Lda, The Julia* [1949] AC 293.

The general rule is that if the variations from the normal cif terms are far-reaching, they may have the effect of destroying the cif nature of the contract: see *DI Henry* v *Clasen* [1973] 1 Lloyd's Rep 159.

c) *The obligations of the cif seller*

The duties of a seller under a cif contract are relatively onerous than under fob contracts and may be summarised in the following terms.

   i)   Shipment of the goods

In general, under a cif contract the seller is required to ship the goods unless the terms of the contract relieves him or her of this obligation. Shipment of the goods is also the reference point at which the performance of the seller's obligations in relation to the conformity of the goods to the express or implied terms of the contract is tested.

The seller is required to load the goods on a vessel nominated by himself. Failure of the nominated vessel to arrive at the port of loading in time amounts to a repudiatory breach of the contract by the seller unless the breach is waived by the buyer: see *Nova Petroleum International Establishment* v *Tricon Trading Ltd* [1989] 1 Lloyd's Rep 312.

Unless the parties agree otherwise, the seller's shipment obligations are as follows:

- the seller must ship the goods on a ship which departs from the port of shipment on the date, or within the period, specified in the contract. In the absence of a specific date, the choice rests with the seller;

- if the vessel is specified by the buyer, the seller is required to use this vessel only;

- if a specific port of loading is required, the seller must ship from that port;

- the seller must ensure that the goods are stowed aboard the vessel according to the terms of the contract;

- the ship must be one bound for the agreed port of destination and follow the contractual route or, if none is specified, use the usual or reasonable route;

- unless there is a provision for deviation, the seller is in breach if the ship in fact deviates. The buyer can reject the goods on this basis and the seller's recourse is against the carrier provided that the contract of carriage prohibits deviation.

ii) The shipping documents

In the absence of stipulations to the contrary, the cif seller is bound to tender three documents to the seller or his agents: a bill of lading, a policy of insurance and an invoice.

The bill of lading

The bill of lading is a document issued by or on behalf of the actual carrier of the goods to the person with whom he or she has contracted to transport the goods to the port of destination. The bill of lading performs three functions:

- It is evidence that the goods described in it have been received by the carrier and, if a shipped bill of lading, that they have been shipped.

  Hence, a shipped bill of lading is evidence that the goods have in fact been shipped on the date specified. Similarly, a statement that the goods were shipped in apparent order and condition is evidence of that fact: see *Grant* v *Norway* (1851) 10 CB 665.

- It is evidence of the contract of carriage.

  In common law, the bill does not actually contain the contract of carriage and hence the existence of a bill of lading does not necessarily mean that a contract of carriage has been made or that the terms stated in the bill actually reflect the true contractual position: see *The Ardennes* [1951] 1 KB 55.

- Provided that it satisfies certain requirements, it is a document of title to the goods in both common law and by statute.

  Possession of the bill of lading gives its possessor constructive possession of the goods and, if transferred with the intention of passing, the transferor's property in the goods will also give the transferee that property: see *Lickbarrow* v *Mason* (1787) 2 Term Rep 63.

A carrier is not bound to part with possession of the goods except on production of the bill and is liable to the holder of the bill if he wrongfully delivers the goods to someone else. Similarly, a carrier's failure to deliver the goods to the holder of the bill renders him liable in tort for conversion under the Torts (Interference with Goods) Act 1977 and he will also usually be liable for breach of contract of carriage.

The bill must be tendered by the seller to the buyer in a reasonable time after shipment in the absence of contractual stipulations to the contrary. Late delivery of the bill of lading may have an effect on the contract of sale and if there is an express stipulation that time for tendering of the document is of the essence, failure to comply with this term amounts to a repudiatory breach for which the buyer may reject the goods.

The other types of documents which are commonly substituted for a shipped bill of lading, provided that the terms of the contract so permit, are as follows:

- a ship's delivery order;
- a delivery warrant;
- an ordinary delivery order;
- a container bill of lading;
- a through bill of lading;
- a mate's receipt;
- a combined transport document.

The policy of insurance

Unless otherwise agreed between the buyer and the seller, the buyer is entitled to a policy of marine insurance covering the goods against the usual marine risks, and such other risks as may be specified in the contract.

The buyer is entitled to reject the policy if it covers goods other than those comprised in the bill of lading.

Where the contract allows, a certificate of insurance may be substituted for delivery of a specific policy but if there is no such provision the buyer can reject such documents because they do not give the holder a direct right of action against the insurer: *Wilson* v *Belgian Grain & Produce Co* [1920] 2 KB 1.

A policy of marine insurance is assignable by indorsement and delivery, or in any other customary manner: s50 Marine Insurance Act 1950.

The commercial invoice

A commercial invoice describes the goods and their price. It is required by the buyer to clear the goods through customs since it is on the price charged that customs duties are usually assessed.

The commercial invoice should identify the buyer's order and should set out the full details of the parties, the goods, the price and payment terms, shipping marks and numbers, and the shipment itself including the port of loading, the route and the port of discharge.

Other documents required by the buyer

Other documents may be required by the express terms of the contract, the most common being export and import licences and certificates of quality.

d) *The obligations of the cif buyer*

Since the seller bears so many obligations under a cif contract, the obligations of the buyer are relatively few. Nevertheless, it should be borne in mind that the buyer will pay a greater price to the seller in return for the seller fulfilling his obligations under the contract.

i) To pay the seller on tender of the documents

In a cif contract, the duty of delivering the goods, which rests with the seller, in return for making payment of the price, which rests with the buyer, are separated which amounts to a deviation from the presumption set out in s28 of the SGA 1979. Payment of the price becomes due when the documents are delivered to the buyer.

The buyer must pay the price if the documents conform and cannot delay until he has examined the goods. If the buyer knows that the goods are not in accordance with the contract, he must nevertheless pay against the documents if they are in accordance with the contract. This is subject to two exceptions:

- the rule does not apply where the non-conformity of the goods can be attributed to fraud on the part of the seller: see *Gill & Duffus SA* v *Berger & Co Inc* [1984] AC 382; and

- where the goods actually shipped differ fundamentally from those that have been sold, the buyer need not pay against the documents.

The position is fundamentally different where the documents do not conform with the requirements of the contract. This may arise in two ways:

- the documents may indicate on their face that they are not in conformity with the contract, ie the bill of lading is claused or the shipping date is outside the contract period; or

- the documents may contain a latent defect, ie the terms of the documents are false so as to appear consistent with each other and with the requirements of the contract.

If the documents are correct, the buyer must pay the price in the manner specified by the contract. This is usually a strict obligation and the unauthorised use of another mode of payment will enable the seller to reject the buyer's purported performance.

Where the goods have been properly shipped and the requisite documents tendered to the buyer, the subsequent loss or deterioration of the goods is at the buyer's expense. In such an event, the buyer's remedies are not against the seller but against the carrier, insurer or guilty third party depending on the circumstances of the case.

ii) To take delivery of the goods

Unless the buyer has rejected the documents, he or she is required to take delivery of the goods. At this point, the buyer has rights, under ss34 and 35 of the SGA 1979 to inspect the goods and to reject them if he or she can show that the goods did not conform when the seller shipped them.

iii) Additional duties

A cif contract may impose other duties on the buyer. For example, if the contract specifies several potential destinations for delivery of the goods, the buyer must notify the seller of his choice of destination. Such a notice must reach the seller within a reasonable time before the beginning of the shipment period in order to allow the seller an opportunity to comply.

e) *Buyer's right to reject the goods or the documents*

The buyer has the right to expect that both the goods and the documents conform to the terms of the contract and accordingly has two separate rights of rejection: (a) the right to reject the goods; and (b) the right to reject the documents.

The difference in these two rights was lucidly expressed by Devlin J in the following terms:

'There is a right to reject the documents and a right to reject the goods and the two things are quite distinct. A cif contract puts a number of obligations on the seller some of which are in relation to the goods and some of which are in relation to the documents. So far as the goods are concerned he must put on board at the port of shipment goods in conformity with the contract description, but he must also forward documents and these documents must comply with the contract. If he commits a breach, the breaches may in one sense overlap in that they flow from the same act. Thus the same act can cause two breaches of two independent obligations. A right to reject is merely a particular form of the right to rescind, which involves the rejection of a tender of goods or of documents': *Kwei Tek Chao* v *British Traders & Shippers Limited* [1954] 2 QB 459.

f) *Passing of property*

Section 17 of the SGA declares that property in goods passes according to the intention of the parties expressed in the contract. In cif contracts, the presumption is that property does not pass until delivery of the shipping documents to the buyer or his authorised agent.

g) *Risk*

Although property prima facie passes to the buyer when he makes payment against the documents, in a cif contract the presumption is that the risk in the goods passes as from the time of shipment: *Johnston* v *Taylor Bros* [1920] AC 144. This is because the parties have regulated the prospect of loss or damage in transit and covered it by the contracts of carriage and insurance which the seller is required to take out and subsequently transfer to the buyer.

The divorcing of the passing of risk in the goods from the passing of property is an example of where the parties have agreed to disapply the general rule stated in s20 of the SGA 1979.

3.3 Recent cases and statutes

Compagnie Commerciale Sucres et Denrées v *C Czarnikow Ltd, The Naxos* [1990] 1 WLR 1337: the buyers successfully sued the sellers for breach of contract for failure to deliver the goods and damages for having to purchase more expensive goods as a result.

Attorney-General of Ghana v *Texaco Overseas Tankships* (1994) The Times 16 February: the damages for non-delivery of goods are assessed by reference to the market value of the goods at the time and place at which they ought to have been delivered.

3.4 Relevant materials

Sassoon, *CIF and FOB Contracts* (3rd edition, 1984).

Benjamin, *Sale of Goods* (3rd edition, 1988), pp1072–1309.

C M Schmitthoff *The Law and Practice of International Trade* (9th edition, 1990), pp16–55.

3.5 Analysis of questions

Questions on both these topics are extremely common and yet, as will be seen from the forthcoming selection, the same issues arise time and time again. This means simply that, with proper reading of this sample of questions, no novel issues should arise to surprise a well prepared candidate.

3.6 Questions

Question 1

By virtue of a sales contract dated 14 February 1994, Wright Limited sold to Wrong Limited 1,000 tonnes of tomatoes fob Southampton (UK). The contract, which was expressly subject to English law, contained the following terms as regards nomination:

a) the buyers are required to give provisional notice of eight clear days of the date on which the vessel will arrive at the port of lading;

b) the nomination must identify the vessel by name, its itinerary and the approximate quantity of goods to be loaded;

c) the provisional notice must be confirmed by a definite notice of four clear days from the date of presentment of the vessel for loading;

d) in the event of the buyer's failure to give definite notice he will be deemed to be in default and the buyer entitled to cancel the contract.

On 12 February 1994 Wrong Ltd gave a provisional notice nominating *The Rusty Nail* or substitute with an estimated time of arrival on 20 February, and on 15 February gave a definite notice that *The Rusty Nail* would arrive on 23 February 1994. Wright acknowledged receipt of the definite notice of *The Rusty Nail* and confirmed they would accept *The Rusty Nail* provided she complied with all the terms and conditions of the contract.

On 16 February Wrong gave definite notice substituting *The Black Russian* with an estimated date of arrival of 19 February. Wright rejected this notice on the grounds that definite notice had already been issued in respect of *The Rusty Nail*.

The Black Russian arrived at Southampton and gave notice of her readiness to load on 19 Febuary, but Wright refused to load the goods on the ship on the grounds that she was not the contractual vessel, since she had not been nominated in accordance with the contractual terms. Wright consider themselves to have acted correctly and that Wrong are in default. Hence they have cancelled the contract.

Wrong wish to seek a remedy against Wright in the form of an action for non-delivery. What do you advise in relation to their prospects of success?

Question prepared by the Editor
April 1994

General comment

This question is designed to test the student's knowledge of the responsibilities of the parties under a fob contract where the contract has been modified by an express term. However, the question itself is relatively straightforward and students with a good knowledge of this aspect of the law should be able to score quite well.

Skeleton solution

Duty of the seller to nominate a vessel under a strict fob contract.

Construction of an express term of the contract regarding notice.

Nomination as a condition of the contract.

Right of substitution.

Right of the buyer to claim damages for non-delivery of the goods.

Suggested solution

The sales contract between Wright and Wrong requires delivery of the goods fob Southampton (UK). In such a contract, the seller, in this case Wright, is required to place the goods aboard the nominated vessel for onward transmission to the buyer. The seller's duties require that the goods are placed on the nominated vessel, but the seller is not required to arrange the vessel to carry the goods or for the procurement of insurance. Once the goods are safely on board the ship, the seller's duties are at an end.

The purchaser is required to nominate the vessel on which the goods are to be placed by the seller. In the present case, the sales contract expressly regulates the duty of nomination. The buyer is required to give eight clear days provisional notice of the estimated time of arrival of the nominated vessel at the port of loading. Thereafter, a final notice of four clear days is required prior to arrival of the vessel.

While this clause clarifies the purchaser's duty to nominate, it does not alter or negate the duty to nominate and therefore the contract remains a strict fob contract.

As such, Wrong is required to nominate a suitable vessel and to do so within a reasonable time, bearing in mind the terms of the contract. The peculiarity of this contract is that no month is stated as to the time for delivery, ie shipment to take place in February 1994, and instead the time of delivery is left open-ended.

On the facts stated in the question, Wrong gave provisional notice nominating *The Rusty Nail* or substitute with an estimated date of arrival of 20 February 1994, which was subsequently changed by definitive notice with respect to *The Rusty Nail* to 23 February 1994.

Later, Wrong attempted to change the nominated vessel to *The Black Russian*, which was due to arrive on the 19 February 1994 and which did in fact arrive on that date. The question is whether Wright was entitled to refuse to load the goods on *The Black Russian* on the ground that the vessel was not the one originally nominated.

In a fob contract, any contractual stipulation as to the time to nominate a suitable ship is considered to be a condition and as such is a matter that is of the essence of the contract. A seller is normally entitled to treat the contract as repudiated if the buyer fails to nominate a ship within the stipulated time or, if there is no express stipulation as to time, within a reasonable period: see *The Osterbeck* (1972).

Can it be said that Wrong failed to nominate a suitable vessel within the required time? This depends on whether Wrong were entitled to substitute *The Black Russian* for *The Rusty Nail* which itself turns on the construction of the notice clause.

According to the terms of the clause, Wrong was required to give provisional notice, of the nominated vessel's estimated time of arrival, the vessel's name, its itinerary and the approximately quantity to be loaded.

As an ancillary obligation, Wrong was obliged to provide a final or definitive notice but only of the date of the presentment of the vessel for loading. In other words, Wrong was not required under this condition to give definitive notice of the name of the nominated vessel.

It should also be noted that the term allowing the buyer to cancel the contract in the event of failure to give definitive notice does not give Wright the right to consider the contract terminated because of Wrong's substitution of the nominated vessel. The final notice given by Wrong gave four clear days of the date of presentment of a vessel for loading, which was the only express stipulation in the clause as regards final notice.

Naturally, it would be open to Wright to put forward an interpretation of the clause that restricted the right of Wrong to nominate a substitute vessel. For example, Wright could claim that the requirement of naming the nominated vessel in the provisional notice could be construed as a term implying that the vessel in the final notice should be the same vessel.

Since the issue of the right to substituted a vessel is not expressly regulated by the contractual terms, it falls to be determined by the general principles of the common law. In *Agricultores Federados Argentinos* v *Ampro SA* (1965), the court held that if a contract of sale provides that the buyer must nominate a vessel within a particular time, a substitute vessel can be nominated if the substitution takes place within the stipulated period of delivery and there is no contractual provision to the contrary. In this case, *The Black Russian* arrived prior to the date for loading of the originally nominated vessel which was stated as the 20 February.

If the vessel had arrived after the 20 February, then Wrong would have been in default because the substituted nomination would have meant that loading would have taken place after the nominated date.

Wrong was not in breach of the contract by substituting *The Black Russian* as long as the nominated vessel arrived within the contractually specified period. Since Wrong was not in breach, Wright had no right to refuse to load the goods onto the ship.

It therefore appears that Wright are liable for non-delivery because there was no justification for refusing to load the contractual goods on board the nominated vessel. Wrong nominated a suitable ship which was available for loading within the contractual period.

Wrong is therefore entitled to claim damages from Wright for non-delivery of the goods, but cannot claim the purchase price since it did not pay for the goods. Its claim would be confined to injury sustained, such as loss of profit on the resale of the goods to a third party.

Question 2

Samuel ships 50,000 tons of oil from Texas to Southampton aboard the mv *Lenuf*.

He sells the 20,000 tons in No 1 Hold to Boomer fob US port, taking a bill of lading to his own order, payment to be made by Boomer's bank cash against documents on arrival. After the vessel arrives, the bank pays on tender of the documents and the oil is pumped into Boomer's storage tanks. Boomer then discovers that the documents presented included a certificate and not a policy of insurance, that the total volume of oil in the hold and pumped into his tanks was only 18,000 tons, and that the oil is not of the quality agreed in the contract.

The master of the *Lenuf* also issues a bill of lading to Samuel for the 30,000 tons of oil stores in No 2 Hold. Samuel sells 25,000 tons of this to Cuthbert cif Southampton, payment to be under a letter of credit to be issued by Cuthbert's bank. The bank accepts a bill of exchange on Samuel's tender of documents which include a delivery order for the 25,000 tons. The remaining 5,000 tons are sold des *Lenuf* to Dirk. Dirk informs Cuthbert that the oil he has bought is of inferior quality, so Cuthbert declines to take delivery of his 25,000 tons and instructs his bank not to pay Samuel.

University of London LLB Examination
(for External Students) Commercial Law June 1987 Q6

General comment

This question essentially concerns the remedies of a buyer whose goods are defective or where non-performance of the contract has been made. The involvement of the bank is a side issue and should be treated as such in the answer.

Skeleton solution

Obligations of parties under Fob contracts.

Breach of s14(2) as to quality?

Defects in bill of lading.

Cif contracts.

Duties of parties under cif, especially as to delivery and tender of documents.

Suggested solution

a) *Boomer*

Boomer bought 20,000 tons of oil on fob terms. We are not told any details of the fob contract and, in particular, it is not known whether it was strict fob or fob and additional services. Since Samuel appears to have arranged for insurance, so it seems that it is probably a form of fob and additional services.

The goods sold were specific goods, being identified and agreed upon as the oil in Hold No 1 (s61(1) Sale of Goods Act (SGA) 1979). That there were only 18,000 tons there and not 20,000 is something which, prima facie, places Samuel in breach, because he described the specific goods as '20,000 tons'. This breach, accordingly, is of the condition implied by s13 of the Sale of Goods Act 1979.

There appears to have been a breach of the condition implied by s14(2) as well in that the oil was not of the quality agreed. This agreement could, of course, have made the requirement that the oil meet a particular quality an express condition of the contract, but it makes no difference to Boomer's position whether the failure to match that quality is seen as breach of an express or implied condition.

Boomer had the right to inspect the oil on arrival in order to see whether it matched the required description and quality (s34 SGA 1979). There appears to be little difficulty, on the limited facts given, in finding that Boomer may still reject the oil. Provided the bill of lading has been made over to Boomer, property has passed to him – it passed when the bill of lading was indorsed. But if he rejects the goods then he must also reject the bill of lading and on doing this property will revest in Samuel. The acceptance of the bill of lading by the bank will not estop Boomer from rejecting it when it is discovered that it does not properly state the quantity of goods, because its acceptance was not with knowledge of the deficiency.

It is the buyer's duty to arrange marine insurance of goods sold on fob terms, and if the seller takes out insurance he does so as agent of the buyer. We are not told whether the method of payment here required Samuel to present an insurance policy. It is unlikely that it did because there was no documentary credit as such, but merely payment against documents. Provided he took out insurance which in fact covered Boomer's marine risk then Samuel will not be in breach by tendering only a certificate of insurance.

Boomer may, in the alternative, choose to take action against the ship owner, whoever he may be. Whether such an action is open depends upon facts which are not given, but it would be open if the shipowner falsely represented on the bill of lading that there were 20,000 tons in Hold No 1, or if he falsely represented anything about the quality of the oil (s4 Carriage of Goods by Sea Act 1992). It is unlikely that he would have said anything about this second matter, but likely that the bill would have named the quantity.

b) *Cuthbert*

Cuthbert has bought a quantity of unascertained goods on cif terms to be paid for by documentary credit. The bank paid against a delivery order rather than the bill of lading which would normally be required. Whether this was a good tender by Samuel depends upon the terms of the credit, about which there is no information. It may be that because the sale is of a part of a bulk quantity so it can be inferred that a delivery order would be good tender under the cif contract, but this would have to be a delivery order issued by the ship otherwise Cuthbert would have no contractual right to demand delivery from the ship (*Comptoir D'Achat et de Vente du Boerenbond Belge SA* v *Luis de Ridder Lda, The Julia* (1949)). It cannot be said with any certainty whether the delivery order was a ship's delivery order or was a document emanating from Samuel himself.

On the assumption that the delivery order was not a valid document under the contract of sale it is highly unlikely to have been valid under the documentary credit either. The normal practice is that the bank has a dual role when accepting cif documents, firstly it acts as the agent of the buyer for the purpose of the cif contract and secondly it acts on its own account and is contractually liable to pay the seller on presentation of the correct documents. The acceptance of the bill of exchange by the bank amounted to payment under the credit. But it did not amount to acceptance of the cif documents by Cuthbert, because the bank acted outside its authority in accepting documents which did not comply with the cif contract and Samuel had notice of this want of authority.

Samuel's position, therefore, is that he has received payment from the bank but has not had the documents accepted by Cuthbert. Therefore Cuthbert is still entitled to reject the documents, provided he has not accepted them either expressly or by delaying in rejecting (*Biddell Bros* v *E Clemens Horst Co* (1912)). It appears that there may have been acquiescence here because Cuthbert has refused to accept the goods and they would only have been physically delivered after the documents had been accepted by the bank. If there has indeed been physical delivery of the oil to the port of destination (Southampton) and if Dirk was correct in saying that the oil was of poor quality then Cuthbert would be entitled to reject it for breach of the implied condition of merchantable quality. An attempted rejection prior to arrival would not be effective because the right to reject only crystallises on arrival (*Gill & Duffus SA* v *Berger & Co Inc* (1984)).

c) *Dirk*

Dirk's position can be stated quite simply, although we are not told whether he has received delivery of the oil or whether his stated complaint about quality is justified. A sale des requires the seller to deliver the goods from the ship on arrival directly to the buyer who is the obliged to pay unless he can find a breach of condition in which case he may reject, like any other buyer who finds goods to be a breach of condition (*Yangtsze Insurance Association* v *Lukmanjee* (1918)). On the assumption that Dirk is right about the poor quality of the oil he would be entitled to reject the oil tendered and would not have to pay.

Question 3

Arnold sells to Bert fob Liverpool 200 computers and 400 radios. Bert arranges for shipment on Carver's ship Danko and asks Arnold to load the goods and forward to him one bill of lading for the computers and one for the radios. After loading, Bert pays for the bill of lading for the radios but rejects the bill for the computers as he has heard that they have been stowed alongside a cargo of magnets, which are liable to have damaged them.

Hearing that the Danko has collided with another ship, the Ergo, and that the Danko has sustained a leak, Bert contracts to sell 200 radios to each of Fred and George cif Cape Town. Fred's bank issues a letter of credit to Bert but (when Bert presents it with a delivery order, insurance certificate and invoice) it refuses to pay, having heard about the collision. George pays Bert for similar documents but his radios are dropped and damaged on unloading, so he demands his money back.

Advise the parties.

University of London LLB Examination
(for External Students) Commercial Law 1992 Q7

General comment

The combination of sale of goods, international sales and bills of lading is a recurring theme in examinations over the years. Like many previous similar questions, the wording is deliberately ambiguous and so a whole series of alternatives need to be considered. Basically a fairly easy question to answer, it is necessary to keep in mind all the various possibilities and permutations to cover the whole question comprehensively.

Skeleton solution

Passing of title in the goods.

Risk fob contracts.

Risk cif contracts.

Antecedent impossibility/misrepresentation.

Bank's act in repudiating documents – liability.

Suggested solution

When English law applies to a contract of international sale, then relevant legislation such as the Sale of Goods Act 1979 (SGA) will apply. Although we are not specifically told that this is the case, the rubric on the examination paper requires this approach and so we shall proceed on that assumption. It appears from the wording of the question that the contract between Arnold and Bert is for specific goods, though the possibility exists that the goods may be unascertained. The initial question is as to passing of title. In the case of specific goods, ss17–18 of SGA are relevant. Section 17 states:

1. 'where there is a contract for sale of specific goods ... property in them is transferred to the buyer at such times as the parties ... intend it ...'; and

2. to ascertain the intention of the parties 'regard shall be had to the terms of the contract, the conduct of the parties, and the circumstances of the case'.

If no intention can be ascertained under s17, then resort must be had to s18 which contains a number of rules or guidelines.

To invoke s17 first therefore, is any assistance to be found in ascertaining the parties' intentions by the fact that the goods are being sold fob? The initials stand for free on board. Normally property in the goods passes to the buyer the moment the goods go on board, and once the goods go over the ship's rail the buyer assumes responsibility for any damage done to the goods. However, this can be subject to certain important exceptions. Firstly, if the parties expressly or impliedly make it clear in the contract that property is intended to pass at some other time, this will take priority over the normal rule on fob contracts. Thus, for example, under s19 SGA the seller may expressly reserve title to the goods in one of a number of ways. One possibility is by a so-called 'Romalpa' clause. Or, by s19(2) where goods are sent by sea and by bill of lading the goods are deliverable to the order of the seller or his agent, the seller is prima facie to be taken to reserve rights of disposal. Or, by s19(3) if the seller makes the passing of property through the bill of lading conditional on the buyer honouring a bill of exchange in payment. One must take into account, also, the fact that by the Carriage of Goods by Sea Act 1992 s1, property will not pass until transfer of the bill.

If the goods are unascertained, s16 SGA applies which states 'Where there is a contract of sale for unascertained goods, no property in the goods passes to the buyer unless and until the goods are ascertained.' As to when property in unascertained goods passes if they never are ascertained, s18 rule 5 is relevant – the main criteria being the time of unconditional appropriation of the goods to the contract (see below).

Which of the above might be said to apply to Arnold and Bert? Firstly, there is no indication in the wording of the question that Arnold has reserved rights in the goods by any sort of Romalpa clause. Does s19(2) apply? Certainly Bert asks Arnold to arrange for a bill of lading to be forwarded, rather than Arnold, the seller, directing when payment is to be made. Nor does s19(3) seem appropriate, there is no indication that passing of property is conditional on the buyer honouring a bill of exchange. All in all, it seems that s17 of SGA, combined with the use of an fob contract, would seem to indicate that property and hence risk passed to Bert when the goods were put on the ship.

Does this mean Bert has no redress for the damaged computers? Firstly, one point should be clarified: the meaning of 'stowed alongside'. If the computers were placed, for example, in containerised storage, alongside the magnets, even before being placed on board ship this will be the responsibility of Arnold, the seller. If the goods were placed in such a way, on the ship, as to be damaged, then under the normal rules for specific goods shipped under fob contracts, risk will have passed to Bert, the buyer, and he will bear the responsibility. However, if the goods are faulty, he will not lose the right to reject, even though property has passed, until such time as he accepts the goods (s11 SGA).

This damage has been caused in transit and so it could not be argued that the implied conditions of SGA as to fitness for purpose or merchantability have been breached. Bert therefore has no right to reject the bill of lading and Arnold has the normal rights of an unpaid seller.

The next problem is the question of Bert's sale of the radios to Fred and George. Bert makes the sale, knowing full well that the Danko has collided with another ship and sprung a leak, though in fact it is not clear whether he thinks the radios are damaged or not. One problem to dispose of early on in this part of the question is whether the goods are specific or unascertained, as this will have important repercussions with regard to the passing of title and of risk. At first sight, since there are 400 radios, and Bert sells them in two batches of 200, it is tempting to describe them as specific. But it seems more likely that initially the goods will be unascertained, at least until the first lot of 200 radios is separated out and off-loaded. The remaining 200 – George's – will at this point become ascertainable by exhaustion.

Sections 6–7 of SGA have very specific rules on antecedent impossibility and frustration, depending on whether the goods are specific or not, but the main problem is that although the Danko has collided and been damaged this does not seem to have affected the radios at all. We are concerned with antecedent impossibility rather than frustration here, because Bert knows about the collision when he sells the radios. Section 6 provides that where specific goods perish, the contract will be voidable. It seems clear that 'perish' can refer not only to absolute destruction, but to a reduction in the quality of the goods (*Asfar & Co v Blundell* (1896)). But at this point the goods were unascertained and apparently did not perish so s6 has no application.

Cif contracts almost invariably mean that risk passes to the buyer the moment the goods are on board ship, but property does not pass until the shipping documents are presented to the buyer and the buyer has paid against them.

The normal rule with regard to payment is that a bank has a dual role when accepting cif documents. Firstly, it acts as the agent of the buyer for the purpose of the cif contract and, secondly, it acts on its own account and is contractually liable to pay the seller on presentation of the correct documents. Note, in this context, that Bert's presentation of, inter alia, an insurance policy certificate that may not be valid, raises the question of whether the seller in this case has presented the correct documents (see final paragraph). All the provisions in the SGA are subject to the overriding right of the parties to indicate when they wish property to pass.

Because the goods are, initially, unascertained there must come a point when they become ascertained. Section 18, rule 5 of the SGA mentions the point of appropriation. This occurs most usually when the seller tenders the relevant documents to the buyer or buyer's agent. It is not clear whether Fred's bank have refused to pay on Fred's instructions, or on their own account. If they believe the cargo to have perished entirely, they might be justified in avoiding the contract, but this is not the case. There are still some radios aboard, because we are told that George's quota is off-loaded. While goods are unascertained, which these are until the moment of appropriation, it is considered that impossibility and/or frustration cannot operate to destroy the contract, because other similar goods are still available.

If the rejection of the goods is the bank's own act, Bert will have a right of action under s40 Bills of Exchange Act for dishonour of the letter of credit. If Fred is rejecting the goods, then Bert will have an action against him as unpaid seller for breach of contract, and may sue for the agreed price.

With regard to George's radios, dropped and damaged on unloading, it seems clear that they were not damaged by the collision. Since with cif contracts risk normally passes once the goods go on board ship and property passes on presentation of the appropriate documents and payment, then there seems little doubt that George is the owner and must bear the loss. He may, of course, have an action in negligence against other parties, for example the stevedore company responsible for unloading.

One final point needs to be mentioned and that is whether or not there may be an element of misrepresentation in Bert's contracts with Fred and George, and/or whether the implied terms (s14(2) and (3) of SGA) as to fitness have been breached. We are told that Bert contracts to sell the radios only after he hears the ship has collided and sprung a leak. Does he know some radios are damaged, and more importantly does he conceal this fact? If so, there may be an element of misrepresentation and export sale of goods contracts are no different in this respect from any other: If the misrepresentation is sufficiently serious, the buyers will have the appropriate remedies, both under common law and by virtue of s2 Misrepresentation Act 1967.

Question 4

Gavin agrees to sell 50,000 litres of high quality olive oil from his farm in Spain to Scott. The terms of the sales contract are cif Birmingham (UK), shipment in January 1994. The terms of the contract expressly declare that English law is to apply.

Accordingly, Gavin charters a ship for the voyage of the olive oil from Spain to Birmingham and sends a fax to Scott confirming that the name of the vessel is *La Bonne Chance*. In fact, the olive oil is loaded on 12 January aboard *The Good Luck*. However, the bill of lading, which identifies the vessel as *The Good Luck*, incorrectly gives 7 January as the date of shipment.

Scott accepts delivery of the olive oil when it arrives in Birmingham. Later, the shipping documents arrive, by which time the price for that particular quality of olive oil has declined sharply. Scott then discovers that the true date of shipment was 12 January 1994.

In order to avoid his obligation to pay, Scott seeks your legal advice. What would your advice be?

Question prepared by Editor
April 1994

General comment

The question is quite typical and seeks to test the student's knowledge of the different types of international sales contracts. Relatively high marks may be scored in answering this question by students capable of ascertaining the relevant legal principles.

Skeleton solution

Duty of the seller to provide goods of the contractual description.

Stipulations as regards time and place of delivery.

Duty to deliver the shipping documents.

Right to reject shipping documents.

Suggested Solution

The contract of sale is cif Birmingham (UK), shipment in January 1994 and the contract is governed by English law.

In the absence of express terms to the contrary, the seller in a cif contract is bound to fulfil five main obligations. First, to make out an invoice for the goods sold. Second, to ship goods fitting the description of the contractual goods to the named port. Third, to secure a contract of carriage for the goods under which the goods will be conveyed to the destination agreed in the contract within the time agreed, if any. Fourth, to arrange for the insurance of the goods. Fifth, to dispatch the shipping documents to the buyer, namely the invoice, the bill of lading and the insurance policy: *Johnston* v *Taylor Bros* (1920).

The duties of the buyer are to accept the documents tendered if these are in conformity with the contract of sale, to receive the goods at the agreed port of destination and to pay the agreed price on the tender of the proper documents.

Gavin is therefore required to supply goods fulfilling the contractual description. In the sales contract, the contract goods are described as 'high quality olive oil'. However, the commodity actually procured is 'olive oil'. Naturally there is a difference in the quality between the goods contracted for and those actually dispatched.

But, it is unlikely that this discrepancy will allow Scott to refuse to pay against the tendering of the documents because, so long as the documentation conforms to the contract, the duty to pay is virtually absolute. The only exceptions to the obligation to pay against the documents is in the case of fraud on the part of the seller or where there is a dramatic difference between the goods shipped and those agreed in the contract of sale. However, while Scott may not be entitled to reject delivery, he may have a right to raise an action for breach of contract on the ground that the goods delivered were not those agreed in the sales contract.

Gavin is required to arrange the contract of carriage. Stipulations in cif contracts relating to the time and place of shipment are normally conditions of the contract, breach of which allows the buyer to refuse to accept the goods: see *Aruna Mills Ltd* v *Dhanrajmal Gobindram* (1968). There is no term in the contract regarding the nomination of a particular ship, but there is a term requiring shipment in January 1994. This condition appears to have been satisfied because the goods are in fact shipped in January 1994.

The fact that the vessel was the *The Good Luck* and not *La Bonne Chance* is not relevant under a cif contract in the absence of an express stipulation to the contrary. The position would have been different had the agreement been a fob contract in which the purchaser is required to nominate a particular ship.

Gavin is also required to tender the shipping documents to Scott against which payment is required. The relevant documents are the invoice, the bill of lading and the insurance policy but the main dispute concerns the bill of lading. The bill of lading is defective on two counts. First, it gives the incorrect date of shipment and second, it names a different ship from that notified to Scott as the chartered vessel.

A wrongly dated bill of lading amounts to a breach of a condition in a cif contract and entitled the buyer to reject the bill itself and to treat the contract as repudiated. This is the case, even if the goods in question were in fact shipped within the contract time which is the situation in the present case: see *The Almak* (1985). The defect lies in the inaccuracies in the bill of lading and not in the failure to deliver the goods within a particular period.

The fact that the wrong ship is notified to Scott is probably irrelevant quite simply because this error itself does not vitiate the bill of lading. The bill is a document identifying the ship on which the goods were carried and in this particular case the goods were transported aboard *The Good Luck*. The bill is therefore accurate in this respect.

The purchaser in a cif contract is entitled to reject both the documents and the goods. The right to reject the goods arises when the goods arrive in the nominated port while the right to reject the documents arises at the time the documents are tended: see *Kwei Tek Chao* v *British Traders & Shippers Ltd* (1954). Usually the right to reject the documents arises before the right to reject the goods because the documents generally arrive at the purchasers before the goods, but in this case the opposite is true. Scott has accepted the high quality olive oil and is now attempting to reject the documents, although it is not clear how he could have obtained the goods without the relevant shipping documents.

The right to reject the goods arises when the purchaser inspects the goods and they are found to be not in accordance with the terms of the sales contract. Typically, this means that the goods are of an inferior quality, damaged during transit or are an insufficient quantity.

But, since Scott has taken physical possession of the goods, he cannot now reject them. His only other recourse is therefore to reject the documents on the ground that the bill of lading is defective. This right is not affected by the fact that he has accepted the goods.

The right to reject the documents is lost if payment of the contractual price has been made by the purchaser even if the documents subsequently proved to be defective. If a purchaser accepts the documents he or she is precluded from afterwards complaining on the basis of late shipment or a defect in the bill of lading. The only exception to this rule is the fraud of the seller.

The rejection of the documents must also be clear and unequivocal. Rejections that are ambiguous are ineffective and will not act to prevent the purchaser from being liable to pay the price.

On the basis of the facts presented in the question, Scott will be able to reject the goods because of the right to reject the documents.

4 BILLS OF EXCHANGE

4.1   Introduction

4.2   Key points

4.3   Recent cases and statutes

4.4   Relevant materials

4.5   Analysis of questions

4.6   Questions

4.1   Introduction

One of the most common means of financing an international sale is by using a bill of exchange. These instruments can be used as a means of making immediate payment, but more commonly as a mechanism for providing the buyer with a period of credit. By specifying that a sum is payable on the expiry of a period of time after a bill of exchange has been tendered for payment, the buyer is given additional time to make payment instead of having to settle immediately once the goods have been delivered or the documents of title tendered by the seller.

The law recognises that such arrangements are an important means of conducting international business and accordingly has created a special body of rules to regulate the use of bills of exchange. These rules are contained in the Bills of Exchange Act 1882 (BEA 1882). This statute provides the answers to most of the questions raised in relation to the use of such instruments.

In this chapter, we shall first consider the definition and attributes of a bill of exchange as properly constituted. Then the procedure for transferring rights under a bill will be described together with the rights and duties of the parties in such a transfer. Finally, we shall consider the prerequisites for the enforcement of rights under a bill and the remedies available in the event that a bill is dishonoured.

4.2   Key points

a) *The statutory definition of a bill of exchange*

Since the law confers special privileges on bills of exchange, any instrument which does not fall within the statutory definition of a bill of exchange is not entitled to the protection granted by the law. The statutory definition of a bill of exchange is contained in s3(1) of the BEA 1882 which provides:

'A bill of exchange is an unconditional order in writing, addressed by one person to another, signed by the person giving it, requiring the person to whom it is addressed to pay on demand or at a fixed or determinable future time a sum certain in money to or to the order of a specified person, or to bearer.'

It can be seen from the definition that a bill of exchange is essentially a promise in writing to pay a sum of money, framed in the form of an order, which must be addressed to someone other than the person making out the bill.

Section 3(2) of the statute specifically states that an instrument which does not comply with these conditions, or which requires any act to be done in addition to the payment of money, is not a bill of exchange. This means that the criteria specified in the statutory definition are critical to identifying whether or not an instrument is truly a bill of exchange.

b) *The parties to a bill of exchange*

Each of the different parties to a bill of exchange has separate rights and duties and therefore it is important to differentiate the various parties. The parties to a bill of exchange are as follows:

i) The drawer: the person who gives the instruction to pay the order. Normally, this is the seller in a sales contract.

ii) The drawee: the person to whom the order is addressed and must, of course, be someone other than the drawer. Again, in general, in an international sales contract this is either the buyer himself or the buyer's bank.

iii) The acceptor: the person who accepts the obligation to pay the order which is embodied in the bill. Acceptance of the bill differs from paying the order; it will occur before the bill matures and requires the holder of the bill to present it to another person, usually the drawee. If the bill is accepted when presented the acceptor will become liable to pay the bill at its face value at the time specified.

iv) The payee: the person who is to be paid by the drawee or the acceptor is the payee and in normal circumstances this will be the seller.

v) An indorser: where the bill gives the drawee a period of credit, a holder may transfer the bill through indorsement and delivery. The transferor of the bill is known as the indorser.

vi) The indorsee: is the person to whom the bill is negotiated.

vii) The holder: this party is defined in s2 of the 1882 Act as 'the payee or indorsee of a bill who is in possession of it, or the bearer of it'.

c) *The necessary elements in a bill of exchange*

The statutory definition of a bill of exchange identifies seven essential requirements which must be met before an instrument will be deemed to be a valid bill of exchange.

i) The instrument must be an unconditional order.

There is no room in bills of exchange for conditions to be attached for payment. If the order is conditional on some identified contingency, the occurrence of the event will not validate the bill: s12 BEA 1882. However, reference to the commercial transaction which has given rise to the bill of exchange does not make the order conditional. It is important to note that bills of exchange drawn under a documentary credit are not rendered conditional by such a reference: *Guaranty Trust Co of New York* v *Hannay* [1918] 2 KB 623.

ii) The order must be in writing and preferably in ink.

iii) The order must be addressed by one person to another person.

The drawee must be named or otherwise indicated on the bill with a reasonable degree of certainty. Joint drawees are permitted but alternative drawees are not: s6 BEA 1882.

iv) The bill must be signed by the person giving the order.

The drawer's signature on the bill is essential. A forged signature is a nullity and therefore not a signature. A bill signed by a person authorised to sign on behalf of the drawer is valid and operates as the drawer's signature.

v) The date when the bill is to be paid must be certain.

A bill will satisfy this requirement if it is (a) payable on demand or (b) payable at a fixed or determinable future date.

A bill is payable on demand, under s10 of the BEA, when:

- it is expressed as such;

- it is expressed to be payable on sight;

- no time for payment is expressed at all; or

- a bill is accepted or indorsed after maturity it is deemed to be payable on demand.

A bill is payable at a fixed or determinable future date if:

- payable at a fixed period after date;

- payable at a fixed period after sight (meaning that the bill has to be presented for acceptance but there is no requirement that the bill is actually accepted); or

- payable on or at a fixed period after the occurrence of a specified certain event even if the date of its occurrence is uncertain (ie on someone's death): see *Korea Exchange Bank* v *Debenhams (Central Buying) Ltd* [1979] 1 Lloyd's Rep 548; and *Claydon* v *Bradley* [1987] 1 All ER 522.

vi) The sum specified for payment under the bill must be certain.

Specification of a sum of money is necessary under the BEA 1882. A bill is invalid if the consideration is non-monetary, such as the rendering of services in exchange for goods.

It is irrelevant that the sum is payable with interest, or is payable in a particular way (ie by instalments). Naturally, payment must be specified in a legal currency.

vii) The bill must be to, or to the order of, a specified person or bearer.

The various possibilities permitted under the definition are as follows:

- a specified person;
- the order of a specified person; or
- the bearer.

d) *Computation of time in bills of exchange*

While a date on a bill is obviously desirable, the omission of a date is not fatal. When a bill is expressed to be payable at a fixed period after date, but is issued with the date missing, or where the acceptance of a bill payable at a fixed period after sight is undated, any holder may insert the true date and, if acting in good faith, the date inserted will be taken as the true date even if incorrect: s12 BEA 1882.

The manner in which time is to be computed in a bill of exchange transaction is regulated by s3 of the Banking and Financial Dealings Act 1971, which repealed s14 of the BEA 1882.

A bill is deemed due and payable on the last day of the time fixed by the bill for payment. Where a bill of exchange is payable on a fixed period after sight, or the happening of a certain future event, the time for payment is determined by excluding the day from which time is due to run but by including the day of payment.

When a bill is due payable at a fixed period after sight, the period is deemed to run from the date of acceptance of the bill or, if the bill was not accepted, from the date of noting or protesting the bill.

e) *The procedure for transferring a bill of exchange*

Under s31 of the BEA 1882 'a bill is negotiated when it is transferred from one person to another in such a manner as to constitute the transferee the holder of the bill'. Whether or not a bill has been validly transferred depends on the type of bill.

If the bill is payable to bearer, there is a valid negotiation by mere delivery: s31(2) BEA 1882. The person who possesses the bill is the 'bearer' and therefore the holder and is entitled to sue on the bill in his own name.

In the event that the bill is an order bill, there is a valid negotiation if two requirements have been satisfied: (i) there has been an indorsement by the prior holder; and (ii) the bill has been delivered to the possessor: s31(3) BEA 1882.

i) Indorsement

Two types of indorsement are authorised under s34 of the BEA 1882. The first is special indorsement where the name of the new indorsee is specified on the reverse of the bill. Where special indorsement has been made, only the person to whom the bill has been indorsed can present the bill for payment. The second is indorsement in blank where the intended transferee is not named, and the prior holder simply signs his name on the reverse of the bill. The bill becomes a bearer bill until converted back into an order bill by special indorsement.

Where an order bill is delivered without indorsement the transferee is not the holder of the bill as there has not been a proper negotiation of the bill. Nor can he or she be the bearer of the bill as the bill was never a bearer bill. In such circumstances s31(4) provides that the transfer gives the transferee such title as the transferor had on the bill – in other words, the bill is taken subject to equities.

ii) Delivery

Physical possession of the bill must also be given to the transferee for the rights and duties under the bill to become effective.

f) *The categories of holders*

The right to enforce payment of a bill is only available to the holder of the bill specifically defined in the BEA 1882 as 'the payee or indorsee of a bill or note who is in possession of it, or the bearer thereof': s2 BEA 1882.

In the case of a bearer bill, possession of the bill is sufficient to constitute the possessor a holder for the purposes of the statute.

If the bill is an order bill, in addition to possession the possessor must show that he is the person named on the bill, ie that the last special indorsement was to him or was in blank. Where an inchoate instrument is delivered, the transferee has prima facie authority to complete the bill and thereby make himself or herself a holder, although he or she cannot obtain the status of a holder in due course: s20(1) BEA 1882: see *National Park Bank* v *Berggren & Co* (1914) 110 LT 907.

There are two separate types of holders under a bill of exchange: (i) a holder for value; and (ii) a holder in due course.

i) A holder for value

A holder for value has, not surprisingly, given an adequate consideration for the bill. As a general principle, adequate consideration is merely enough to support a simple contract and the value of the consideration is immaterial.

Such a holder can:

• Retain possession of the bill and can sue on it in his or her own name.

- Give a valid discharge to a drawee or acceptor if the payment has been made in due course.

- Convert an order bill into a bearer bill by indorsement in blank and convert such a bill back into an order by special indorsement.

ii) A holder in due course

The requirements necessary to achieve the status of a holder in due course are outlined in s29(1) of the Act which provides:

'A holder in due course is a holder who has taken a bill, complete and regular on the face of it, under the following conditions, namely:

a) that he became the holder of it before it was overdue, and without notice that it had been previously dishonoured, if such was the fact;

b) that he took the bill in good faith and for value, and that at the time the bill was negotiated to him he had no notice of any defect in the title of the person who negotiated it.'

Only a holder in due course can acquire title to the bill free from equities and defects in the title of his transferor and therefore take the full benefit of the negotiability of the bill of exchange which operates as an exception to the nemo dat principle. The only limitation on the rights of the holder in due course is that where a signature on the bill has been forged, or is otherwise of no legal effect, he or she has no rights against those who were parties to the bill prior to the ineffective signature. Vis-à-vis these parties, the purported holder in due course is no holder at all.

A holder in due course of a bill takes the bill free from defects in the title of prior parties and free from any personal defences that third parties might raise against those prior parties: s38(2) BEA 1882.

The defences which can be raised against a holder in due course are therefore limited. In general, these are (a) that the bill does not comply with the definition set out in s3; (b) the signature through which the holder claims was a forgery and therefore a nullity.

g) *The effect of forged signatures*

The general principle with regard to forged signatures is stated in s24 in the following terms:

'Where a signature on a bill is forged or placed thereon without the authority of the person whose signature it purports to be, the forged or unauthorised signature is wholly inoperative, and no right to retain the bill or to give a discharge therefor or to enforce payment thereof against any party thereto can be acquired through or under that signature unless the party against whom it is sought to retain or enforce payment of the bill is precluded from setting up the forgery or want of authority.'

This principle is subject to the rules concerning estoppel particular those contained in ss54 and 55.

h) *Acceptance of a bill*

Acceptance is defined as 'the signification by the drawee of his assent to the order of the drawer': s17(1) BEA 1882. Acceptance is not formally complete until the bill has been delivered, ie handed back, to the person who presented it for acceptance.

An acceptance is formally invalid unless it complies with the following conditions, namely:

i) The acceptance must be written on the bill and be signed by the drawee. The mere signature of the drawee without additional words is sufficient.

ii) It must not express that the drawee will perform his promise by any other means other than the payment of money.

After acceptance, the drawee is called the 'acceptor' and is personally liable on the bill if properly presented for payment. To be properly accepted the following material conditions must be satisfied:

i) A bill can only be accepted by the drawee who must be named on the face.

ii) The bill should be presented within the period specified for acceptance. However, a bill may be accepted under s18(2) when it is overdue or after it has been dishonoured by a previous refusal to accept or by non-payment. A bill when overdue is payable on demand in accordance with s10(2) of the BEA.

There are two forms of acceptance: (i) general acceptance; and (ii) qualified acceptance.

i) A general acceptance is constituted by the mere signature of the acceptor, or the signature of the drawee with the word 'accepted', or the signature of the drawee together with the date.

ii) Qualified acceptance takes five forms:

- Conditional acceptance, for example, where the drawee agrees to pay the bill only if the underlying goods are of a particular quality or quantity.

- Partial acceptance, for example, where the bill is drawn for £100 and the drawee accepts the bill to a limit of £50 only.

- Local acceptance, for example, where the drawee agrees to pay only if the bill is presented for payment at a particular place.

- A qualification as to time, for example, when a bill accepted payable at six months after date is in fact drawn at three months after date.

- Acceptance by some but not all the drawees.

Under s44 a holder of a bill may refuse to take a qualified acceptance, and if he or she obtains a qualified acceptance, may treat the bill as having been dishonoured by non-acceptance. If the holder agrees to accept a qualified acceptance no prior indorser or the drawer of the bill is bound by the decision of the holder to accept and will be discharged from secondary liability on the bill unless the holder fails to indicate the rejection of the qualified acceptance within a reasonable time of being notified.

Although some bills do not have to be presented for acceptance the following bills must be presented for acceptance:

i) Where a bill is payable after sight, presentment for acceptance is necessary in order to fix the maturity of the bill.

ii) Where a bill expressly stipulates that it shall be presented for acceptance.

iii) Where a bill is drawn payable at a place other than the place of business or residence of the drawee.

A bill which is payable after date does not have to be presented for acceptance by the holder in order to bring the bill to maturity.

i) *Liabilities of the parties under a bill of exchange*

The nature of the drawee's or acceptor's liability on a bill differs from that of the drawer and indorsers of the bill. The drawee/acceptor is the party primarily liable on the bill and the bill must be presented to him when due.

The drawer and indorsers of the bill bear secondary liability on the bill and are treated as sureties or guarantors for the drawee/acceptor's promise to pay. If therefore the drawee/acceptor's liability to pay is altered in any way, the other parties to the bill are discharged unless they consent to the change.

j) *Prerequisites for enforcement*

If a bill is properly presented and acceptance refused, the bill has been dishonoured by non-acceptance and an immediate right to recourse accrues against the other parties to the bill and the bill need not be presented for payment. The right of recourse is lost if the prerequisites for enforcement are not properly fulfilled.

i) Presentment of payment

In general, presentment of the bill for payment is unnecessary where it has already been dishonoured by non-acceptance.

But when the bill is a demand bill which has not been accepted, it must be presented for payment when due in order to render the drawer and indorsers liable. If the bill is not properly presented the drawer and the indorsers are discharged from their liabilities.

The rules for presentment for payment are set out in s45 of the BEA 1882. According to this section, a bill must be presented to the drawee/acceptor or his authorised agent on the due date at the proper place and failure in either of these respects will also discharge the prior parties from liability.

ii) Notice of dishonour

Where a bill has been dishonoured by either non-acceptance or non-payment, a notice of dishonour must, unless excused, be given to the drawer and each indorser to preserve their liability. Any drawer or indorser to whom notice is not given is discharged. Notice must also be served within a reasonable time of dishonour: see generally *Hamilton Finance* v *Coverley Finance* [1969] 1 Lloyd's Rep 53.

Delay in giving notice is excused where the delay is caused by circumstances beyond the control of the party giving the notice and not imputable to his default, misconduct or negligence. When the cause of the delay ceases to operate, the notice must be given with reasonable diligence.

iii) Protest

In the case of foreign bills, s51(4) of the Act requires an additional step after the notice of dishonour; the bill must also be protested by the holder.

Protest is a means of obtaining legal proof of dishonour. The holder first presents the bill for payment to the drawee or acceptor. On dishonour, the holder passes the bill to a notary public who again presents the bill for acceptance or payment as the case may be in order to obtain the legal proof of dishonour. If acceptance or payment is still not forthcoming the notary public will draw up an official certificate evidencing the dishonour.

k) *Remedies for dishonour and the form of action*

When a bill of exchange is dishonoured, whether by non-acceptance or non-payment, the holder can sue all the parties liable on the bill provided that the prerequisites for enforcement have been fulfilled.

The approach of the courts to actions on dishonoured bills of exchange has been summarised by Lord Denning in the following terms:

'We have repeatedly said in this court that a bill of exchange or a promissory note is to be treated as cash. It is to be honoured unless there is some goods reason to the contrary': *Fielding & Platt* v *Selim Najjar* [1969] 1 WLR 357.

The general rule is therefore that the defendant will not be allowed to set off or counterclaim damages for breach of the underlying, or any other, contract and the plaintiff will be entitled to summary judgment unless there is a total failure of consideration or a liquidated partial failure as between the immediate parties: see *Nova (Jersey) Knit Ltd* v *Kammgarn Spinnerei GmbH* [1977] 2 All ER 463.

Order 14 of the Rules of the Supreme Court (RSC) allows a plaintiff who has served a statement of claim, to which the defendant has given notice of intention to defend, to apply to the court for judgement on the ground that the defendant has no defence to the claim: see *SL Sethia Liners Ltd* v *State Trading Corporation of India* [1985] 1 WLR 1398.

4.3 Recent cases and statutes

Clifford Chance v *Silver* (1992) Financial Times 31 July: delivery of a bill of exchange may be shown to be conditional or for special purposes only and not for the purposes of transferring property in the bill.

Strathmore Group v *Alexanders Discount* 1992 SLT 846: where there is a mere allegation of forgery on a bill of exchange, caution must be lodged for the value of the bill as a condition for the interim suspension of payment under the bill.

4.4 Relevant materials

Chalmers & Guest, *Bills of Exchange* (14th edition, 1991).

F Dow, *Understanding Documentary Credits* (1991), pp83–100.

4.5 Analysis of questions

The following selection of questions deals with various aspects of the use of bills of exchange.

4.6 Questions

Question 1

Davidson Ltd, a UK company, sold a consignment of computers to Wright Limited, also a UK company. The terms of the sale were for the goods to be delivered cif Newport (USA) at a price of £30,000. The price was to be paid by a bill of exchange payable 90 days after sight. Davidson Ltd drew up the bill of exchange in the appropriate terms and, once shipment had been made, tendered the shipping documents and the bill of exchange to Wright Ltd for acceptance. The bill was accepted on 1 January 1994 and returned to Davidson Ltd.

Due to a cash flow problem, Davidson Ltd decided to sell the bill, at a discount, to its own bank. Once the bill matured, the bank presented it to Wright Ltd for payment. Payment was refused by Wright Ltd on the grounds that the computers were not of merchantable quality. The bank debited Davidson Ltd's account for the sum which had been credited on the sale of the bill.

Davidson has now sought advice as to whether or not they can pursue a claim against Wright Ltd on the bill of exchange and the prospects of success. What do you advise?

Question prepared by the Editor
April 1994

General comment

The main issue at the heart of this question is whether a company against which a bill of exchange has been drawn can repudiate liability because the goods were defective. The remaining matters concern general points under the Bills of Exchange Act 1882 none of which presents any particularly serious difficulties.

Skeleton solution

Nature of bills of exchange.

Rights against holders in due course.

Underlying obligation in the contract of sale.

Protest and proceedings on bills of exchange.

Suggested solution

Payment for the goods is to be made by bill of exchange payable 90 days after sight. A bill of exchange is simply an unconditional order in writing, addressed by one person to another, and signed by the person issuing it, requiring the person to whom it is addressed to pay a certain sum of money: s3 Bills of Exchange Act 1882.

In this case, the bill issued by Davidson Ltd is a time bill and requires presentation for acceptance. The bill was accepted by Wright Ltd which allows the period of maturity of the bill to be fixed, namely 90 days after acceptance. Wright Ltd is required to fulfil its obligation to pay on the bill 90 days after this date. But, since the bill was not refused at this point, it has not been dishonoured and can validly be passed to holders in due course.

The bill is subsequently sold to the bank. This is known as discounting, whereby the payee is entitled to transfer a time bill to another holder in return for some percentage of the final amount due. This allows Davidson Ltd to obtain most of the sum due under the bill in cash without waiting until the expiry of the period of maturity.

Purchasers of bills of exchange, provided that they act in good faith and without knowledge of any defect in title of previous holders, are entitled to hold the bill free of any defects. The bill should be complete and regular on the face of it, with no essential element, such as a signature, missing. Further, payment under the bill must not be overdue.

Assuming that the bill is regular, the bank is entitled to the rights of a holder in due course because the bill is not overdue and because value had been given for the bill: s29 Bills of Exchange Act 1882. We can also presume from the facts of the case that the bill has been properly endorsed and notice of this has been given to the drawee.

A holder in due course is entitled to proceed against the drawee of the bill as well as any other holders for value. In the present case, this means that the bank can proceed against both Wright Ltd and Davidson Ltd, but only once the bill is dishonoured. The bill is dishonoured at the moment when Wright Ltd refuses to make payment on presentation for payment.

A bill of exchange creates a right of action independent of the commercial transaction for which it has been issued. The fact that Davidson Ltd and Wright Ltd are in dispute as to the quality of the merchandise sold under the sales contract is a separate legal issue from non-payment under the bill of exchange. Wright Ltd is therefore required to fulfil its obligation to pay under the bill of exchange even though there is a dispute as to the quality of the goods: *Nova (Jersey) Knit Limited* v *Kammgarn Spinnerei GmbH* (1977).

The refusal by Wright Ltd to pay at the date of maturity of the bill of exchange means that the bill has been dishonoured and, in order to preserve the rights of the holder against other parties, the bill must be protested. A bill is protested when it is presented for payment for a second time, usually by a notary public, and payment is again refused. The notary public marks on the bill that it has been protested and any answer received as a justification for non-payment.

Once the bill is rejected, the bank is required to give notice of the refusal of Wright Ltd to pay to any holders in due course which it wishes to preserve recourse against. Generally, the dishonoured bill would be returned to Davidson Ltd and this amounts to suitable notice.

Both Davidson Ltd and the bank are entitled to seek a summary judgment against Wright Ltd. Davidson Ltd would be able to claim as the drawers under the bill while the bank's claim against Wright Ltd is derived from the fact that it is a holder in due course. The bank is a holder in due course because it acquired the bill before it was dishonoured, in good faith, and after it had been endorsed by Davidson Ltd.

At the same time, both Wright Ltd and Davidson Ltd are liable to the bank under the bill for payment of the stipulated price. Wright Ltd is liable under the bill as the drawee because it has written its acceptance on it. Davidson Ltd are liable because they are the drawer under the bill as well as being an endorser of the bill in favour of the bank. But it is Wright Ltd that bears primary liability since it is the drawee and Davidson Ltd is only liable in recourse.

If a bill has been protested, a summary judgment may be obtained against Wright Ltd under the Rules of the Supreme Court 1965, Order 14. Bills of exchange are to be treated as cash and, as such, in the absence of exceptional circumstances, even where there is a dispute between the immediate parties to the bill, judgment will not be held up by virtue of a counterclaim. Similarly, the existence of such a claim does not justify staying the execution of a summary judgment.

The only exception to this general rule is that limited defences are available in the event that fraud is averred, or a claim based on the invalidity of the bill, or for failure of consideration: see *Banco Atlantico SA* v *British Bank of the Middle East* (1990). However, there is no evidence to support such a defence in the facts presented in the question.

Question 2

Commercial Suicide (UK) Ltd is a British company whose business is discounting bills of exchange. It has decided to expand its operations into the European market and, as the first stage of this operation, purchases a consignment of bills of exchange, to order, from Sacre Blue, a French company also engaged in discounting, which has an office in London. Two of the bills were drawn on Strathclyde Steel by Firenze Steel, an Italian company and made payable to drawer at the main branch of Banco di Torino, in Florence.

When the bills were presented for payment on the due date, they were dishonoured. Commercial Suicide, after investigation, has discovered that Strathclyde Steel has been engaging in international fraud and that the documents tendered to them, and against which they accepted the bills of exchange, represent non-existent cargoes. It also appears that Strathclyde Steel is now in receivership.

Since it is unlikely that Commercial Suicide will be able to recover any sums from Strathclyde Steel, the company has sought your advice on its position vis-à-vis Sacre Blue. The French company has substantial sums lodged in banks accounts in the United Kingdom. Unfortunately, Commercial Suicide also owes considerable sums to Sacre Blue on a number of other separate discounting transactions.

What is your advice to Commercial Suicide?

Question prepared by the Editor
April 1994

General comment

This is a relatively straightforward factual-type question. Essentially it focusses on the rights of holders of bills against indorsers and the enforcement of bills in the English courts.

Skeleton solution

Commercial Suicide as a holder in due course.

Legal status of a holder in due course.

Primary liability of the drawee.

Noting and protesting of the bill.

Summary judgment.

Suggested solution

A bill of exchange is an unconditional order in writing, addressed by one person to another, signed by the person giving it, requiring the person to whom it is addressed to pay on demand or at a fixed or determinable future date a sum certain in money to, or to the order of, a specified person, or to bearer (s3 Bills of Exchange Act 1882). The obligations contained in a bill of exchange can be transferred by the negotiation of the bill. In the case of a bearer bill, the transfer is effected by mere delivery of the bill. In the case of a bill to order, both delivery of the bill and indorsement are required.

In the present problem, Commercial Suicide has purchased a consignment of bills of exchange, to order, from Sacre Blue. Under s5 of the BEA, a bill of exchange may be drawn to the order of the drawer and is a negotiable instrument under the terms of the Act. When such a bill is drawn in favour of the drawer, it becomes payable to the bearer as soon as the drawer indorses in blank.

Commercial Suicide is therefore a holder in due course of the bills of exchange. A holder in due course is someone who has taken a bill of exchange which is complete and regular on the face of it and which also satisfied two other conditions: (a) that the holder accepted the bill before it was overdue and without notice that it had been previously dishonoured; and (b) that the holder accepted the bill in good faith and for value and that at the time the bill was negotiated to the holder he or she had no notice of any defect in the title of the person who negotiated it: s29(1) BEA. Since the bills drawn on Strathclyde Steel were regular and because Commercial Suicide accepted the bills in good faith and for valuable consideration, it would appear that Commercial Suicide are valid holders in due course.

A holder in due course holds the bill free from any defect in the title of prior parties, as well as free from mere personal defences available to prior parties: s38(2) BEA.

The primary liability to pay a bill of exchange rests with the drawee. The drawer and any indorsers are only liable if the drawee dishonours the bill and they have received a notice of dishonour from the holder or a subsequent indorser. A bill payable to order is dishonoured if it is not paid upon presentation at the specified date. Consequently, although the Banco di Torino in Florence bears responsibility for payment of the bill as the payee, the drawer – Firenze Steel – the drawee – Strathclyde Steel Ltd —and the indorser – Sacre Blue – are also liable for payment under the bill. Since Commercial Suicide believes that it is impractical to claim against Strathclyde Steel on the basis of insolvency problems, a remedy is sought against Sacre Blue.

Sacre Blue endorsed the bills of exchange to Commercial Suicide and are therefore liable under s55(2) of the BEA. This section provides that anyone who endorses a bill of exchange engages that, on due presentation of the bill, it shall be accepted by the drawee and paid according to its tenor. An indorser also undertakes that if the bill is dishonoured, he or she will compensate a subsequent endorser, provided that the requisite procedure after dishonour is respected. Further, any prior indorser is precluded from challenging the authenticity and regularity of any previous indorsement and the signature of the drawer.

Despite the fact that the bills of exchange were originally drawn fraudulently against non-existent cargoes, Sacre Blue has no valid defence against an action raised by Commercial Suicide in the English courts. Any fraud in relation to the underlying contract is no concern of a subsequent holder in due course raising an action for payment against a previous endorser.

However, before Commercial Suicide can proceed against Sacre Blue, the bill of exchange must be duly noted and protested. Immediately upon the dishonour of a bill of exchange at due presentation, whether by non-acceptance or non-payment, a right of recourse against the indorsers accrues to the holder. But in order to avail themselves of this right, holders must give due notice of dishonour and, in the case of a foreign bill of exchange, cause it to be protested: s51(2) BEA. Commercial Suicide must first inform Sacre Blue of the dishonouring of the bill and then protest the bill. Protest of a foreign bill requires the authority of a notary public who verifies that the bill has in fact been dishonoured. A notarial certificate of the protest abroad of a foreign bill is sufficient to establish that fact.

After noting and protest, Commercial Suicide may raise an action in the English courts for non-payment of the sums due under the bills of exchange on the basis that they were endorsers of the bills. However, a summary judgment may only be obtained against an immediate party to a bill of exchange and not an endorser, under the Rules of the Supreme Court, Order 14. An action in the English courts is competent on the basis that Sacre Blue has offices in London, England and also operates bank accounts. But, it would not be possible to obtain an injunction against Sacre Blue to prevent liquidation of their assets in the United Kingdom.

The fact that Commercial Suicide owes money to Sacre Blue will not preclude such an action. In fact, in one case, Lord Wilberforce referred to time bills as 'deferred instalments in cash' and consequently such a bill is an unconditional order in writing: *Nova (Jersey) Knit Ltd* v *Kammgarn Spinnerei GmbH* (1977). English law does not permit cross-claims, or defences to an action for payment on a bill of exchange, except on the limited grounds of fraud on the bill, invalidity or failure of consideration.

Question 3

Once a bill of exchange has been drawn up, discuss the circumstances in which presentment for acceptance must be made.

Question prepared by the Editor
April 1994

General comment

Essay-type questions are not common in this area of the law, but this one has been added to give variety. It requires a narrative answer to describe the procedure for presentment for acceptance.

Skeleton solution

Bills of exchange normally presented for acceptance/payment together.

Section 39 BEA, certain types need to be presented for acceptance separately.

Mode of presentation.

Failure to comply with BEA.

Suggested solution

At some time after the bill has been drawn up, it will be sent to the drawee for acceptance. With the exception of certain limited situations as listed below, which require a bill to be presented for acceptance in advance of payment, most bills are not presented for acceptance until time for it to be presented for payment. Acceptance and payment may thus take place virtually simultaneously.

The drawee will signify his acceptance of the bill by writing on and/or signing the bill.

A bill which must be presented for acceptance will be either one payable a certain number of days after sight, or at a place which is not the drawee's ordinary place of business. See the Bills of Exchange Act 1882, s39(1): 'Where a bill is payable after

4 BILLS OF EXCHANGE

sight, presentment is necessary in order to fix the maturity of the instrument' and s39(2); 'Where a bill expressly stipulates that it shall be presented for acceptance, or where it is drawn payable elsewhere than at the residence or place of business of the drawee, it must be presented for acceptance, before it can be presented for payment.'

Where a holder is in possession of a bill which must be presented for acceptance separately and in advance of payment and does not comply with s39 by obtaining acceptance, the drawer and prior parties will be discharged as to their duties as to the holder if the bill is subsequently dishonoured (s40(2) BEA).

A holder of such a bill must present it within a reasonable time s40(1) and what is reasonable will depend on trade usage s40(3) BEA.

The rules as to presentment for acceptance are to be found in s41(1) and provided the holder has acted in accordance with those rules then if the bill is not accepted, the holder is entitled to treat the bill as dishonoured s42(1) BEA.

It is sometimes found that the drawee will accept, but impose conditions. Should the holder agree to such a 'qualified acceptance' he effectively agrees to vary the effect of the bill as originally drawn. He will to all intents and purposes be waiving his rights to treat the bill as dishonoured. The holder of a bill, provided he complies with the requirements of the Act in presentment is entitled to a 'general acceptance' ie unqualified by any conditions or reservations.

In the event that the drawee dishonours the bill, either by failing to accept it, or offering only conditional acceptance, the holder has immediate rights and need not wait until the bill is subsequently dishonoured by non-payment (s43(2) BEA).

It is important to note however that in order to secure such rights s48 of the Act requires the holder of a bill which has not been accepted to give notice of dishonour by non-acceptance to the drawer and prior parties. Failure to do this will discharge them from liability and lose the holder his rights under s43(2).

Question 4

Barny inspects a sample of zgwerchmeit seed in Sadsack's New York storehouse. Thereafter, Sadsack contracts to sell to Barny 'US $50,000 worth of zgwerchmeit as per sample cif London, payment cash against documents.' On Barny's instructions, the Karkey Bank is to open a letter of credit in favour of Sadsack for payment 'as per terms of sale contract.'

Sadsack ships the goods and presents the shipping documents to the bank and tenders a bill of exchange for US $50,000. The bank states that it will accept the shipping documents but (as it believes that sterling is about to be devalued) will only accept a bill of exchange for the current sterling equivalent of US $50,000. Sadsack objects but, in case he cannot resell the goods elsewhere, gives in to the bank's terms. The following day, sterling is devalued and the bill of exchange loses 10 per cent of its value. Sadsack wishes to recover this loss.

On the voyage, a heatwave causes the temperature in the hold to rise. This stimulates the growth of a fungus which was not detected when Barny inspected the sample at

New York. The fungus makes the seed sterile, although on a visual examination it appears to be in the same condition as when Barny first saw it.

Advise Sadsack and Barny.

University of London LLB Examination
(for External Students) Commercial Law June 1993 Q8

General comment

This is a common form of question where the issue of bills of exchange arises. The legal issues relating to bills of exchange are buried in the text of the question and the question itself primarily deals with other issues, most commonly international sales contracts and the passing of risk in such contracts. The student would be well advised to study this question extremely carefully since this is the form of question most likely to arise in examinations.

Skeleton solution

Goods sold by sample, by description, implied conditions under ss13–15 SGA.

Passing of risk and property in the goods.

Duties of the bank; their dual role.

Unpaid seller; rights and duties.

Right to reject, when lost, and other remedies especially s53 SGA.

Suggested solution

Goods sold in bulk present special problems with regard to implied terms as to fitness and also on the question of the passing of risk and of title from seller to buyer. Those problems are compounded in this instance because the goods are sold by sample.

Where goods are sold by description as well as by sample then, in accordance with ss13–15 Sale of Goods Act (SGA), goods must correspond with description and sample, and if sold in the course of a business they must be merchantable under the provisions of s14. Goods sold by description include goods sold under a trade name (*Azemer v Casella* (1867)) though it is not clear whether 'zgwerchmeit' is a trade name. Goods sold by sample must correspond with that sample – as indeed is the case here. The only problem is that the defect in the seed is not visually apparent; s15(2)(c) excludes the implied condition that the goods should be merchantable where the defect rendering them so could have been ascertained on a reasonable example of the sample. In s14(2) the implied term of merchantability is only excluded if an actual examination has been made. It is assumed that a buyer in a sale by sample will examine the sample – if he does not do so he will have no remedy for defects he could have discovered on examination.

There is a problem in the wording of the question which makes it unclear as to whether the fungus was not detected on Barny's (B's) inspection because it was not then present or whether it was present but undetected in a reasonable examination. In this respect the wording is ambiguous. Obviously if the fungus was not present in the sample, the bulk does not correspond to sample. If it was present even in the sample a good deal depends on what constitutes a reasonable examination. Remember that B inspects the sample in the warehouse, where laboratory tests and microscopic examination would be impossible. For further discussion of what constitutes a reasonable examination, see *Godley* v *Perry, Burton & Sons* (1960) and *Wren* v *Holt* (1903). Ultimately it boils down to the fact that if the defect is latent the buyer may reject goods, whether or not they correspond with the sample, whereas if the defect is patent and could have been detected on examination he will have no right to reject.

There is, however a further complication in that it is the heat on board ship which causes the fungus to grow making the seed sterile. Is the condition of the hold – poor loading, lack of ventilation – the fault of the shipper or his agents? Could it be argued that the seed, even if affected by the fungus, was perfectly merchantable until adversely affected by the heat? This is obviously of considerable importance to Sadsack (S) and B alike.

The next question to look at therefore is exactly when risk would have passed in such a contract. The agreement between S and B is a cif contract, the seller arranges insurance and freight and places the goods on board ship. Seller's risk normally ceases and passes to the buyer when the goods are placed on board ship. This will be the case unless S and B have re-allocated risk and there is no indication that they have. Consequently, if the seed has been adversely affected by the heat and would have been merchantable (with or without the fungus) had it not been for the heatwave, B may not have the right to reject the goods or consider the contract breached. (This is of course the sort of eventuality insurance is arranged to cover.)

Property in goods (as opposed to risk) normally passes in cif contracts on presentation of the documents of title against payment. Here again there are problems. S presents the bill of exchange to the K Bank but is told that the bank will only pay out a sterling equivalent. Under pressure S caves in and loses $5,000 on the transaction. Two distinct questions arise. Does the bank's action in any way affect the passing of property to B and secondly will S have any right of action against B as an unpaid seller?

The normal rule is that the bank has a dual role when accepting cif documents; firstly it acts as agent for the buyer, and secondly it acts on its own account and is contractually liable to pay the seller on presentation of the correct documents. If the bank have executed improper pressure or behave improperly in instigating their own 'condition' that the bill of exchange be for current sterling values, they will of course be liable on their own account. Though, as is normal, they act as agents for B, there is no suggestion that he has so instructed them. Nevertheless in any agency situation where the agent has apparent/ostensible authority, the principal, B in this case, will be liable for the agent bank's action regardless of whether they have disregarded his instructions. Effectively 10 per cent of S's payment is still owing and S will qualify as an unpaid seller with all the rights that status carries. B may of course have a right of action separately against his agent, the bank, for not following his instructions.

Note that S may have a right against the bank to sue for the 10 per cent loss as equally he may have a right against B, but these are alternative courses of action; he may not pursue both. Should he decide to sue he must elect, as is usual in agency situations, to sue one or the other and is then bound by that choice.

Thus S may be able to recover, either from the bank or from B, the difference in sterling values. But what of B's rights? As already stated, if the fungus is harmless and has only mutated because of the heatwave on board ship, then since the goods are travelling (presumably) under normal cif rules at the buyer's risk, B will have to rely on insurance of the goods to make good the loss he has suffered.

If on the other hand the defect in the seed, ie the presence of the fungus would sooner or later have rendered the seed sterile and thus unmerchantable, then B will have the right to reject the goods and/or compensation. We have already discussed the problem of latent/patent defects and the assumption is that the presence of the fungus could not, at the point B examined it in New York, have been detected. Of course if it was apparent and B missed it, he loses his protection under the SGA.

Transfer of property in the goods takes place in cif contracts (unless the parties indicate to the contrary) on payment of cash against documents. Two questions arise in this case. S has lost about 10 per cent of the total price – does this count as 'payment'? And secondly, if property has been transferred, does this mean B has lost his right to reject?

Unless a seller is paid in full the assumption would normally be that no property has passed. This will be of considerable significance to S. It is only after property has passed that a seller can maintain an action against the buyer for the purchase price (or part of it). While the property lies in the buyer this remedy can only lie in damages. This means that he must try and mitigate his loss by selling elsewhere and the question notes that S anticipates he might have difficulty doing this. In any case the goods are now known to be unmerchantable; to try to re-sell them would of necessity involve a degree of deception on S's part. For convenience, even if because of some financial hiccup payment is not made, or not made in full, property is normally assumed to pass when the seller tenders the documents of title. This is the case even if for some reason cash payment is not made (*Arnold Karlberg* v *Blythe* (1916)).

But if property has passed to B, will it avail S to begin an action for the 10 per cent unpaid? B will have far greater rights, he has after all received a ship-load of seed which is unmerchantable.

If a buyer exercises his right to reject the goods as being in breach of ss13, 14 and 15 SGA, then he can either decline to pay the price, or if he has paid he may recover it as being paid for a total failure of consideration by the seller. He is not required to return the goods to the seller (s36 SGA). In certain circumstances, however, the buyer may lose the right to reject – has this happened to B? The passing of property no longer affects the right to reject, but acceptance of the goods by B may mean he loses his right to reject. What would constitute acceptance? Sections 34–35 SGA govern the rules as to when acceptance will be deemed to have occurred. Section 34 in particular provides that until such time as the buyer has had a reasonable opportunity to examine the goods, he cannot be deemed to have accepted. It is not clear whether B has yet had such an opportunity. Section 35 says that if the buyer intimates acceptance or otherwise performs some act consistent with ownership (eg selling on goods) then acceptance will have occurred. Section 34 however takes priority; a buyer will sometimes sell-on goods before having an opportunity to examine them. Obviously if a buyer has such an opportunity to inspect and does not avail himself of it then he will lose the protection of s34. It is not clear whether B has either inspected the goods or acted in a way indicating acceptance. It may be in any event that discovery of the defect would be considerably delayed, because we are told that visually the seed looks perfect, but its sterility would presumably be only discovered after being sown.

Merely because B accepts the goods, thereby losing the right of rejection, does not mean that he is bereft of any other means of redress. Section 53 of the SGA provides that, in the event of a breach of warranty (such as a defect in the quality of the goods) the dissatisfied buyer may sue for damages. The measure of damages is the difference in the value of the goods as they presently are (presumably nil in this case!) and the value they would have had if they had fulfilled the warranty. Particularly in the case of seeds etc, a breach of s14(2) as to merchantable quality means that the potential gain from the seeds if they had grown properly can be taken into account. But, it should be noted that sub-sales to other buyers are generally not included in these damages (*Slater v Hoyle and Smith* (1920)).

So even should S, in the interval before the defect in the seeds is noted, be able to recover the amount still outstanding, once the sterility of the seeds becomes apparent B will have a corresponding right either to reject (if it is not too late and it probably is) or to sue under s53. The limitation period of course starts to run from the period when the defect giving rise to the cause of action first becomes apparent.

5 DOCUMENTARY CREDITS

5.1   Introduction

The documentary credit system is intended to give both buyer and seller a degree of protection which they would not otherwise have, given the fact that they will usually be separated by great distances; and since they are in different countries different currencies would apply.

The seller will primarily want to be sure that, having shipped the goods, he is paid for them. The buyer will want to ensure that, if he pays, the seller will comply with his requirements (because of transit problems it may be some time before he can actually check the goods for himself).

To reach a compromise between these concerns, a buyer can open a credit facility, usually through a bank in his own country in favour of the seller. This offers the seller an assurance that payment will be made, provided the seller can in return prove that he has performed his side of the contract. Payment under the credit facility will not, however be made, unless and until, the necessary documentation (evidencing contractual performance by the seller) has been presented to the bank.

The sort of documents likely to be involved will vary. The buyer himself may if he wishes dictate documentation requirements, but the list is likely to include a combination of any or all of these: bill of lading, invoice, insurance policy, and/or bill of exchange.

5.2   Key points

a) *Uniform Customs and Practice (UCP)*

The Uniform Customs and Practice for Documentary Credits is a set of rules issued by the International Chamber of Commerce and intended to regulate the operation of the system of documentary credits. The edition currently in force is the UCP 500 which came into effect on 1 January 1994. When the terms of the UCP 500 are incorporated into a documentary credit, the respective rights and duties of the parties are determined by its terms.

It should be noted that, under English law the use of UCP is not mandatory and will only apply where expressly incorporated into the credit arrangements by the parties. Nevertheless, in practice, incorporation of the terms of the UCP into credit arrangements is extremely common.

b) *The parties*

Briefly the parties may be listed as:

i) The applicant for credit – usually the buyer by whom the contract price is owed.

ii) The issuing bank – the buyer's own bank opens the credit, probably having received some form of collateral from the buyer.

When the credit facility is open the bank will notify the seller and issue instructions as to how the seller must act to obtain payment.

iii) The correspondent bank – usually the seller's bank.

This bank may act in an advisory or confirming capacity and its powers will vary accordingly.

iv) The beneficiary – the seller.

Provided the seller presents the proper documents he will be entitled to payment regardless of any disputes that have arisen over the underlying contract of sale.

c) *Varieties of credit*

The simplest form of credit is the straightforward letter of credit, also known as a documentary credit, for a single non-recurring transaction. The following are common but more intricate varieties of credit:

i) back to back credit;

ii) packing credit;

iii) revolving credit;

iv) negotiation credits;

v) transferable credits.

In many cases the name of the type of credit is indicative of the way it operates.

It should be noted that credits as such are non-assignable although the beneficiary may assign the proceeds of the credit provided the assignment is made according to the provisions of s136 of Law of Property Act 1925.

d) *The mandate*

The instructions given by the buyer or applicant for credit to his bank comprise the buyer's mandate.

The mandate must be clear and precise stating those documents against which the bank is to make payment to the seller or beneficiary (and sometimes listing those documents which if tendered will be unacceptable).

Where the mandate is ambiguous the common law allows the bank to interpret in the light of what is 'reasonable'.

Alternatively the bank may simply refer back to the buyer for further instruction. If, however, the bank proceeds and pays, despite the ambiguity they will lose their right to be paid by the buyer if they have exceeded their mandate.

e) *Revocable/irrevocable and confirmed/unconfirmed credits*

i) Revocable/irrevocable credits

Whether a credit is revocable or irrevocable depends on whether the issuing bank has made an undertaking to the beneficiary (the seller). If the credit is revocable the issuing bank may withdraw the credit at any time and without prior notice being given to the beneficiary. Conversely, if the credit is irrevocable, the issuing bank cannot cancel the credit at its discretion but must honour the obligation until the expiry of the duration of the credit.

The UCP 500 provides an Article 6b that a credit should clearly indicate whether the credit is revocable or irrevocable. In the absence of any such indication the credit is deemed to be irrevocable: Article 6c.

ii) Confirmed/unconfirmed credits

When the correspondent bank adds its own undertaking to honour the credit, the credit is described as a confirmed credit. The correspondent bank is then known as the confirming bank.

The legal effect of confirmation is the creation of a contractual relationship between the confirming bank and the beneficiary. As Diplock J observed, a confirmed credit is a 'direct undertaking by the banker to the seller that if he presents the documents as required in the required time, he will receive payment': *Hamzeh Malas & Sons* v *British Imex Industries Ltd* [1958] 2 QB 127. This dictum has been directly incorporated into the UCP 500 in Article 9a.

An unconfirmed credit is simply one to which the correspondent bank has not added its own undertaking to honour the terms of the credit. Where the credit is not confirmed, the correspondent bank is known simply as the advising bank.

iii) The three variations of credit

Although technically four variations in type of credit are possible, in practice revocable credits will not be confirmed by a correspondent bank and are therefore not used in commerce. The remaining three variations are:

- revocable and unconfirmed credits;
- irrevocable and unconfirmed credits;
- irrevocable and confirmed credits.

Revocable and unconfirmed credits are an extremely unsatisfactory method of financing an international sales transaction from the point of view of the exporter, while irrevocable and confirmed credits are the most secure. Again in practice irrevocable and confirmed credits are the most common means of payment for international sales contracts.

f) *The principle of the autonomy of the credit*

Letters of credit are most often used to make payment under international sales agreements and in such contracts payment by a particular type of letter of credit is frequently expressly stipulated. Nevertheless, from the point of view of the contractual relationships created by a letter of credit, the underlying contract of sale is absolutely distinct from the functioning of the credit. This principle is succinctly stated in Article 3a of the UCP 500 which states:

'Credits, by their nature, are separate transactions from the sales or other contracts on which they may be based and banks are in no way concerned with or bound by such contracts, even if any reference whatsoever to such contracts is included in the credit.'

As a result, in the event of a dispute between the buyer and the seller as to the goods which are the subject of the sale – ie a dispute as to merchantable quality, delivery, performance of the terms of the contract, etc – a bank cannot refuse to pay the beneficiary if the credit is valid simply because the buyer tries to invoke the contractual dispute. The only exception to this rule is in the case of fraud which is considered later.

This principle is also behind the rule contained in Article 4 of the UCP 500 that, in credit operations, all parties concerned deal with documents and not with goods, service or the other performances to which the document may relate.

g) *The doctrine of strict compliance*

A correspondent bank, whether acting in the capacity of an advising or confirming bank, is the agent of the issuing bank and as such is required to act within the mandate created by that relationship. The most important aspect of that function is to accept only those documents from the seller that are specifically identified by the issuing bank for payment under the credit. Failure to observe this duty will render the correspondent bank liable to the issuing bank.

The rigorous nature of this duty requires the correspondent bank to refuse to make payment against presentation of the documents where either: (i) not all the documents specified in the credit are presented for payment; or (ii) the particular documents presented are not exactly those described in the credit.

More often than not, documents are rejected because they do not conform to the description set out in the credit. The UCP 500 sets out certain guidelines for some types of documents which may be deemed equivalent, and for the cross-reference of specific terms to others, in Articles 20 to 34. But frequently guidance cannot be obtained from this source. In such cases, the correspondent bank is entitled to reject documents which do not contain all the particulars contained in the credit: see *Soproma SpA v Marine & Animal By-Products Corporation* [1966] 1 Lloyd's Rep 367.

h) *Taking up the seller's documents*

The most likely documents to be required to be presented by the seller have already been noted.

When the seller tenders those documents required to the bank, the bank must examine all documents with reasonable care to ascertain, inter alia, that they are correct, consistent and the content is as required. The bank's liability is to take 'reasonable' care. They need not, for example, investigate a document's background if it is apparently in order, and if a document appears to be the original they need not set up tests to detect forgery. Obviously, however if the bank has any grounds for suspicion they must probe more deeply.

However, should a bank delay unnecessarily in examining the documents presented, it may be liable to the issuing bank, at the very least to pay interest and any additional costs incurred by the delay: see *Co-operative Centrale Raiffeison v Sumitomo Bank* [1988] 2 Lloyd's Rep 250. Also, when the documents are correct and the bank refuse to pay or delays payment, it may find itself liable to the seller.

i) *The expiry of the credit*

Article 42a of the UCP 500 requires that all credits must specify an expiry date and a place for presentation of the documents for payment and acceptance. In addition, an expiry date stipulated for payment, acceptance or negotiation will be construed as an expiry date for the presentation of the documents.

j) *Payment under reserve*

Where a correspondent bank has concerns as to whether or not the documents tendered by the seller conform to the terms of the credit it may make payment under reserve. Payment under reserve has been explained in the following terms:

'Payment made under reserve [means] that the beneficiary would be bound to repay the money on demand if the issuing bank should reject the documents whether on its own initiative or on the buyer's instructions'; per Kerr LJ in *Banque de l'Indochine et de Suez SA v JH Reyner (Mincing Lane) Ltd* [1983] QB 711.

Factors which are taken into account by a correspondent bank in deciding whether or not to make payment under reserve include:

i)   the financial standing of the beneficiary;

ii)   the discrepancies found between the documents and the instructions;

iii)   the likelihood of the issuing bank and the buyer accepting the documents.

An advising bank is entitled to recover sums paid under reserve to a beneficiary in the event that the documents are eventually rejected by the issuing bank or the buyer.

k) *Effect of fraud*

The single exception to the duty of the correspondent bank to make payment against the tendered documents is in the case of fraud. In such circumstances an advising or confirming bank is entitled to refuse to honour its undertaking to pay the beneficiary against the documents.

Equally, proof of fraud may provide grounds on which a buyer may obtain an injunction to prevent a bank paying the beneficiary. To obtain such a court order, it is necessary for the buyer to establish the existence of fraud and knowledge on the part of the bank as to the fraud.

5.3   Recent cases and statutes

Bankers Trust Co v *State Bank of India* [1991] 2 Lloyd's Rep 443: an important decision relating to the apportionment of liability between the issuing bank and the confirming bank after payment has been made against inconsistent documents.

Rafsanjan Pistachio Producers Co-operative v *Bank Leumi (UK) Ltd* [1992] 1 Lloyd's Rep 513: an illustration of the effect of fraud by the beneficiaries on the liability of a confirming bank to pay.

Seaconsar Far East Limited v *Bank Markazi Iran* [1993] 1 Lloyd's Rep 236: a case concerning the right of a plaintiff to serve proceedings out of the jurisdiction under RSC Ord 11 on the basis of a dispute concerning the operation of a letter of credit.

5.4   Relevant materials

ICC, *Uniform Customs and Practice for Documentary Credits 1993 Revision* (UCP 500).

F Dow, *Understanding Documentary Bills and Credits* (1991).

C Schmitthoff, *The Export Trade* (9th edition, 1990), pp400–445.

J Crabtree, *International Sale of Goods* (1991), pp83–101.

5.5   Analysis of questions

Questions as to documentary credits have cropped up several times in University of London's past papers and are usually fairly straightforward.

Essay-type questions on the subject are relatively rare and the focus is normally on problem-type questions based on hypothetical factual situations.

5.6 Questions

Question 1

Give a general account of the *legal* position where an international sale governed by English law is financed by a banker's irrevocable and confirmed documentary credit.

University of London LLB Examination
(for External Students) Commercial Law June 1983 Q1

General comment

This is the exception to the rule: an essay question requiring a straightforward narrative answer.

Skeleton solution

Revocable/irrevocable credits.

Additional security for seller provided by irrevocable credit.

Buyers mandate.

Doctrine of strict compliance.

UCP rules.

Suggested solution

The legal position where an overseas sale is financed by an irrevocable and confirmed documentary credit reflects the fact that the system is designed to provide security for both parties which the actual contract of sale itself can never do and to raise credit – a problem which arises primarily because no seller or buyer will wish to commit working capital to goods in transit. Essentially, a third party (in the form of two banks) agrees to be the drawee of the seller's draft and promises to honour it provided that the seller discharges his duties under the contract of sale. It is important to note that the legal position under the documentary credit system and the seller's right to claim payment thereunder is not subject to the seller performing all his duties under the contract of sale.

Firstly, from the point of view of the seller his legal rights conferred by the confirmed and irrevocable credit presents him with the most acceptable way of financing the sale. Provided the documents are tendered in conformity by the seller, the corresponding bank guarantees that it will pay against them, and it cannot withdraw that guarantee, even if the buyer subsequently instructs that that be done. The credit is irrevocable. Whether a documentary credit is confirmed or unconfirmed depends upon the role assumed by the correspondent bank. The correspondent bank may only act to notify the seller about the opening of the credit by the issuing bank and if that is the position, then the credit is unconfirmed although it may be irrevocable on the part of the issuing banker. In that case the correspondent bank is essentially an agent. However, often the seller will seek to bind the correspondent bank with an irrevocable guarantee and in that case the correspondent adds his own guarantee to that of the issuing banker and the credit is confirmed. Each bank's undertaking is as principal, although the issuing bank's role is analogous to that of a commission agent, authorised to conclude a contract with the seller but on his own account. In practice a correspondent bank will never confirm a revocable credit.

Seller/buyer

Legal consequences ensuing from the credit begin when buyer and seller agree to insert into the contract of sale a documentary credit clause. The buyer is then under an obligation to have a documentary credit opened in favour of the seller. It is a condition precedent to the seller's duty to deliver the goods, but need not necessarily be such for *all* the seller's obligations under the contract – for the seller may be under a duty to perform some act prior to the buyer's duty to furnish the credit. If the documentary credit clause stipulates an irrevocable confirmed documentary credit then that is what the buyer must provide. If no stipulation is made then it has been suggested that the contract of sale is incomplete: *Schijveschuurder and Others* v *Canon (Exports) Ltd* (1952).

The buyer's duty to furnish the credit is absolute within the time stipulated. This duty is not negated by factors beyond the buyer's control. In *Lindsay & Co* v *Cook* (1953) an inter-bank communication delay, entirely independent on the fault of the buyers, nevertheless entitled the seller to repudiate the contract of sale. As against that strict duty, however, it is always open to the seller to waive the breach where a buyer has either failed to open a credit in time, or has opened one which deviates in some way from that specified in the contract. This, of course, may constitute a *strict waiver* (cf, Lord Denning in *W J Alan & Co* v *El Nasr Export and Import Co* (1972) or a *variation* of the contract. Whether one or the other applies depends upon the circumstances of the case, but the majority of the Court of Appeal in *Alan* v *El Nasr* opined that the waiver doctrine would not apply in cases where the buyer had not detrimentally relied.

With respect to payment, the seller is under a duty to claim payment from either the issuing bank or the corresponding banks – depending upon the term of the credit, and only in the rare instance of default of the relevant bank will he be entitled to claim from the buyer. If the seller fails to present the documents to the relevant bank – preventing him from claiming payment, the buyer will be absolutely discharged from his payment obligation. From the buyer's point of view, however, merely opening the credit itself will not operate to discharge the buyer. This was confirmed by Lord Denning in *Alan* v *El Nasr* who said that ordinarily when the contract of sale stipulates for payment to be made by confirmed irrecoverable documentary credit, then when that is issued and accepted by the seller, it operates as a conditional payment of the price. It did not operate as an absolute discharge.

This was also the ratio of the decision in the *Maran Road Saw Mill* v *Austin Taylor* (1975) where it was held that the opening of a credit operated only as a conditional discharge so that if an issuing bank failed to perform its undertaking given in the irrevocable credit, the buyer's duty to pay the price revived. The unusual feature of *Maran Road* was that there the question of discharging the buyer from a payment obligation arose *after* the buyer had placed the issuing bank in funds. The argument rejected was essentially that the buyer had already performed by remitting the stipulated amount to the bank. However, because the buyer had to *pay* by credit and not just *provide a documentary credit*, since the sellers had not been paid, the buyer's obligation revived. This has been criticised on the basis that it constitutes, essentially, a buyer's guarantee of the issuing bank's solvency, but against that it could simply be argued that the irrevocable credit constituted a security furnished by the buyer, for the seller and if that security fails, the buyer ought to bear the resultant loss.

These considerations affect the relationship between the seller and the buyer. But the irrevocable and confirmed result brings into existence four more contractual relationships – those between the buyer and the issuing banks, the issuing bank and the correspondent bank, the issuing bank and the seller and the correspondent bank and the seller.

There is no privity of contract between the buyer and the correspondent bank. However, for any default of the correspondent bank causing the buyer loss, the buyer has a remedy against the issuing bank – an action for liability for the acts/omissions of its agent.

Issuing bank/buyer

The relationship between the buyer and issuing bank is simply that of banker and customer, formed by a unilateral contract in which the buyer submits an application which constitutes an offer, the issuing bank accepts by issuing the letter of credit. As we have seen, acceptance of such a letter of credit does not discharge the buyer. So if the bank dishonours the draft by not paying, the seller may have recourse to the buyer. In that case, the buyer may have to pay twice – one to the seller and once to the Mercantile issuing bank. However, the court may release the buyer from any obligation assumed by him towards the defaulting issuing bank as in *Sale Continuation* v *Austin Taylor & Co* (1967) where Paull J released the buyer from his obligation to the bank. The case has been criticised on the ground that by accepting the documentary credit in the first place the banker has *partially performed* its duties under the contract with the buyer and therefore there is no total failure of consideration when the bill is subsequently dishonoured and on the basis Gutteridge suggests that the buyer be *obliged to perform*. However, as Ackner J pointed out in *Maran Road* the main object is payment of the seller and this type of credit is simply to provide the buyer with short-term credit.

It is therefore wrong to regard the bank's act of accepting the seller's bill as performance of the bank's duties to the buyer *in any way*, and so there is a total failure of consideration. On that basis, *Sale Continuation* is quite acceptable.

The issuing bank is protected by the UCP against the risks that attach with the engagement of a correspondent banker. Article 9 of the UCP 500 protects the issuing bank against liability for delivery, and generally under Article 11 of the UCP, if the issuing bank utilises the services of a correspondent banker, he does so at the buyer's risk and, accordingly, he therefore assumes no liability if the correspondent banker does not carry out his instructions. This applies even if the issuing bank has taken the initiative and selected the correspondent.

Issuing bank/seller

Now, as between the issuing bank and seller an irrevocable credit creates a legally binding contract. It can therefore be enforced by the *seller*. The added element of confirmation means that the correspondent banker is jointly and severally bound with the issuing bank towards the seller – the two banks are therefore under similar obligations.

Now, it has been said that the issuing bank/seller contract is established as soon as the documentary credit reaches the hands of the seller, but this analysis is difficult to accept because it is by no means easy to find consideration moving from the seller at that time. However, Greer J in *Dexters* v *Schenkers* (1923) said that there was full and ample consideration because until the seller has got a banker's credit, the seller is not bound to send the goods at all. This depends upon reasoning that the seller becomes bound to ship only when the credit reaches his hands. Alternatively, it could be argued that consideration is furnished by the seller, on the basis of the irrevocable credit, to *demand payment from the buyer.*

The substance of the contract is an undertaking by the issuing bank that payment will be made on presentation of the documents. It is given as *principal*, not as agent of the buyer – like the issuing bank/buyer contract, the issuing bank's contract with the seller is completely *independent. It cannot be modified by the terms of the main buyer/seller contract.* Now, the question of whether the seller is to look for payment to the issuing bank first, or the correspondent bank defends his terms of the credit. The correspondent bank, adding its own name to the 'guarantee' to that of the issuing bank, in a sense becomes *both principal* to the seller and *agent* to the issuing bank. By informing the seller of the opening of the credit he acts as agent of the issuing bank but by conforming the credit he assumes towards the seller the role of principal.

Correspondent bank/seller

Finally, as has been noted, there is a contract between the correspondent bank and the seller, with the former adding its name to the payment undertaking as *principal*. It is not joint and several liability but independent undertakings, so if the terms of the correspondent banker's confirmation are more restricted than those of the original credit, then the correspondent bank's liability to the seller is correspondingly more limited.

Question 2

Gracechurch Supplies Ltd bought the following goods under separate contracts governed by English law:

i)   from Simpson Ltd

    20,000 microwaves cif London.

ii)   from Hart Ltd

    15,000 video records fob Singapore for delivery in Beirut, Lebanon.

iii) from Young Ltd

    2,000 word processors cif London.

Each contract stated (inter alia) that

i)   Payment was to be made by irrevocable letter of credit at South Eastern Bank on presentation of the shipping documents;

ii)   shipment was to take place in January/February 1986; and

iii) liability 'for breach of any express or implied warranty was excluded'.

The directors of Gracechurch Supplies Ltd consult you and state:

1) *Ovens*

We opened the credit in favour of the sellers on January 3, 1986. The bank paid on presentation of the invoice, the marine insurance policy and a 'received for shipment' bill of lading. When the ovens reached us, we found that the hinges on the doors were faulty but could be put right at a minimal cost. We sold 2,000 of them to Rees Ltd on the same terms. They returned them to us one month later on discovering that fault. The packing cases in which the rest of the ovens were packed were stolen property.

2) *Video recorders*

The credit was opened on December 28, 1985. We contacted the sellers and said that we wanted to inspect the recorders before shipment, but they would not allow us to do so. The bank paid on presentation of the shipping documents. On the arrival of the vessel at Beirut she and all her cargo were a total loss by shell fire in the civil war. We find that the recorders were shipped on February 3, but we knew nothing of this until after the loss.

3) *Word processors*

The bank paid on presentation of the shipping documents including bills of lading showing shipment on February 28. We had instructed the bank not to pay because there were some newer models on the way. On arrival 700 of the word processors had keys in the Greek instead of the English alphabet and were useless for our purposes as we intended to sell them to our customers in England. We spent £30,000 in advertising the word processors and our goodwill has been damaged. The bills of lading were forged and shipment took place on March 1.

Advise the directors of Gracechurch Supplies Ltd in relation to all the matters stated above.

University of London LLB Examination
for (External Students) Commercial Law June 1986 Q3

General comment

This is a problem based on rather intricate hypothetical circumstances. In reality, the letter of credit issue is interwoven into the fabric of the question along with issues relating to liability under the underlying sales contract. For the sake of completeness, all the legal issues involved, including those relating to the sales contracts, will be addressed here.

Skeleton solution

UCP 500.

International supply contracts not governed by UCTA 1977.

Cif and fob contracts.

Documentary credits.

Bills of lading.

Faulty goods – Sale of Goods Act – export sales.

Rights and remedies of parties.

Suggested solution

We are told that the contracts are governed by English Law. It will be assumed, where relevant, that the documentary credits incorporated the current UCP (Uniform Customs and Practice for Documentary Credits 1993 Revision) because it is the standard practice of the banks to issue credits on these terms. One other issue can be dispensed with at this stage, namely that because the contracts are international supply contracts they are not subject to regulation by the Unfair Contract Terms Act 1977 (see s26). All discussion of the exclusion clause, therefore, will revolve around the common law only.

1) *The ovens*

The credit ought to have been opened a reasonable time before the beginning of the shipment period (*Sinason-Teicher Inter-American Grain Corporation* v *Oilcakes & Oilseeds Trading Co* (1954)). The failure to do this was a breach of a condition in the sale contract. There is some authority for the proposition that this is breach of a condition precedent to the very formation of the sale contract (*Trans Trust SPRL* v *Danubian Trading Co Ltd* (1952)), but nothing revolves around that because it is clear from the facts given that the sellers, Simpson Ltd (S), did not attempt to discharge the contract for this breach but affirmed it by shipping the goods. This will prevent any remedy being available unless S can prove that a loss resulted from the credit being opened late; which on the facts given they will not be able to do.

The documents presented to the bank included a received for shipment bill of lading. Such a document is not good tender under the cif contract because it does not assure the buyer that the goods have been loaded (*Diamond Alkali Export Corporation* v *Fl Bourgeois* (1921)). Under the UCP 500 a received for shipment bill can sometimes be accepted by the bank (article 23) and at other times a received for shipment bill can be transformed into a shipped bill. In the absence of agreement to the contrary a cif contract can only be performed by the presentation of a shipped bill and the credit contract is likely to be read in this light. In principle the credit contract is a

95

separate thing from the sale contract which it finances and therefore it should be possible for the cif contract to require one document and the credit contract another. But, in the context of a normal cif contract, the credit and sale contracts will be read together. The position here, then, is that the bank accepted a received for shipment bill in breach of its mandate. This has two consequences, firstly the acceptance of documents by the bank is not acceptance by the buyer under the cif contract and secondly the buyer is not obliged to reimburse the bank.

As regards the first point, the bank is the agent of the buyer to accept the cif documents (*Donald H Scott & Co Ltd* v *Barclays Bank Ltd* (1923); *Panchaud Frères SA* v *Etablissements General Grain Co* (1970)), and all the circumstances are known to the seller; therefore if the seller tenders documents which are not in compliance with the requirements of the cif contract and the bank accepts them then the seller knows that the bank is acting outside its authority. In such circumstances the buyer can ratify the wrongful act of his agent, the bank, and on ratification it is deemed that the acceptance of the documents was valid as from the beginning. As regards the second point, once the buyer ratifies the acceptance of the documents by the bank he is obliged to reimburse the bank the amount of the credit (and the bank's fee), but has a right of action against the bank for any loss arising from the wrongful acceptance of the documents (the buyer has a contract with the issuing bank; any wrongful acts by the bank will amount to a breach of that contract. It is assumed that South Eastern Bank was the only bank involved and worked through one of its branches when accepting the documents). The manner of ratification is a matter for the buyer, but physical acceptance of the goods by the buyer will amount to ratification (*Panchaud Frères SA* v *Etablissement General Grain Co* (1970)).

Therefore, on the facts we are given, the bank acted outside its authority when accepting a received for shipment bill of lading, but that wrongful act has been ratified and no loss has resulted from the bank's breach. Acceptance of the documents does not preclude the buyer from rejecting the goods if a breach of condition in relation to the goods can be proved which was not apparent on the face of the documents (*Kwei Tek Chao* v *British Traders & Shippers Limited* (1954) and *Panchaud Frères* (above)).

Three matters fall for discussion in relation to the goods. Firstly the effect of the hinges being faulty, secondly the effect of the sale of 2,000 to Rees and thirdly the effect of the packing cases being stolen goods.

Faults in goods which are sold as new goods render those goods unmerchantable provided the faults did not arise at a time when the goods were at the risk of the buyer. In a cif sale risk passes as from shipment (*Kwei Tek Chao* v *British Traders & Shippers Limited* (1954)), which means at the time the goods cross the ship's rail, so if the hinges were damaged in transit then GS must look to the ship for compensation because there will be no right of action against the sellers. GS will have a contract with the ship either by virtue of the Bills of Lading Act 1855 or by virtue of the parallel rule in *Brandt* v *Liverpool, Brazil and River Plate Steam Navigation Co* (1924); an action will be available in negligence provided GS had property in the goods at the time damage occurred, *The Aliakmon* (1986). On the other hand, the occurrence of this damage prior to shipment will give GS a remedy for breach of s14(2) of the Sale of the Goods Act 1979 against S. The fact that the hinges could be put right at minimal cost does not prevent the ovens from being unmerchantable because they will not be reasonably fit for their normal purposes. Furthermore there will be a breach of s14(3) because the purchase of 2,000 ovens makes known to the seller that they are being bought for a resale and they are not reasonably fit for resale if they have damaged hinges.

The remedy for breach of s14(2) and 14(3) is rejection of the goods and damages. Rejection will not be available for those of the goods which have been accepted. In most sales the contract will be entire and the buyer will lose the right to reject if he sells on any of the goods supplied. But if the contract is severable, a partial acceptance will not preclude rejection of the rest. The main factor determining whether a sale contract is entire or severable is, usually, whether there is delivery in instalments with each instalment being paid for separately (*J Rosenthal & Sons Ltd v Esmail* (1965)). In cases like the present where delivery of all the goods occurs at the same time, then there is no clear rule about how one judges whether it is severable or entire. The presumption is that where goods are shipped all in one consignment, the contract is entire, though the House of Lords accepted that the presumption is weak); but we are told that the 2,000 which were sold to Rees Ltd (R) were sold on the same terms, which indicates that the original sale was severable (the *Rosenthal* case is distinguishable because it is always a matter of fact whether a contract is or is not severable and in that case it was the course of dealings between the parties which prevented the shipment under two bills of lading from rendering the contract severable). We are told that the bank accepted 'a' received for shipment bill of lading, which indicates that there was only one bill; a matter which would normally make a resale of part of the goods difficult, but we are not told of any problems in effecting the sub-sale.

The question now is whether the goods have been accepted by GS. There is a long line of authority which holds that a resale and delivery of goods by a buyer amounts to acceptance because it is an act inconsistent with the ownership of the original seller (*Perkins v Bell* (1893)). Therefore, when GS sold and delivered 2,000 ovens to Rees Ltd (R) that was acceptance of those 2,000. R rejected one month after delivery and in many domestic sales this would be too late, but in a CIF sale, which usually involves an international element, this would not be such a long time that the right to reject for the breach of s14(2) was lost (*Kwei Tek Chao v British Traders & Shippers Limited* (1954)). So there was acceptance by GS of the 2,000 sold to R.

But, there is an added complication caused by the third issue outlined above; the fact that the packaging of the rest of the ovens was stolen. Packaging is part of the goods supplied (*Wormell v RHM Agriculture (East) Ltd* (1986)) and if there is a defect in packaging this can be a breach of s14(2); it can also be the case that s12(1) can be breached. In the present case part of the goods delivered have turned out to be stolen which necessarily means that S did not have the right to sell them. The doctrine of acceptance does not arise where there is a breach of s12(1) arising from the sale of stolen goods, therefore the 18,000 ovens and their packaging can be rejected. It has been stated above that this contract is severable and so the acceptance of 2,000 will not preclude rejection of the 18,000 remaining (s11(4) Sale of Goods Act 1979 would not prevent rejection because that only applies to non-severable contracts).

In addition to having the right to reject goods for breach of condition, damages can also be claimed. GS will be able to claim the difference between the value that 18,000 ovens would have had if delivered on time and in the proper condition, and the contract price – in other words they can claim their loss of bargain, if any. It will not, however, be possible to claim any substantial sum to cover losses arising from resale because we are told that the hinges could be repaired at minimal cost and the failure of GS to effect such repairs before delivery to R means that the rejection by R could have been avoided and, therefore, that they have not reasonably mitigated their loss (*The Solholt* (1983)).

The exclusion clause in the contract will not help S because it only attempted to exclude liability for breach of warranty and the breaches here were breaches of condition. The fact that in relation to the 2,000 sold on to R the breach of condition falls to be treated as breach of warranty does not affect this because it only falls to be treated as a breach of warranty, it is still a condition which is breached.

2) *The video recorders*

The opening of the credit on 28 December 1985 was not too late, but may have been too early. Documentary credits do not remain open indefinitely and if they are opened too early the seller can be prejudiced by expiration occurring before he has had time to present documents to the bank (*Trans Trust SPRL* v *Danubian Trading Co Ltd* (1952)). However, on the facts given it appears that Hart Ltd (H) had ample time to present documents and so nothing revolves around the date of opening of the credit.

In sales on fob terms risk passes to the buyer at the time of shipment (*Pyrene & Co* v *Scindia Navigation Co* (1954)), therefore, prima facie, any damage done during the voyage was at GS's risk. But it may be possible to shift this loss onto H if it can be proved that inspection of the goods 'before shipment' would have led to GS rejecting them.

The contract provided for shipment January/February; this allowed H to ship at any time within that period on the vessel nominated by GS (*J & J Cunningham Ltd* v *RA Munro & Co Ltd* (1922)). There is nothing to indicate that the bank was acting wrongly in paying against the documents. The only thing which went wrong was that H refused to allow GS to inspect the goods before shipment. This matter is of importance in the fob contract only and does not affect the operation of the credit contract (*Hamzeh Malas & Sons* v *British Imex Industries Ltd* (1958)).

Section 34(2) of the Sale of Goods Act 1979 provides that the seller must on request allow the buyer an opportunity to inspect the goods at the time that delivery is tendered. The time of tender of delivery in fob sales is the time of shipment (*Bragg* v *Villanova* (1923)). There is nothing to indicate that GS would have found anything wrong at that time so as to justify rejection, but the inspection of goods bought under an fob sale may be in order to discover matters necessary for the buyer to take out effective insurance (this is the buyer's job unless otherwise agreed and there is nothing in the facts given to indicate that the seller had agreed to take out insurance for the buyer). Therefore, on the assumption that GS were unable to take out effective insurance because they did not have sufficient information about the goods we must ask whether H are responsible for the loss resulting.

It has been held that s32(3) of the 1979 Act applies to fob contracts, so that H should have given GS notice of all matters necessary to allow the goods to be insured during transit. Failure to do this means that the goods are at the risk of the seller during transit (s32(3)). In cases where the seller fails to give the buyer the opportunity to inspect the goods to which he is entitled, s32(3) puts the goods at seller's risk during transit because unless the buyers were in a position to insure the goods from their own knowledge then the obligation remained on the sellers to furnish this information. It is not clear on the authorities how this matter affects the performance of the sale contract. In the present case the goods have not been physically delivered to the buyers at the port of destination and it may be that failure to give GS the chance to inspect means that delivery to the ship will not be construed as delivery to GS. On the other hand it may be that delivery to the ship was still delivery to GS, but that GS can complain about any damage occurring between that time and physical delivery to them; if this is correct then GS can sue for damages for breach of s14(2). The better view is that there is no delivery to the buyer until the goods arrive and therefore that GS can sue for damages for non-delivery since the video recorders have been destroyed (s51 SGA 1979).

GS are entitled to recover the purchase price as money paid for a consideration which has totally failed (s54 SGA 1979) and also damages assessed under s51(3) of the 1979 Act to cover the difference between the available market value the goods would have had on arrival and the purchase price.

The exclusion clause fails to help H for the same reason that it failed to help S under the CIF sale discussed above.

3) *The word processors*

The sellers, Young Ltd (Y), committed a breach of condition by shipping the goods late (the breach is of a s13 SGA 1979 because a March shipment is of a different commercial description to a January/February shipment). Unless the bank knew that Y were personally involved in a fraud, the payment against apparently correct documents was a good payment within the terms of their mandate (*United City Merchants (Investments) Ltd* v *Royal Bank of Canada* (1983); UCP Article 15, *Gian Singh & Co Ltd* v *Banque de l'Indochine* (1974)). Therefore in the absence of clear evidence of the bank's knowledge of fraud, GS are obliged to reimburse the bank (*United City Merchants case* (1983)). Furthermore, once an irrevocable credit has been opened the buyer is not entitled to instruct the bank not to pay (*Hamzeh*

Malas & Sons v *British Imex Industries Ltd* (1958)). The position of the bank is that it is liable to the seller (the beneficiary under the credit) once the credit has been opened, even though there is no consideration given by the seller, and will be liable in damages for wrongfully withdrawing the credit (see Benjamin's Sale of Goods). The buyer is not allowed to force the bank to incur liability to a third party, so once the credit is opened the bank is entitled to pay on presentation of apparently conforming documents.

We have already seen that Y have committed one breach of condition by shipping the goods late. This entitles GS to reject all of them on arrival. Seven hundred of the word processors may have been unmerchantable or not fit for the buyers' particular purpose, but even though the contract may have been severable GS were not obliged to accept the other 1,300 because all 2,000 were shipped late. GS, therefore, are entitled to reject all 2,000 word processors; on the evidence we have the time for rejection has not yet passed.

In addition to being able to reject the word processors, GS are also entitled to damages for non-delivery and will be able to recover in damages for other losses provided it can be proved that Y knew of circumstances which would reveal to a reasonable man that such losses were not likely. The £30,000 spent on advertising and the loss of goodwill are only recoverable, therefore, if Y knew that they were not unlikely to arise as a result of late shipment. It is unlikely that the full £30,000 will be recoverable because GS could have mitigated their loss by accepting the 1,300 which were late but merchantable, so that less than the full £30,000 was lost. Damage to goodwill is only rarely recoverable and not in the circumstances of this case.

The exclusion clause is of no effect for the same reason given in relation to the other contracts.

Question 3

Theodore, a UK exporter, concluded a contract for the sale of 10,000 tonnes of 'good old oats' to Lillian, a Greek importer, at a price of US$ 20 per tonne. Payment for the goods was to be made by irrevocable and confirmed letter of credit to be opened by Lillian with the Bank of Athens and confirmed by Barclays Bank in London. Under the terms of the credit, which was regulated by the provisions of the UCP 500, payment was to be made against tender of three separate documents: (a) a bill of lading; (b) an invoice for the goods; and (c) a certificate of quality attested to by two experts from the relevant department of the Ministry for Agriculture, Fisheries and Food (MAFF).

In fact, Theodore tendered the following documents: (a) a received for shipment bill of lading; (b) an invoice for '10,000 tonnes of old oats in good condition', and (c) a certificate of quality signed by one expert from MAFF and another person.

Barclays Bank refused to accept the documents which Theodore tendered because of the defects in the bill of lading and the certificate of quality. Although Theodore claimed that the documents were in order, he did obtain a shipped bill of lading and evidence from MAFF that a second signature on the certificate of quality was that of a person recently assumed as an expert into the MAFF.

Nevertheless, on re-tender of the documents, the bank again refused to make payment this time because of the defects in the invoice. The day immediately after the re-tender of the documents, the credit expired.

Advise Theodore whether or not he has grounds of action against the Barclays Bank for wrongfully refusing to accept the documents.

Question prepared by the Editor
April 1994

General comment

This question involves another popular area of examination, namely the doctrine of strict compliance for letters of credit. Students must be familiar with the details of the Uniform Customs and Practice for Documentary Credits where the answers to most of the issues raised in the question are to be found. However, the case law in this area remains useful as a source of examples with which to illustrate the application of the relevant principles.

Skeleton solution

Concepts of revocable/irrevocable and confirmed/unconfirmed credits.

Principle of strict performance.

Documents: bill of lading, invoice and certificate of quality.

Notice of rejection.

Resubmission of the documents after the expiry of the credit.

Suggested solution

Payment of the contractual price by Lillian to Theodore is by irrevocable confirmed documentary credit payable on the tender of documents. The credit itself incorporates the Uniform Customs and Practice for Documentary Credits (UCP 500) and therefore falls to be construed in light of the terms of that code.

The credit is irrevocable and confirmed. An irrevocable credit is one which cannot be withdrawn by the bank until the expiry of the period of its validity. If a letter of credit is expressed to remain irrevocable until a certain date, the beneficiary is entitled, upon satisfying the terms of the credit, eg presentation of documents, to payment from the bank. A bank is not entitled to withdraw from its liability under an irrevocable letter of credit even if instructed by the purchaser to cancel the credit: see *Hamzeh Malas & Sons* v *British Imex Industries Ltd* (1958). This is known as the doctrine of the autonomy of the credit.

A credit is confirmed if an issuing bank arranges with an advising bank in another country to open a letter of credit for a beneficiary. If the local bank undertakes to make direct payment to the beneficiary on presentation of the required documents, the credit is a confirmed one. The fact that the credit is confirmed means that the bank confirming the credit is directly liable to the beneficiary of the credit to pay him on receipt of the relevant documents.

Theodore is required to tender a bill of lading, an invoice and a certificate of quality against payment under the credit. However, the documents he in fact tendered were slightly different.

The presentation of documents for payment under a letter of credit is subject to the principle of strict performance. Since the confirming bank will have no idea as to the nature of the underlying sales contract, its position is protected against fraud by the requirement that payment can only be made against the documents specified in the letter of credit. If these documents are not tendered, or if they vary from those required, the bank can refuse to pay and the principle of strict performance protects the bank from liability to an unpaid seller.

At the same time, the confirming bank is an agent of the issuing bank and if it exceeds the authority of the principal, namely the issuing bank, it would be unable to recover sums paid for breach of its duties as an agent.

The letter of credit required presentation of a bill of lading and instead Theodore tendered a 'received for shipment' bill of lading. A 'received for shipment' bill of lading merely confirms that the goods have been delivered into the custody of the shipowner and not actually placed upon the vessel itself.

Whether a 'received for shipment' bill of lading suffices for payment falls to be decided by the terms of the UCP 500, Article 23(a) of which states that a bill of lading will be acceptable as long as the bill appears on the face of it to have been signed by the carrier or his agent and which indicates that the goods have been loaded on board or shipped on a named vessel. However, there is no evidence to suggest that this is in fact the case with the bill of lading presented by Theodore and, consequently, the bank would be entitled to reject it: see *Yelo* v *SM Machado & Co Ltd* (1952).

The second document presented by Theodore, the invoice for the agreed price, describes the quantity, the nature of the goods and their quality.

According to Uniform Credit rules, the description of the goods in the commercial invoice must correspond with their description in the letter of credit. Presumably the invoice required for payment under the credit identifies the contractual goods as 'good old oats'.

It is unlikely that the invoice describing the goods as 'old oats in good condition' is acceptable. The courts have tended to protect banks who have refused to accept documents that are considered to be almost the same as those requested or which will do just as well. Thus, in *Bank Melli Iran* v *Barclays Bank DCO* (1951), the courts held that an invoice raised for trucks identified as being 'in a new condition' in the credit, should be rejected when the invoice described the goods as 'new and good'. Therefore, the bank is within its rights to reject an invoice which describes the goods in different terms from those required under the invoice.

The third document required under the credit is a certificate of quality signed by two experts from MAFF. The presentation of this document is rejected on the grounds that one of the experts signing the certificate presented, is not listed as a member of MAFF.

Again the bank is probably entitled to reject the certificate of quality since it has no way of establishing that the second signature is in fact that of an expert other than to consult the official list of members. If that list does not disclose the name, there is a presumption that he or she is not a member. The fact that he or she has not been included on the official list because of an oversight of the MAFF is not a concern of the bank.

Theodore subsequently resolves the problems concerning the bill of lading and the certificate of quality, but when the documents are represented, the bank refuses to pay this time claiming that the invoice is defective. If a bank decides to reject documents, it must specify the discrepancies in the notice of rejection: see Article 14d of the UCP 500. The reason for this rule is to allow a beneficiary an opportunity to represent the documents after having cured the defects in the documentation.

The defect in the invoice is not raised by the bank as a ground for rejection until the second presentation of the documentation. Therefore, it is reasonable to conclude that, in the notice of rejection issued after the first submission, the bank failed to draw this to the attention of Theodore. In these circumstances, there is an argument that the bank is personally barred from challenging the validity of the invoice because it did not raise the matter at the original presentation. Theodore was therefore deprived of the opportunity to remedy the deficiency.

Clearly, it is not possible to resubmit the documents after the letter of credit has expired: see *Soproma SpA* v *Marine & Animal Bi-Products Corporation* (1966). Any tender of documents after a credit has expired is irrelevant and has to be rejected.

The correct course of action would have been for Barclays Bank to have rejected all the documents at the time they were presented for the first time. The failure of the bank to do so deprived Theodore of the opportunity of correcting any discrepancies and to receive payment. Consequently, the bank is liable in damages to Theodore for failure to pay the contractual price: see *Ozalid Group (Export) Ltd* v *African Continental Bank Ltd* (1979).

Question 4

Craig and Klaus agree the terms of three separate contracts for the sale cif of 100 best quality bicycles. The contracts differ from each other principally because the ports of discharge are identified as Hamburg, Bremen and Copenhagen. Each contract specifies payment is to be made by letter of credit opened by the Bank of Scotland but no reference is made to whether or not the credits are to be irrevocable or confirmed.

Craig instructs the Bank of Scotland to open three irrevocable credits in favour of Klaus negotiated with the Hamburg Bank in Germany. The Bank of Scotland opens three irrevocable credits in Klaus' favour undertaking to accept bills of exchange drawn by Klaus.

The credit for the Hamburg consignment does not state whether it is revocable or irrevocable but the credits in respect of the other two consignments are expressly stated to be irrevocable. Each of the three credits stipulates that payment is to be made against a clean bill of lading, a certificate of insurance and a commercial invoice.

The Hamburg Bank advises Klaus of the opening of the new credits and adds its own confirmation to the credit relating to the Bremen consignment but not the other two. Each of the credits is expressly subject to the terms of the UCP 500 and is governed by English law.

Klaus tenders three clean bills of lading along with the other required documents to the Hamburg Bank for payment. The Hamburg Bank considers the documents to be in order and makes payment to Klaus on the value of the bills of exchange tendered.

Before the Hamburg Bank sends the documents to the Bank of Scotland for payment, the Bank of Scotland sends the Hamburg Bank a telex informing it that it will not honour any of the undertakings made in respect of the three documentary credits.

The Bank of Scotland now consults you as their legal adviser as to their liability to the parties involved in the transaction.

Advise the Bank of Scotland.

Question prepared by the Editor
April 1994

General comment

A simple question requiring the student to state the rights and duties of instructing and responding banks under revocable and irrevocable commercial credits.

Skeleton solution

Difference between revocable and irrevocable letters of credit.

Implications of confirming the credit.

Obligation to reimburse disbursements.

Doctrine of strict compliance.

Documents required for presentation for payment.

Suggested solution

Three separate contracts have been made between Craig and Klaus each of which specify payment by bankers' documentary credit, but there are no conditions in the contracts relating to whether or not the credit is to be irrevocable or confirmed. However, Craig did in fact instruct the Bank of Scotland to open three irrevocable credits.

The first credit opened by the Bank of Scotland does not state whether or not it is revocable and is not confirmed. In the absence of an indication whether a credit is revocable or otherwise, the credit is deemed to be irrevocable: Article 6c UCP 500.

The second credit is expressly stated to be irrevocable, and confirmed by the Hamburg Bank. The third credit is also irrevocable, but has not been confirmed by the Hamburg Bank.

The Bank of Scotland, as the issuing bank, has a number of obligations. It is first obliged to pay against the tender of documents. If the credit is revocable, the bank may only refuse to pay against the documents if the seller has not drawn on the credit prior to the revocation of the credit. If the confirming bank has paid the seller before the credit is revoked, then in the absence of a defect in the tender of documentation, the issuing bank must reimburse the foreign bank. The issuing bank is, however, under no obligation to inform the seller of the revocation: *Cape Asbestos Co Ltd* v *Lloyds Bank Ltd* (1921). Therefore, the Bank of Scotland must reimburse the Hamburg Bank for disbursements made before the credit was revoked.

A credit which is expressly declared to be irrevocable cannot be cancelled or modified and must be honoured provided the seller presents the correct documents to the issuing bank within the contract period.

The Hamburg Bank is liable to Klaus for the credit that it added its confirmation to, but not those which it did not confirm. An unconfirmed credit is one under which the correspondent bank merely advises the seller of the opening of the credit, but does not itself undertake any obligation.

The sole means by which the Bank of Scotland can avoid making payment under the credit is if the tendered documents do not conform to those specified in the credit. This is known as the doctrine of strict compliance, according to which the issuing bank is required to ensure that the documents against which payment is made are identical to those specified in the credit.

In the present case, payment is to be made upon presentation of: (a) a clean bill of lading; (b) a certificate of insurance; and (c) a commercial invoice. According to the question, Klaus tendered the bills of lading along with the shipping documents. If no certificate of insurance was required by the Hamburg Bank, then the Bank of Scotland is not required to make payment.

But, if the documents tendered to the Bank of Scotland comply with those specified, it will be liable for the value of the disbursement made by the Hamburg Bank to Klaus. This liability is in addition to that to Craig for failing to properly establish the credit as instructed.

6   BILLS OF LADING

6.1   Introduction

A bill of lading is a document issued by a shipowner or his representative once goods have been shipped on board a vessel. It is an extremely important legal document in the law of the carriage of goods by sea, being both a document of title for the goods loaded aboard a vessel and a receipt from the carrier for the goods.

In addition, a bill of lading is the legal link between the buyer of the goods and the carrier of the goods if the bill has been validly transferred to the buyer by the seller. At the same time, the bill of lading is one of the most important documents in the operation of documentary credits and international sales transactions in general.

6.2   Key points

a) *Definition of a bill of lading*

A statutory definition of a bill of lading can be found in s1(4) of the Factors Act 1889 which provides:

'The expression "document of title" shall include any *bill of lading*, a dock warrant, warehouse-keeper's certificate and warrant or order for delivery of goods and any other documents used in the ordinary course of business as proof of possession or control of goods.'

A bill of lading may be of several different types, the most common being:

   i)   a 'complete form' bill of lading, which contains all the clauses relating to the contract of carriage;

   ii) a 'short form' bill which contains only the most important clauses;

   iii) a containerised bill, which is used when the shipped goods are packed into containers; or

   iv) a combined transport bill, which is required when the shipment involves carriage of goods by ship as well as by other modes of transport.

Another important distinction is between a 'received for shipment' bill and a 'shipped' bill. A 'received for shipment' bill indicates that the goods have only been accepted by the carrier and held under his control, whereas a 'shipped bill' indicates that the goods have actually been loaded aboard the ship.

The law relating to bills of lading was originally contained in the Bills of Lading Act 1855, but this statute has been repealed and replaced by the Carriage of Goods by Sea Act 1992. However, common law principles still continue to play a significant part in the law regulating the operation of bills of lading.

b) *The functions of the bill of lading at common law*

At common law a bill of lading has three distinct functions: (i) as a document of title; (ii) as a receipt for the goods; and (iii) as evidence of the contract of carriage between the shipper and the carrier.

i)   A document of title

A bill of lading is a document of title under common law which entitles the holder to take possession of the goods loaded aboard the vessel from the carrier.

Transfer of a bill of lading amounts to symbolic delivery of the goods. Even if the goods are in transit, constructive possession can be validly transferred on the tender of a bill of lading to another party: see *Clemens & Horst* v *Biddel Bros* [1912] AC 18. Once transferred, the party in possession of the bill can claim the goods when these arrive at the port of destination. The transfer is of all the contractual rights and liabilities under the bill.

The manner in which a bill can be validly transferred depends on the way in which the consignee is designated and on whether or not the bill is an 'order' bill or a 'bearer' bill. The basic distinction is that an order bill is non-negotiable whereas a bearer bill is negotiable.

An order bill is one made out to a named consignee and therefore not transferrable; it can only be given to the named consignee. In contrast, a bill made out to 'consignee', as a general term, to 'shipper's order' or to 'bearer' is negotiable and can be transferred.

Where a transfer of a bill is validly effected, the transferee cannot acquire a better title than the transferor. Therefore the transfer is only good if the transferor's title is good.

ii) A receipt for the goods

A bill of lading constitutes a receipt for the goods by the carrier. In fact, it is a receipt certifying three separate qualities: (i) the quantity or volume of the goods; (ii) the leading marks on the goods; and (iii) whether or not the goods are in apparently good order and condition.

Statements on the face of a bill of lading as to these qualities are only prima facie evidence and it is open to the carrier to challenge these statements by evidence to the contrary. However, the carrier in these circumstances will have the onus of rebutting the evidential presumption constituted by his own statements or statements made on his behalf on the bill: see *The Saudi Crown* [1986] 1 Lloyd's Rep 255.

A carrier may be vicariously liable for any misrepresentations on the bill made by one of his or her employees. The position of shipmaster in such circumstances is slightly different since he is not always the employee of the carrier. Unless the shipmaster is an employee of the carrier, he will be deemed to be the agent of the carrier.

If acting as an agent of the carrier, the shipmaster has authority to sign a bill of lading on behalf of a carrier but only for goods in fact loaded. If he signs for non-existent goods, he acts outside his actual authority and cannot bind his principal, although he becomes personally liable for non-delivery to the holder of the bill: *Grant v Norway* (1851) 10 CB 665. However, less significant misrepresentations, such as misdating the bill, may be within an agent's apparent authority: *The Ocean Frost* [1986] 2 Lloyd's Rep 109.

Where a bill of lading states that the goods have been 'shipped in apparent good order and condition', this is known as a clean bill of lading. Prima facie a clean bill of lading indicates that the goods are in their proper condition. Where the goods are not in good order and condition, and the carrier marks this fact on the bill of lading, the bill is known as a 'claused bill of lading'.

The statement that goods have been shipped in apparent good order and condition binds the carrier and he is estopped from claiming the contrary under the Carriage of Goods by Sea Act 1971.

A clean bill of lading relates only to the condition of the goods when they were placed aboard the vessel and does not cover any damage sustained by the goods in the course of the voyage: see *The Galatia* [1980] 1 WLR 495.

iii) Evidence of the contract of carriage between the shipper and the carrier

The third function of a bill of lading is as evidence of the contract or carriage between the shipper and the carrier. This function is discussed in more detail in section (f) below.

c) *The functions of the bill of lading under statute*

The Bills of Lading Act 1855 was originally enacted to remedy a lacuna in the law which prevented a buyer in an international sales contract from suing the carrier for loss or damage to the goods under his control. Because of the doctrine of privity of contract, the buyer had no direct contractual relationship with the carrier, only with the seller of the goods. The statute created a legal nexus between the carrier and the buyer which allows the buyer to sue the carrier for breach of the contract of carriage as long as the requirements of the Act are met.

As noted above, the Carriage of Goods by Sea Act 1992 (COGSA 1992) repealed the Bills of Lading Act 1855 by replacing its terms with new principles to update the prior law. The COGSA 1992 is more extensive than the 1855 Act and covers not only bills of lading but also sea waybills and other similar documents.

Previously, under the 1855 Act, a holder of a bill of lading was required also to have taken property in the goods before a transfer of rights under a bill of lading could take place. This had the effect of denying consignees or endorsees in lawful possession of the bill, for example as security, to rely on the contractual rights contained in the bill.

This rule has been changed by the 1992 Act, s2(1) of which provides:

'A person who becomes ... the lawful holder of a bill of lading ... shall (by virtue of becoming the holder of the bill or, as the case may be, the person to whom delivery is to be made) have transferred to and vested in him all rights of suit under the contract of carriage as if he had been a party to that contract.'

The effect of this section is to break the link between the transfer of contractual rights and the acquisition of property by reason of consignment or indorsement which was required under the 1855 Act. Lawful possession of the bill of lading, rather than having property in the goods, becomes the key to the transfer of contractual rights to the holder.

This divorce of rights of suit from the passing of property has the practical effect that pledgees and other parties, such as banks, who take the bill of lading as security, will be able to sue on the contract embodied in the bill of lading; such parties no longer have to rely on the fiction of the implied contract.

d) *Good tender of a bill of lading*

A good tender of a bill of lading means that the bill satisfies a number of specified criteria. These are as follows:

i) the bill is in shipped form, which means that it indicates that the goods have been actually loaded on board and not merely received by the carrier for shipment.

ii) the bill is clean and does not indicate on its face that there are any apparent defects in the goods on shipment.

iii) the bill shows the proper date on which the goods were received and the place they were received.

iv) the goods covered by the bill are only those contracted in the contract of sale.

v) the bill is a through bill of lading, which means that the bill must cover the voyage of the goods from the port of loading to the port of destination.

In the event that the tender of the bill from the shipper to the consignor meets these conditions, it will be a good tender, but any failure to comply with even one of these conditions will mean that the transfer of the bill is not a good tender.

e) *Indemnities*

At common law, it is perfectly possible for a carrier to insert into a bill of lading a clause relieving him, or even exempting him completely, from liability for statements made in the bill. Provided the terms of such an exemption clause cover the statement in question, the clause may serve as evidence that any damage cannot be imputed to the carrier if it occurred before shipment. Indemnity clauses need not be linked only to physical deficiencies, but may also be used to indicate a carrier's immunities concerning, for example, a buyer's rights to possession.

Whether or not the courts will apply such an indemnity clause depends largely on the circumstance of each case.

f) *The contract of carriage*

The seller/shipper and the carrier are quite free to negotiate any terms they wish to regulate the shipment of the goods. In practice, the bill of lading is not the entire contract of carriage because the terms of the agreement are not only to be found in the bill of lading; they may, for example, have been agreed orally in advance of shipment or even implied by trade usage. However, a bill may be useful evidence as to the existence of the terms of the contract of carriage negotiated by the parties.

At common law, there is an implied rule that if the bill conflicts with any prior agreement, the bill will be superseded by any clear rights, agreements or obligations expressly negotiated by the parties.

Problems may arise, however, when the bill is transferred to a third party who has no knowledge of the terms of any agreement between the shipper and the carrier. The basic rule is straightforward enough; the bill of lading becomes, as far as third parties are concerned, the sole contract of carriage.

Alternatively, in some cases, a bill of lading may refer to the agreement between the shipper and the carrier and specifically state that the terms of this agreement will apply to any third party transferee of the bill. In such situations, the general rules relating to the incorporation of these types of terms into contracts with third parties are applicable.

6.3   Recent cases and statutes

Carriage of Goods by Sea Act 1992: this statute came into force on 16 September 1992 and replaces the Bills of Lading Act 1855. The principal change is to remove the difficulties raised to claims by holders (ie consignees or endorsees in lawful possession of a bill of lading) against the carrier who issued the bill.

The Future Express [1992] 2 Lloyd's Rep 79: this is a pre-1992 Act case where a bank attempted to sue the shipowners under a bill of lading in which the bank was named as consignee but the bank was not an original party to the contract of carriage contained in, or evidenced by, the bill. The court held that the bank did not have a valid security over the goods as against the shipowner. Although Diamond J expressed concern that a consignee named in a bill of lading was unable to sue on the bill this shortcoming has since been rectified by the 1992 Act.

6.4   Relevant materials

C M Schmitthoff, *The Export Trade* (9th edition, 1990), pp561–564.

J Crabtree, *International Sale of Goods* (1991), pp168–171.

6.5   Analysis of questions

The significance of bills of lading is evidenced by the fact that questions relating to the law of bills of lading very frequently arise as ancillary points in general questions. In the following selection, we have opted mainly for problem-type questions to illustrate this fact.

6.6   Questions

Question 1

Steven agrees to sell to Tinks 100 boxes containing 50 copies each of the book *Seditious Voices* to be shipped on or before 1 May 1989, cif Basra, payment to be by letter of credit 'on tender of documents to Barcoutts Bank'. Steven then contracts to obtain an import licence for Tinks. The books are put on board mv *Rushmoor* on 30 April but a fire breaks out of the vessel on the following day and some of the boxes containing the books are wetted while the fire is being extinguished. The boxes are therefore unloaded and the books repacked in 50 boxes, each containing 100 books. They are reloaded on 2 May. The master of the *Rushmoor* signs a bill of lading for '50 x 100 *Seditious Voices* shipped by 1 May 1989'.

Tinks sends a copy of the sale contract to Barcoutts, instructing it to pay on tender of the correct documents. Tinks then hears of the events connected with the fire and telephones Barcoutts to ensure that the bill of lading is for 100 boxes of 50 books each, since boxes of 50 books each are more easily sold to sub-buyers. When Steven presents the documents, Barcoutts therefore rejects them. Steven takes the bill of lading back to the owner of the *Rushmoor*, who agrees to have the books repacked on the voyage and issues a fresh bill of lading for 100 boxes of 50 books each, which Steven then presents to Barcoutts. However, Tinks has heard that Steven has been unable to obtain an import licence, so instructs Barcoutts not to pay under the credit.

Advise the parties.

University of London LLB Examination
(for External Students) Commercial Law June 1989 Q6

General comment

This question involves discussion of the rights, duties and liabilities of parties to a cif contract which has, at its heart, a potentially defective bill of lading. After we are told that Barcoutts rejected the original bill, there is no statement as to what the parties' actions were. The answer, therefore, will have to look at the alternative courses of action which may be taken and the consequences of each.

Skeleton solution

Cif contracts – rights + duties of parties.

Application of SGA 1979 to cif.

Bills of lading – accuracy – right to reject documents.

Terms of contract – innominate terms – breach.

Right to reject goods.

Suggested solution

Steven has sold the books to Tinks on a cif basis. This means that the obligation of shipping the good and all the costs involved in their shipment, will be borne by the seller, this expenditure being included in the amount paid by the buyer. Cif means cost, insurance and freight. These are the main items of expenditure met by the seller. Cif contracts are essentially contracts for the sale of goods, so the Sale of Goods Act 1979 (SGA) will apply to the transaction.

Under s17 SGA, property in specific or unascertained goods passes when the parties intend it to pass. If no such intention can be discovered, property passes according to the rules in s18 of the Act. By s20, whoever has property in the goods also bears the risk of those goods being accidentally damaged or destroyed. A cif contract, however, is a contract for the sale of documents and property in the goods represented in the documents will pass when the seller tenders the bill of lading to the buyer or to the buyer's agent, in this case, Barcoutts Bank (*Arnold Karlberg* v *Blythe* (1916)). When the fire breaks out on the mv *Rushmoor*, therefore, the goods are still at the risk of the seller, Steven.

The fire and its consequences, however, appear not to have harmed the books. The problem arises in relation to the way in which the books are packed. The contract requires them to be delivered in 100 boxes of 50 books each. After the fire, they are re-packed in 50 boxes, each containing 100 books. The way in which the goods are packed could be argued to be outside the scope of s13 SGA in that they are not necessary to identify the nature of the goods (*Ashington Piggeries Ltd* v *Christopher Hill Ltd* (1972)), nor do they state or identify an essential part of the description of the goods (*Reardon Smith Line* v *Hansen-Tangen* (1976)). The way in which the books are packed, however, is an express term of the contract which the seller has broken. If the buyer had stressed the importance of this term when the negotiations for the contract were being undertaken, it will be a condition. If, however, it is not possible to categorise the term in this way, it will be treated as an innominate term and the court will 'wait and see' the effects of its breach. On the facts of the problem it would appear that the effects could be serious for the buyer. In either case, therefore, if the books are delivered incorrectly packed it would appear that Tinks could reject them for breach of the express term.

The date on which the goods are to be shipped under a cif contract is part of the description and therefore falls within s13 SGA. It is therefore an implied condition that the goods will be shipped by the agreed date and if they are not, the buyer will be entitled to treat the contract as repudiated and claim damages for any loss suffered as a consequence. By shipping the books after the date required by the contract, Steven is in breach of an implied condition.

Tinks, the buyer, has two rights of rejection. He may reject the documents or he may reject the goods. The documents tendered to Barcoutts do not comply with the contract. This is breach of the doctrine of strict compliance as stated in *Equitable Trust Co of New York* v *Dawson Partners* (1927). Barcoutts, therefore, is entitled to reject the documents in the form in which they were originally submitted. When the document is re-written to comply with the contract, Barcoutts, as Tink's agent, may accept it. There is no duty to do so. See also *Proctor & Gamble Philippine Manufacturing Co* v *Kurt A Becher GmbH* (1988) for details as to misdated bills of lading.

If Barcoutts does accept the new documents Tinks may have a further remedy if the wrong date of shipment is still shown. If, when the goods arrive, it is clear that the date must have been inaccurate, Tinks can sue Steven for loss of the right to reject the documents (*Kwei Tek Chao* v *British Traders and Shippers* (1954)). The measure of damages will be the loss arising directly and naturally from the breach, s51 SGA. If there is an available market for the books, the measure of damages will prima facie be the difference between the contract price and the market price of the goods at the time of delivery. In *Sharpe* v *Nosawa* (1917) it was held that in a cif contract, the time of delivery is the time of tender of the documents. Tinks will also be able to claim damages on this basis if Barcoutts accepts the revised bill of lading but, when the books arrive, it is discovered that they have not been repacked as required under the contract. Tinks has the right to examine the goods on arrival (s34 SGA).

Steven is also in breach of his undertaking to obtain an import licence for Tinks. From the wording of the question, it appears that this promise is not part of the original contract of sale. Under a cif contract, the seller's obligation is to help the buyer obtain such a licence. If Stevens has not helped, then he will be in breach of the original contract. If there is no breach of the contract for the sale of the books, Tinks will have to pay for them and bring a separate action against Steven for breach of the separate contract to obtain an import licence.

If the promise to obtain an import licence is part of the contract, then this imposes an absolute duty on Steven. His failure to obtain such a licence, therefore, will constitute a breach of the main contract and Tinks could treat the contract as repudiated.

Question 2

Sandra ships from Buenos Aires 3,000 tons of corned beef aboard Oasis' ship the mv Sturmer, bound for Liverpool and Glasgow. Sandra receives from Oasis three bills of lading, each for an unspecified 1,000 tons. She contracts to sell 1,000 tons to Kelvin cif Liverpool and 1,000 tons each to Lynda and Miranda cif Glasgow. Sandra instructs Oasis to discharge 1,000 tons at Liverpool and 2,000 tons at Glasgow.

Sandra delivers one bill of lading to Kelvin's bank, under a letter of credit, in return for the bank's acceptance of a bill of exchange payable on 1 June. When Sandra presents the bill of exchange for payment on 1 June, the bank refuses to pay it. Sandra therefore instructs Oasis that the 1,000 tons to be discharged at Liverpool is not to be released to Kelvin but is to be held to Sandra's order. However, Kelvin agrees to resell the 1,000 tons for cash to Norma, to whom he delivers a bill of lading.

After the ship leaves Liverpool, Sandra delivers one bill of lading each to Lynda and Miranda on payment of cash. The following day the Sturmer collides with the ss Drongo and sinks. Ignorant of the collision, Lynda sells her part of the cargo to Miranda, to whom she endorses her bill of lading.

Advise the parties.

University of London LLB Examination
(for External Students) Commercial Law June 1991 Q7

General comment

This combination of sale of goods, international sales and bills of lading is a common one. The question is not an ideal one to answer, being so drafted as to be rather ambiguous, and a number of assumptions need to be made in answering it. But if at the end of the day the answer is less factual than one would like, it is a typical example of its type. The student should not be deterred merely because there is more than one variation possible in interpreting the question; the subject matter in itself is straightforward enough, the only difficulty being to keep in mind all the alternatives so as to cover every eventuality.

Skeleton solution

International sale contracts and Sale of Goods Act 1979.

Bills of lading.

Bills of exchange; dishonour; duties of bank.

Rights of the unpaid seller; insolvent buyers.

Impossibility and frustration; SGA 1979 ss6 and 7.

Suggested solution

Where English law applies to a contract of international sale, then relevant legislation, in this case the Sale of Goods Act 1979 (SGA), will apply. We are not told in this instance whether English law does apply, but it seems very likely and the rubric on the examination paper confirms this, and we shall proceed on that assumption. While all the usual implied terms as to title, fitness and so on apply as provided for by ss12–15 SGA, these are not really at issue here. What is important is the question of the passing of title especially since the goods are unascertained, or would appear to be. There is nothing in the wording of the question to indicate that each separate 1,000 tons is in a separate hold of the ship or crated up separately. Indeed, we are told in the second sentence that the bills of lading are each for an 'unspecified' 1,000 tons of corned beef.

The basic rule as to unascertained goods is laid down in s16 SGA which states: 'Where there is a contract for the sale of unascertained goods, no property in the goods will pass to the buyer unless and until the goods are ascertained.' Goods will be ascertained by their appropriation, or possibly by exhaustion. Also to be taken into account at this point is rule 5 of s18 SGA which provides in part: 'where there is a contract for the sale of unascertained goods by description ... and goods are unconditionally appropriated ... either by the seller with the consent of the buyer, or the buyer with the assent of the seller, the property in the goods passes to the buyer ...'.

Like all the rules of s18, rule 5 is subject to any contrary intention evinced by the parties and this is important because cif contracts have their own rules as to the passing of property; title normally passes when the documents are handed over to the buyer. All the provisions in SGA 1979 as to the passing of property are subject to an overriding right of the parties to indicate that they wish property to pass at some point other than that provided for by statute; the provisions are guidelines only.

Property thus passes when the parties intend it to pass, and if no such clear intention can be found property passes according to the rules of s18 SGA 1979, the most important of which, rule 5, has already been noted. Rule 5 mentions the point of 'appropriation' of the unascertained goods and because this is a series of cif contracts it is possible to say with some degree of certainty that appropriation occurs when the seller tenders the bill of lading for payment to the buyer or the buyer's agent (*Arnold Karlberg* v *Blythe, Green, Jourdain & Co* (1916)). There is no indication in the question that either Kelvin or Sandra had any other intention. A seller can indicate that he is reserving a right of sale by one of several methods (*Mitsui & Co Ltd* v *Flota Mercante Grancolombiana SA* (1989)), but no such reservation of title would seem to apply in the contract as between Kelvin and Sandra. The prima facie presumption in a cif sale is that when the seller tenders the appropriate documents, invoice, certificate of insurance and bill of lading to the buyer or buyer's agent this will be evidence of unconditional appropriation. If need be the bill of lading alone may be sufficient (Bills of Lading Act 1855) especially if supported by other circumstances. Clearly Kelvin's conduct in reselling the 1,000 tons to Norma indicates that he considers appropriation to have occurred.

The normal practice is that in cif contracts, a bank has a dual role when accepting documents: firstly it acts as agent for the buyer and, secondly, it acts on its own account and is contractually liable to pay the seller on presentation of the correct documents. Acceptance of the bill of exchange will amount to payment, but the bank has refused to pay it. It is not clear whether this is on Kelvin's instructions, or because of some negligent act on the part of the bank. Certainly in issuing a bill of exchange in return for the bill of lading and then dishonouring it, it would appear that Sandra has not been paid. Moment of payment, and hence moment of appropriation, is the point at which the bill of exchange is honoured. It might be argued, assuming both the presentation date of the bill and its dishonouring on the instructions of Kelvin, that he is indicating his rejection of the goods. If, of course, the fault is entirely that of the bank Sandra will be able to obtain redress under s40 Bills of Exchange Act.

If Sandra's instruction to Oasis, on learning that the bill of exchange has been dishonoured, is taken as an indication that title has not yet passed and Sandra is reserving her property in the goods then problems arise as to Kelvin's purported resale to Norma. It is obviously an act incompatible with Sandra's rights as seller and indicates that Kelvin at least considers appropriation in the goods to have taken place and title in them to vest in him. He will be deemed to have accepted the goods under s35 SGA even if his dishonouring of the bill of exchange (assuming this to be Kelvin's act) means that no payment has been made.

The question of the passing of property will be of significance in assessing Sandra's rights and remedies. It is only after property has passed that the seller can maintain an action against the buyer for the purchase price of the goods. While the property remains in the seller, his action for the buyer's breach of contract can only lie in damages. This means that the seller must try to mitigate his loss by selling elsewhere (if there is an available market). The measure of damages will be the difference between the contract price and the available market price, regardless of how much the seller has actually obtained on resale. If property has passed to the buyer however, the seller may argue that mitigation in the form of resale is no longer possible and may thus sue the buyer for the agreed price.

Apart from these rights, if the seller is unpaid he will be able to exercise the right of lien – stoppage in transit – even though property may have passed. The important thing here is to discover whether Sandra has retained physical possession, at least in a constructive form, in that the goods are still in the hands of the carrier. It would seem from Sandra's instructions to Oasis that she is effectively exercising this right of lien, (coupled with a right of resale, possibly – the carriers are told to await Sandra's instructions). This right of stoppage in transit would obviously, assuming the goods have not through some error been released to Kelvin, take priority over Kelvin's sale to Norma.

Because the price has fallen due and Sandra has not been paid Kelvin will, by virtue of s61(4) SGA 1979, be judged insolvent. Insolvency is not in itself repudiatary (*Ex parte Chalmers* (1873)), but obviously specific failure to pay as a deliberate act may be so.

To progress further, to the situation after the ship leaves Liverpool. Firstly we are told that Sandra delivers one bill of lading each to Lynda and Miranda on payment of cash. Under normal cif rules, and unless Sandra has in some way indicated her intention of reserving title, then property, and risk, will pass to the buyers.

The SGA makes some provision for impossibility and frustration, but in each case (ss6 and 7 respectively) the SGA applies only to specific goods. Since there are two separate orders of corned beef aboard the 'Sturmer', these goods are initially unascertained. In any event the sections will apply only before risk passes to the buyer. So, will the contract between Lynda and Miranda be for specific goods? We are told that Lynda sells her part of the corned beef to Miranda as against an endorsed bill of lading. When the two cargoes are joined together they become, presumably, ascertained by a process of exhaustion. In other words there is now only Miranda's corned beef on board the 'Sturmer' and presumably the goods are now ascertained or specific. But when does property pass? The basic rule is that property passes on transfer of the bill, unless any contrary intention can be found. Transfer of the bill of lading is a symbolic delivery of the goods. Without further details of Lynda and Miranda's agreement it is difficult to be sure, but it would seem likely that delivery has been effected when the bill of lading is endorsed.

Section 6 SGA provides that, where there is a sale of specific goods and without the knowledge of the seller those goods have perished at the time the contract was made, then the contract is void. Section 7 provides that where there is an agreement to sell specific goods and subsequently the goods, without fault on the part of the buyer or seller, perish before the risk passes to the buyer, the contract is void. Self evidently therefore the exact sequence of events is important. We are told that Lynda is 'ignorant' of the collision – the clear implication being that the contract was made after the goods perished. This would bring Lynda and Miranda within s6, which deals with antecedent impossibility, rather then s7 which deals with subsequent impossibility.

So, to sum up, Sandra's redress may be against the bank, if there is negligence on its part, otherwise she must proceed against Kelvin. As already stated her exact rights will depend on exactly when property passed. Norma, Kelvin's purported customer, would similarly depend on this factor. By delivering a bill of lading as against cash, Norma would appear to have title to the goods. But two important qualifications must be borne in mind. Firstly property may never have passed to Kelvin himself and secondly whether or not this is so, as an unpaid seller Sandra has a lien and a right of stoppage in transit and ultimately a right of resale that will take priority. Norma may have to seek redress against Kelvin under ss51 and 53 SGA. Such steps might include suing for damages for non delivery of goods, or for breach of implied condition as to title (s12 SGA).

The contracts between Sandra and Lynda/Miranda seem to have been performed straightforwardly enough. Risk has passed to them as buyers. Since the subsequent contract between Lynda and Miranda is probably void, each must bear the loss of her individual cargo.

7 CHARTERPARTIES

7.1	Introduction
7.2	Key points
7.3	Recent cases and statutes
7.4	Relevant materials
7.5	Analysis of questions
7.6	Questions

7.1 Introduction

Charterparties are the contracts used when the hire of a whole ship is required for a particular voyage or period of time. The shipowner gives control of the vessel to another person for the purposes of carrying out an endeavour. As such, charterparties can be distinguished from specific contracts of carriage for particular consignments of goods where the shipowner retains control over the vessel being used for the carriage.

The legal relationship between the shipowner and the hirer of the vessel is governed by the charterparty. This document stipulates the obligations of the shipowner and the rights and duties of the hirer of the vessel. It sets out the fee for the hire, the period of hire, the availability of the vessel and the identity of the vessel being used. These issues will be considered in this chapter, along with related issues such as lay time, demurrage and the function of a bill of lading in a contract of charterparty.

7.2 Key points

a) *Definition of charterparty*

A charterparty is a contract for the hire of a vessel for the duration of a specified voyage or a series of voyages or, alternatively, for a particular definite period of time. These contracts are most commonly used where the quantity or bulk of goods being shipped require that the whole ship is hired. In contracts of charterparty, the individual hiring the vessel is known as the 'charterer' and the contract is made between the charterer and the shipowner.

A major distinction in the nature of charterparties is between charterparties by way of demise and charterparties not by way of demise. In a charterparty by way of demise, the ship's master and crew become the servants of the charterer for the duration of the charterparty. In a charterparty not by way of demise, the master and crew remain the servants of the shipowner.

This distinction is important because, when the charterparty is by way of demise, if bills of lading are issued by the ship's master to third parties for goods carried, the contract of carriage is between the shipper and the charterer. On the other hand, if the charterparty is not by way of demise, the shipowner is the carrier and bills of lading constitute the contract of carriage between the shipper and the shipowner.

Charterparties not by way of demise are by far the most common form and the remaining points in this section refer to this type of charterparty.

b) *The stipulations generally contained in a charterparty*

The charterparty regulates the contractual relationship between the shipowner and the charterer. It is usual for the charterparty to contain the following stipulations:

   i)   identification of the name, nationality and class of the vessel being chartered;

   ii) the carrying capacity and registered tonnage of the vessel;

   iii) the date on which the vessel will be ready to load;

   iv) a clause specifying that the vessel will proceed forthwith to the port of loading;

   v)   the sum payable in respect of the hire;

   vi) the formulae for calculating demurrage and lay time;

   vii) a mechanism to facilitate the return of the vessel to the possession of the shipowner;

   viii) a cesser clause which is a provision intended to relieve the charterer from certain liabilities after the time of loading.

The charterparty also usually contains provisions excepting the shipowner from liability in respect of the usual excepted perils.

Penalty clauses may be included in a charterparty, but it should be noted that such clauses, if true penalty clauses, may be void under the common law: *Watts, Watts & Company* v *Mitsu & Co* [1917] AC 227.

c) *Distinction between voyage and time charterparties*

In terms of form, there are two main types of charterparties:

   i) a time charter – this is contract for the hire of a ship for a definite period of time.

   ii) a voyage charter – this is a contract of hire for a specified voyage or a particular series of voyages.

In both cases, the ship's crew remain the employees of the shipowner but the charterer has certain rights and responsibilities. As a general principle, the division of responsibilities between the charterer and the shipowner has been summed up as follows:

'The charterers might direct where the vessel is to go and with what she is to be laden but the shipowner remains in all respects accountable for the manner in which she may be navigated': *Omaha Coal* v *Huntley* (1877) 2 CPD 464.

d) *Time charterparties*

Donaldson J succinctly described a time charter in *The Berge Tasta* [1975] 1 Lloyd's Rep 422 as a charterparty:

'in which the shipowner undertakes to make the vessel available to the charterer within a specified area over a specified period. The shipowner's remuneration is at a fixed rate for a unit of time regardless of how the vessel is actually used by the charterer. The shipowner meets the costs of maintaining the vessel and paying the crew's wages but the cost of fuel and port charges fall on the charterer.'

The usual obligations of the shipowner under a time charterparty can be summarised as follows:

   i)   to provide a particular vessel for the period of the hire, although occasionally substitution clauses allow the shipowner to supply another vessel during the currency of the charterparty;

   ii) to ensure that the vessel is seaworthy and to maintain the vessel in an efficient state for the period of the hire.

The charterer is required to redeliver the vessel at the end of the period of hire and the shipowner is entitled to redelivery of the vessel in like condition as when hired subject to normal wear. The vessel must also be returned to the shipowner on the specified date and usually at a specified location. Where a date is fixed for redelivery of the vessel, the courts will allow a reasonable margin or tolerance in the case of late delivery. However, if the parties have agreed an express margin or tolerance no further margin will be implied: see *Hyundai Merchant Marine Co Ltd* v *Gesuri Chartering Co Ltd, The Peonia* [1991] 1 Lloyd's Rep 100.

e) *Voyage charterparties*

Voyage charterparties may be for a single voyage or a series of specified voyages. In this type of charter the ship is hired to travel on the agreed customary routes for the specified voyage(s).

In a voyage charterparty, the shipowner impliedly undertakes the following obligations unless expressly specified to the contrary in the charterparty:

   i)   to provide a seaworthy ship;

   ii) that the ship will proceed with reasonable despatch; and

   iii) that the ship will proceed without unjustifiable deviation.

The main obligations on the part of the charterer are the following:

   i)   not to ship dangerous goods; and

    ii)   to redeliver the ship at the end of the voyage, or series of voyages, in like condition to that when hired.

f) *Demurrage and lay days*

A charterparty normally specifies that a number of days, termed 'lay days', will be made available to allow the vessel to be loaded and discharged. In the event that the number of lay days is exceeded, 'demurrage' is the term used for the sum payable by the charterer as liquidated damages for the delay of the vessel beyond the permitted number of lay days. The rate of demurrage payable is generally expressly stated in the charterparty. Usually the maximum number of permitted lay days is specified, together with a fixed rate per day for demurrage. The charterer of the vessel is liable to the shipowner to pay the demurrage.

A shipowner is entitled to raise an action for detention of the vessel in the event that:

    i)   the lay days have expired and demurrage has not been expressly agreed;

    ii)   the period for loading or discharging has not been agreed and a reasonable period of time for loading or discharge has expired; or

    iii)   demurrage has been agreed for a specific period but that period has been exceeded.

A claim for damages for detention is an unliquidated claim. It is for the courts to decide the injury suffered by a shipowner as a result of the vessel being detained in port.

g) *Liability of the parties to load and discharge the goods*

The respective rights and duties of the shipowner and the charterer to load and discharge the goods are, unless altered by the terms of the charterparty, the same as those which apply to the loading and discharge of the goods of shippers not under contracts of charterparty.

The most obvious question in the loading or discharge of the goods is which party is liable if the goods are damaged or destroyed during these processes? In such situations, the following principles apply:

    i)   damage by stevedores – stevedores are normally not employees of either the shipowner or the charterer but independent contractors hired by the charterer. Damage to the goods, if caused by the negligence of stevedores, may render their employer liable to the party which contracted for the service.

    ii)   damage by the charterer or his employees – liability for damage or destruction of the goods in this situation rests with the charterer, and where the damage is to the vessel he or she will be liable to compensate the shipowner.

    iii)   damage by the shipowner or his employees – the shipowner will be liable for damage caused to the goods unless liability is successfully excluded for such injury in the charterparty.

h) *The function of the bill of lading in charterparties*

In both voyage and time charterparties, if the charterer is transporting his or her own goods, he or she will normally request the shipowner to issue a bill of lading for the cargo. In a charterer's hands a bill of lading is merely a receipt for the goods and a document of title. It does not have any contractual function. As a general principle, it is the charterparty that governs the rights and obligations of the charterer and the shipowner in respect of the carriage of the goods.

As the court elaborated in *Temperley* v *Smythe* [1905] 2 KB 791:

'The broad distinction between the position of the charterer who ships and takes a bill of lading and an ordinary holder of a bill is ... that in the former case there is the underlying contract of the charterparty which remains till it is cancelled, and taking the bill of lading does not cancel it in whole or in part unless it can be inferred from the inconsistency of the terms of the two documents that it was intended to do so.'

However, where the bill is subsequently transferred to an indorsee, the holder of the bill is no longer the charterer and the bill becomes the contract of carriage between the shipowner and indorsee.

i) *Inconsistencies between the bill of lading and the charterparty*

The terms of a charterparty may vary from those contained in a bill of lading issued in respect of goods carried. Such inconsistencies are resolved by considering whether the charterparty or the bill of lading has contractual force between the relevant parties.

In the case of the charterer and the shipowner, the charterparty is the sole measure of the legal obligations between these parties since it is their contract for carriage: see *The C Joyce* [1986] 2 All ER 177. In the event of inconsistencies between the charterparty and the bill of lading, the terms of the charterparty prevail.

Between an indorsee or consignee and the shipowner, it is the terms of the bill of lading which embody the contract between the parties and therefore its terms prevail. Hence, for example, if the bill of lading does not incorporate an exclusion of liability for negligence, even though such a clause is contained in the charterparty, a consignee or indorsee can succeed against the shipowner if his employees have been guilty of negligence in the execution of the contract for carriage: *Kruger* v *Moel Tryvan Ship Co* [1907] AC 272.

j) *Distinction between a charterparty and a contract of carriage on a general ship*

Where a shipper chooses to send goods on a general ship, his or her goods will normally be shipped with other merchants' consignments on the same vessel. In such cases, the shipper will generally not enter into a charterparty with the shipowner. Instead the contract is one of carriage on a general ship. Once the goods have been placed on board the vessel, the shipowner, who is both the legal and actual carrier of the goods, will issue the shipper with a shipped bill of lading to cover his goods and no others.

The legal rights and duties of the shipper/seller in a contract for carriage on a general ship are regulated by statute and international convention. These obligations are the subject of the next chapter of this book.

7.3   Recent cases and statutes

Elpis Maritime Co Ltd v *Marti Chartering Co, The Maria D* [1991] 2 WLR 330: a case discussing the charterers obligation to pay demurrage and freight.

The Al Battini [1993] 2 Lloyd's Rep 219: a case confirming that the contract of carriage is contained in the charterparty notwithstanding that bills of lading have been issued by the charterers.

Century Textile and Industry v *Tomoe Shipping Co (Singapore) Pte* [1993] 1 Lloyd's Rep 63: a case concerning the obligation to supply the vessel in a condition fit for loading.

Mendala III Transport v *Total Transport Corporation, Total International Limited and Addax Limited, The Wilomi Tanana* [1993] 2 Lloyd's Rep 41: resolution of conflict between dates on bills of lading issued under a charterparty.

Torvald Klaveness A/S v *Arni Maritime Corporation, The Gregos* [1993] 2 Lloyd's Rep 335: the legitimacy of an order for the last voyage in a voyage charterparty prior to redelivery has to be established at the date the order is given taking into account the reasonableness of the estimated duration of the voyage.

7.4   Relevant materials

L D'Arcy, *Ridley's Law of the Carriage of Goods by Land, Sea and Air* (7th edition, 1992), pp175–191.

E R Hardy Ivamy, *Carriage of Goods by Sea* (13th edition, 1989), pp8–80.

7.5   Analysis of questions

Questions in this area of the syllabus are complicated by the involvement of separate different legal concepts. For example, the legal consequences of issuing bills of lading in charterparty arrangements is a common theme, but answering questions of this nature also require additional knowledge of the law relating to shipowner's liability for damage to goods.

The first question in this section is a general essay-type question which is then followed by a series of three problem-type questions requiring the application of the relevant legal principles to hypothetical legal situations.

7.6 Questions

Question 1

Outline the principal obligations of a shipowner and a charterer under a standard time charterparty.

Question prepared by the Editor
April 1994

General comment

This is a straightforward question requiring the student to list the principal clauses under a standard charterparty. It is only necessary, however, to refer to those clauses which are particular or relevant to a time charterparty.

Skeleton solution

The general clauses; providing the vessel, stipulating the port, payment of the fee, etc.

Period of hire.

Seaworthiness of the vessel.

Use of safe ports only.

Loading and discharge obligations.

Excepted perils.

Obligation of redelivery

Suggested solution

Time charterparties are contracts in which a shipowner allows a charterer to hire his vessel for a particular period of time. Although the shipowner and charterer are, of course, free to agree on the specific terms of their charterparty, in practice standard forms of charterparties are used. For example, the 'Transtime Form' or the 'Baltimore 1939 Form' are commonly used standard time charterparties. These documents contain the principal clauses to regulate a time charterparty, but the parties are free to amend these standard forms as they see fit.

In the charterparty, the shipowner agrees to provide a vessel for a stipulated period of time and the name, size and speed of the vessel are designated together with her fuel consumption and present fuel status. There is also a provision to deal with the port of delivery for the vessel and the time when the vessel will be delivered to the charterer.

While the charterparty will normally identify a particular ship, often the contract will allow the shipowner to substitute another vessel during the currency of the charterparty. This freedom is permitted unless excluded under the terms of the charterparty: *Terkol Rederierne* v *Petroleo Brasileiro SA, The Badagry* (1985).

The charterer will agree to pay a specified amount for the period of the hire and there is normally provision for a certain number of permitted lay days and for payment of demurrage in the event that the vessel is detained during loading or discharge. Certain events are usually stated to relieve the charterer of the obligation to pay for the hire of the vessel, the most obvious being its destruction or repairs being effected.

In normal circumstances, the period of hire will be expressed in days or months or will be deemed to expire on a certain date. In some charterparties, the charterer is granted an option to extend the period of hire after the normal expiry date.

The payment for the hire can be expressed as a single lump sum, a per day rate or a rate calculated in relation to a standard scale. Certain charterparties also include a clause entitling the hire payment to be reduced if the vessel cannot accommodate all the goods intended to be shipped. A similar clause may be inserted to reduce the payment in the event that the vessel falls below the stated performance, such as in respect of her speed.

One of the most important duties on the part of the shipowner is to ensure that the vessel provided is seaworthy. This obligation is normally expressed as a warranty on the part of the shipowner that the vessel is properly fitted for ordinary cargo service. A vessel is not fit if, for example, it has an incompetent crew or does not have the necessary certificates to establish seaworthiness. The requirement to provide a fit vessel is not absolute; the standard of care is that of reasonable diligence.

Whether or not a vessel is fit is a question of fact to be determined in the circumstances of each case. If there is some inherent defect in the condition of the vessel this fact will raise a presumption of unseaworthiness. However, on the other hand, if a facility in the vessel is defective, but the facility does not affect the vessel's capability to complete the voyage, it will be deemed fit for service: see *Athenian Tankers Management SA* v *Pyrena Shipping Co, The Arianna* (1987). Nevertheless, if the charterer is aware that the vessel is in a damaged condition when entering into the charterparty, it may be shown that the charterer has waived any claim against the shipowner for breach of the duty to provide a seaworthy vessel.

The obligation is not only to provide a fit vessel, but also to ensure that the vessel remains in an efficient state for the period of the hire. He must take reasonable steps to rectify defects as soon as these are brought to his notice. If the shipowner does not maintain the vessel in an efficient state, the charterer is entitled to sue for damages, but he is not entitled to repudiate the charterparty as a whole.

Next, the responsibilities for the day-to-day running of the vessel during the period of the charterparty are divided between the shipowner and the charterer. In general, the shipowner will agree to pay the crew's wages, the vessel's insurance and to maintain the vessel in an efficient state for the period of the hire. In turn, the charterer agrees to provide and pay for the fuel necessary for the voyage, to pay dock and harbour dues and to arrange and pay for all loading and discharge dues.

During the period of hire, the charterer will also undertake to engage only in lawful trades and to carry only lawful merchandise. In addition, it is generally agreed that the use of the vessel will be restricted to safe ports where there will be no threat of damage or destruction to the vessel. There is also an indemnity in favour of the shipowner for loss or damage to the vessel caused by the negligence of the charterer or his employees and agents and for careless loading or discharge which causes injury to the vessel.

The requirement to use safe ports merits closer consideration. The normal clause in the charterparty for this obligation states: 'The vessel will be employed between good and safe ports or places where she can safely lie always afloat.' The vessel must never be sent to a destination where it may be at risk from stranding or damage from unusual sea or weather conditions. If the charterer orders the vessel to an unsafe port, and damage to the vessel occurs, he will be required to indemnify the shipowner for the injury suffered.

The charterer is relieved of this duty if the vessel is ordered to sail to a port which is safe at the time the order is given but subsequently becomes unsafe. If some unexpected or abnormal event occurs which creates unsafe conditions the charterer will not be liable for any damage which falls on the vessel. Similarly, the charterer is relieved of liability if the master of the vessel acts unreasonably in a safe port with damaging consequences.

A further important clause is the excepted perils clause. This states that the shipowner will be liable for delay in delivery of the vessel and for loss or damage to the goods on board only if the delay or loss is caused by want of due diligence on the part of the owners or their employees in making the vessel seaworthy and fitted for the voyage or any other personal act or omission. The same clause excludes the liability of the shipowners for all other forms of loss or delay even if caused by the neglect or default of their employees.

Careless loading or discharge of the goods causing damage to the ship is the responsibility of the charterer, who will be liable for any damage caused by improper bunkering, loading, stowing or discharge of the goods by the charterer or his servants.

Once the charterparty expires the charterer is obliged to redeliver the vessel on a specified date and at a specified location. The journey which the vessel takes to be redelivered is known as the last voyage of the charterparty. The vessel must be sent on its last voyage in adequate time to allow for redelivery within the contracted period. When a charterparty specifies redelivery on a stated date, without any express margin or allowance, the court will imply a reasonable margin unless it is expressly stated that no margin or allowance is permitted.

If the vessel is redelivered prematurely to the shipowners, they are entitled to damages: see *Armagas Ltd* v *Mundogas SA, The Ocean Frost* (1986). Similarly, in the event that the vessel is delivered at a location other than that specified in the charterparty, the charterer is liable in damages for wrongful redelivery: *Reardon Smith Line Ltd* v *Sanko Steamship Co Ltd, The Sanko Honour* (1985). The actual measure of damages is to be assessed according to the circumstances of the case.

In normal circumstances, the charterer must redeliver the ship in the same good order as when delivered, fair wear and tear excepted. Breach of this duty entitled the shipowner to damages; he cannot insist on the charterer effecting the repairs before redelivery. Where the vessel is redelivered not in the same good order, and repairs have to be effected to restore her to the proper condition, the shipowner is entitled to the cost of repairs and any loss of profit while she is being repaired. He is not entitled to claim hire for this period.

A standard charterparty also normally contains a clause providing for arbitration in a specified place as well as a proper law for the contract.

Question 2

Tom chartered *The Fred Quimby* from Jerry on a twelve year consecutive voyage charterparty and Tom, in turn, sub-chartered the vessel to Sylvester for a single voyage to carry 10,000 tonnes of cat food loaded in two separate consignments each of 5,000. The vessel has been painted in the colours of Tom's company and the bills of lading signed by the ship's master have been printed on Tom's company stationery.

The head charterparty incorporates the terms of the Hague Rules while the sub-charterparty states that 'the owners are responsible for loss of, or damage to, the goods being carried only if the loss has been caused by their own personal fault'.

The stevedores claim that each consignment weighs 5,500 tonnes when they loaded the consignments but in fact both are actually only 5,000 tonnes each. In any event, the ship's master issues two shipped bills of lading each for 5,500 tonnes but marked 'weight and quantity unknown'.

Both bills contain the following statement: 'All terms and conditions of the charterparty between _____ and ____ dated ____ are incorporated into this agreement.'

Sylvester sells 5,500 tonnes of the cat food to Garfield and indorses one of the two bills of lading in favour of Garfield.

On the voyage, 500 tonnes of each consignment are contaminated by sea water because the vessel was not seaworthy when she sailed. The defect was caused by poor rivets used when carrying out an overhaul of the vessel. The overhaul was carried out by Tweetie Pie & Co which is an independent contractor. The work was carried out on the instructions of Jerry.

Advise Tom and Garfield as to their respective rights in this situation.

Question prepared by the Editor
April 1994

General comment

In this question, the student must be thoroughly with the law of charterparty. The answer turns on the interpretation of the terms of the charter party relating to liability for damage to the cargo.

Skeleton solution

Charter party by demise and the legal principles behind such agreements.

Construction of the terms of the charter party.

Exclusion clauses for liability.

Article VI of the Hague Rules.

Section 1 of the Carriage of Goods by Sea Act 1992.

Suggested solution

Sylvester and Tom have entered into a charterparty arrangement for the carriage of goods. Therefore, as between Tom and Sylvester, the contract of carriage is the charterparty and the bill of lading in the hands of Sylvester is therefore merely a receipt for the goods and a document of title.

From the facts presented, the contract between Jerry and Tom appears to be a charterparty by demise. Control over the vessel, together with its master and crew, have passed to Tom. The owner of the vessel, Jerry, has divested himself of all control over the ship and crew. His sole right is to receive the stipulated hire when the charterparty terminates. During the period of the charterparty, the owner is under no liability to third persons. Jerry is not therefore liable to either Sylvester or Garfield who must look to Tom for a remedy.

Unless expressly prohibited by the head charterparty, Tom is within his rights to sub-charter the vessel to Sylvester. In charterparties by demise, the charterer often exercises such a right and therefore the contract of sub-charter between Tom and Sylvester is perfectly valid.

In common with other mercantile documents, the sub-charter must be construed to give effect, as far as possible, to the intentions of the parties as expressed in the written contract. The charterparty between Sylvester and Tom contains a clause limiting the liability of the owners to loss or damage caused by their personal fault. The loss of the 500 tons is due to the negligence of the master of the vessel. Therefore, in order to establish liability on the part of Tom, Sylvester must show that personal fault includes negligence on the part of employees.

Where exceptions and stipulations are inserted into the charterparty for the protection of one of the parties, such provisions must be construed against the party whom they were intended to protect. Thus, the ambiguous nature of the exclusion clause may allow the courts to hold that the liability of Tom is not limited to his own actual acts, but also those of his employees. This interpretation is supported by the fact that the head charterparty incorporates the Hague Rules which themselves do not excuse the shipowner from liability for negligence on the part of their employees.

It is also likely that the sub-charterparty contains a term which incorporates the conditions of the head charterparty, this being a normal practice. The reason for this practice is to prevent the charterer from becoming liable to the owner for damage or loss by the actions of the sub-charter, but for which the sub-charterer escapes liability while the charterer does not. Therefore the Hague Rules are likely to be deemed part of the sub-charter between Tom and Sylvester.

As observed earlier, as between Sylvester and Tom, the contract of carriage is the charterparty and this document must be examined in order to establish liability for the loss of the goods. According to these rules, Tom is required to exercise due diligence to properly man, equip and supply the ship. In addition, Tom is obliged to properly and carefully load, handle, stow, carry, keep, care for and discharge the goods. Both these duties are relevant in determining whether or not Tom is liable for the loss of the 500 tons of cat food.

But Tom will be able to take advantage of Article VI, rules 1 and 2. Rule 1 states that neither the carrier nor the shipowner is to be liable for loss or damage arising from unseaworthiness unless caused by want of due diligence on the part of the carrier, in this case Tom, to make the ship seaworthy. Equally, rule 2 excludes liability of the carrier for damage or loss arising through no fault of the servants of the carrier.

Since the contamination of the cargo was due to the vessel being unseaworthy due to the use of poor quality rivets by independent contractors engaged by Jerry, it is likely that Tom would escape liability. Further, the fact that the poor nature of the repairs could not be easily discovered by inspection mitigates the prospects of establishing that Tom or his servants were negligent.

The bill of lading itself, however, may expressly incorporate the charterparty terms in which case the indorsee may be affected by the terms. To be effective, the incorporation must be clear and unambiguous and any term thus incorporated must not conflict with any express terms in the bill of lading.

In this particular case, the incorporating provision does not specify either the parties to the charterparty or the date on which the charterparty was negotiated. As it stands, this provision is inchoate and does not expressly refer to any particular charterparty. Consequently, it is unlikely that the terms of the charterparty, including the exclusion from liability, are imported into the bill of lading.

Garfield is allowed to rely on terms of the bill of lading, and, in addition, acquires the rights of Sylvester under the document by virtue of the endorsement: see s1 Carriage of Goods by Sea Act 1992. Garfield may therefore rely on the Hague Rules in order to establish liability on the part of Tom.

The bill of lading was, however, claused by the addition of the terms 'weight and quantity unknown' by the master of the vessel. In effect, Tom is not bound by any statement in the bill of lading with reference to matters specifically excluded by the qualification. It is not clear to what extent the statement qualifies the duty of Tom since the bill of lading also refers to a specific weight. In one case, the court held that, notwithstanding a declaration as to weight, a qualification as to the weight made by the master on the bill of lading deprived the bill of lading of being prima facie evidence of the weight of the cargo: *New Chinese Antimony Co Ltd* v *Ocean SS Co Ltd* (1917).

Question 3

Andy and Craig enter into a time charterparty for the vessel *The Stag* which contains a clause referring all dispute to arbitration in London. Andy wishes to use the vessel to transport consignments of beer from the United State to Liverpool.

A consignment of beer is loaded aboard *The Stag* and a bill of lading issued by the ship's master. This bill states that all disputes are to be settled in the Commercial

Court in London. There is no statement in either the charterparty or the bill of lading as to the governing law of either document.

During one voyage, some of the beer starts to ferment because it has been improperly packed by Ian, an employee of the American Beer Packing Co which has been contracted to put the beer into kegs suitable for exporting the goods. The fermented beer escapes into the holds and stains them. Andy attempts to clean the holds by using a solvent which in fact permanently corrodes the lining of the hold.

Watson, the ship's master also issued an erroneous non-negotiable bill of lading for the consignment. Instead of recording that the stipulated consignment of 500 kegs of beer had been loaded, he issues a bill of lading for 600 barrels. In fact, when the goods are unloaded in Liverpool, 50 kegs of beer have mysteriously disappeared.

The ship is now due to be returned to Craig after this voyage as the time charterparty is near to termination.

Advise both Craig and Andy of their respective rights arising from this situation.

Question prepared by the Editor
April 1994

General comment

The key to answering this question properly lies in familiarity with the terms of a standard charterparty which would normally contain express stipulations governing these eventualities.

Skeleton solution

Proper law of the contract.

Terms of the Baltime 1939 Charterparty.

Duty to return the vessel in proper condition.

Suggested solution

a) *Rights of Craig*

The contractual rights of Craig against Andy are regulated by the terms of the charterparty. The charterparty contains an express clause referring all disputes to arbitration in London and the fact that the bill of lading refers disputes to the Commercial Court in London cannot exclude arbitration in London. Although arbitration is specified in the agreement, it is unclear whether English law or the law of another state will govern the interpretation of the charterparty. Resolution of this question falls to be decided in terms of the Contracts (Applicable Law) Act 1990. According to Article 4(4) of the Convention given force of law in the UK by this statute, in the absence of an express choice of law, a contract is governed by the law of the country with which it is most closely connected. There is a presumption that a contract is most closely connected with the country where the party effecting the performance which is characteristic of the contract is resident. In this particular case, the proper law of the contract will therefore most likely be English law.

Assuming that English law is the proper law of the contract, the rights and obligations of the parties are governed by the terms of the charterparty as construed under English law. Standard terms and conditions are invariably expressly incorporated into contracts of charterparty. In particular, two principal clauses are relevant to this problem: a) the careless loading or discharge clause; and b) the redelivery clause. Both these provisions may also be considered implied terms of a charterparty: see *Ben Shipping* v *An-Board Bainne, The C Joyce* (1986). We can therefore presume that the charterparty between Andy and Craig contains analogous provisions.

A typical careless loading or discharge clause of a charterparty would stipulate that 'the charterers are responsible for loss or damage caused to the vessel or to the owners by goods being loaded contrary to the terms of the charter or by improper bunkering or loading, stowing or discharge of goods or any other improper or negligent act on their part or that of their servants' ('Baltime 1939' form, clause 13). Liability for the damage would therefore depend on whether the actions of the American Beer Packing Co could be attributed to Andy. It is unlikely that Craig could establish that the American Beer Packing Co was an employee, agent or servant of Andy for the purposes of such a clause. Equally, if fault is required, it would be necessary to attribute fault to Andy for negligently using the solvent. Further, if the master of the ship had supervised the loading of the goods and the use of the solvent, liability on the part of Andy will be more difficult to establish: see *MSC Mediterranean Shipping* v *Alianca Bay Shipping, The Argonaut* (1986).

Alternatively, Craig may found upon the duty of the charterer to return the vessel in the same condition, subject to reasonable wear and tear, to establish the liability of Andy. A typical redelivery clause would specify that 'the vessel is to be returned on the expiration of the Charter in the same good order as when delivered to the Charterers (fair wear and tear excepted)' ('Baltime 1939' form, clause 7). This obligation cannot be delegated to another party. Craig would therefore be able to claim damages from Andy on this basis and Andy could not defend the claim by alleging that the damage was caused by the American Beer Packing Co. Whether or not the solvent was used on the instructions of Andy is irrelevant in this determination: *Leigh & Sillivan* v *Aliakmon Shipping, The Aliakmon* (1986). Although the charterer is obliged to return the vessel in the same condition as originally delivered, breach of this duty gives rise to a claim of damages only. The shipowner cannot insist that the charterer effects repairs prior to the redelivery of the vessel. See *Attica Sea Carriers Corp* v *Ferrostaal-Poseidon Bulk Reederei GmbH, The Puerto Buitrago* (1975). The shipowner could therefore claim the costs of repairs and loss of profit from Andy, but would be precluded from claiming hire for the period.

It is extremely unlikely that a remedy in tort can be relied upon by Craig against the American Beer Packing Co. In order for such a claim to be successful, Craig would have to establish that the American Beer Packing Co owed him a duty of care and that the American Beer Packing Co neglected this duty. Injury must also be established on the part of Craig.

b) *Rights of Andy*

The contractual relationship between Andy and Craig is governed by the terms of the charterparty. The bill of lading has no effect on the arbitration clause in relation to jurisdiction for the settlement of disputes between Andy and Craig.

The principal issue is whether or not Andy has a remedy against Craig for the missing goods. Craig would probably not be precluded by the issue of the incorrect bill of lading from adducing evidence that only 500 barrels of beer had been loaded instead of 600 barrels. In the first place, the Hague-Visby Rules do not apply to the carriage of the cargo of beer since the contract of carriage between Craig and Andy is governed by the charterparty. In such a case the bill of lading has no contractual function: see *Rodocanachi* v *Milburn* (1886). Similarly, the Carriage of Goods by Sea Act 1992 does not apply since the document is not a bill of lading for the purposes of the statute, having been marked 'non-negotiable'. Consequently, the Carriage of Goods by Sea Act 1992 is inapplicable to the case, as is the Carriage of Goods by Sea Act 1971. The relationship is therefore governed by the common law.

At common law, the bill of lading is prima facie evidence of quantity. But a shipowner is entitled to show that the goods were never in fact shipped. If this is possible, he escapes liability in respect of them. Further, at common law, the Master of a vessel does not have actual or ostensible authority to sign a bill of lading for goods which have not in fact been shipped: see *Grant* v *Norway* (1851); *The Saudi Crown* (1986). There is, therefore, no possibility of estoppel based on the representations made by the Master that 600 barrels of beer were shipped. But while the bill of lading creates a rebuttable presumption, the onus is placed on Craig to establish that the goods received were incorrect prior to shipping. Consequently, Andy has a distinct advantage in any subsequent litigation.

If Craig is unable to adduce evidence to prove that only 500 barrels of beer were in fact shipped, he will have to prove the existence of one of the four common law exceptions to the duties of a carrier by sea to avoid liability. These are: act of God; act of the Queen's enemies; inherent vice; and jettison. There is no evidence to support the existence of any of these exceptions.

Should the shipowner be able to produce evidence that only 500 barrels of beer were shipped, or if one of these exceptions is applicable, Andy would have to rely on an action against the American Beer Packing Co based on breach of contract.

Question 4

Snoopy, in London, sells Charlie, in the United States, a consignment of peanuts fob English port payment to be made by banker's commercial credit. Charlie nevertheless asks Snoopy to arrange for the carriage of the goods to Virginia. Snoopy arranges for the carriage of the peanuts aboard *The Slide* which is carrying a number of other consignments of peanuts to buyers in the United States.

Charlie requests that the bill of lading is non-negotiable and made out to him as consignee and this is presented by Snoopy to the bank for payment under the letter of credit and, in fact, payment is made by the bank.

The bill is in the form of the Nancy Line and is signed by the loading broker on behalf of the ship's master. Unknown to Snoopy the vessel belongs to the Silus Line and is on a time charter to the Nancy Line.

When the goods are unloaded in Virginia it transpires that 20 per cent of the whole cargo has been damaged by rain during the voyage. It is subsequently discovered that the rainwater has seeped into the peanuts which have excreted an acid-like substance which has corroded the lining of the ship's hold.

Advise all the parties in this situation of their respective rights and liabilities.

Question prepared by the Editor
April 1994

General comment

A short answer is all that is required here, dealing with the mechanics of issuing a bill of lading and the chain of obligations which exists thereunder.

Skeleton solution

Question of who is the carrier?

Liability under a charterparty for dangerous goods.

Duty to properly and carefully load the goods.

Suggested solution

The contract described in this question is not a strict fob as an additional service is requested by Charlie, who would normally be the shipper; that is the seller Snoopy is to arrange the contract of carriage.

In conformity with Charlie's request Snoopy procures a non-negotiable bill of lading naming himself as shipper and Charlie as consignee. Payment for the carriage will be made by Charlie on the arrival of the goods.

The obvious difficulties here are who is the carrier, what duties are borne by the shipper and the carrier and do the Hague-Visby rules apply?

Generally if the contract is between the shipper and the charterer or his agent then the charterer will bear the responsibilities of carrier, but we are told that a loading broker signed 'for the master'. If the shipper took the bill of lading ignorant of the existence of the time charterparty, then he can sue the shipowner, the Silus Line, in the event of an action arising: *Sanderman* v *Scurr* (1913).

In the present case Snoopy clearly believed he was doing business with the Nancy Line, through the Nancy Line's agent, the loading broker. It is submitted therefore that the Nancy Line is the carrier. It was pointed out in the case of *Samuel* v *West Hartlepool* (1957) that it is a question of fact to be determined on the circumstances of the case.

Under a charterparty the shipper must not load dangerous cargo: *Mitchelle Cotts* v *Steel Brothers & Co* (1916). Here we are told that the cargo damaged the ship. If dangerous cargo is loaded without the carrier's knowledge then the shipper will be liable in damages. There is a similar duty not to load dangerous cargo even if the Hague-Visby rules apply: Article 4 r6.

The bill of lading in Charlie's hands is the contract of carriage so Charlie can insist on the terms contained in the bill, the Carriage of Goods by Sea Act 1992 s1. Furthermore Article 5 Hague-Visby rules indicate that the rules will apply to the contract. The ambit of the carrier's liability under the rules means that the carrier is liable for damage caused on the goods during the loading process: Article 3, *Maxine Footwear* v *Canadian Government Merchant Marine* (1959), subject to the exclusions in Article 4.

The carrier must 'properly and carefully load'. He must, therefore, follow a recognised system having regard to everything the carrier knows or ought to know about the cargo: *Albacora* v *Westcott & Laurance Line* (1966). Allowing goods liable to be damaged by rain to be damaged while in transport, is not, it is suggested, 'proper' loading. To rely on any of the exclusions in Article 4 the carrier would have to show he exercised due diligence.

It is not stated whether the 20 per cent of the cargo damaged was entirely in the bulk appropriated to Charlie nor indeed whether there was appropriation. Nevertheless the carrier's liability is limited in a bulk cargo to a maximum value per kilogram of gross weight lost or damaged: Article 4 r5.

Notice of damages must be given immediately or at most within three days, otherwise the carrier will be entitled to assume the consignee has accepted the goods.

8 CARRIAGE OF GOODS BY SEA ACT 1971 AND THE HAGUE-VISBY RULES

8.1   Introduction

8.2   Key points

8.3   Recent cases and statutes

8.4   Relevant materials

8.5   Analysis of questions

8.6   Questions

8.1   Introduction

Originally, bills of lading did not exclude the liability of carriers for damage to goods during transit on ships where the damage caused came about as a result of the negligence or fault of the carrier. In the nineteenth century this situation changed and shipowners relied extensively on exclusion clauses in bills of lading to avoid liability for damaged goods. Eventually it was generally recognised that a balance had to be struck between the rights of cargo owners to compensation for damaged goods and the interests of shipowners.

Since carriage of goods by ship is principally an international activity, the main attempts to strike this balance have been through a series of international conferences. The first successful attempt to introduce rules to regulate the liability of shipowners was the Hague Convention negotiated between 1921 and 1922. The rules embodied in this Convention were given force of law in the UK by the Carriage of Goods by Sea Act 1924.

After almost fifty years, the rules contained in this Convention had become deficient in a number of areas and an amended set of international rules was negotiated in the form of a Protocol signed at Brussels in 1968. The 1968 rules are known as the Hague-Visby Rules and were incorporated into UK law by the Carriage of Goods by Sea Act 1971, which incidentally also repealed the 1924 Act.

Many countries are of the view that the Hague-Visby Rules unreasonably favour the protection of the carrier and accordingly another international convention was negotiated in 1978 known as the Hamburg Rules. This Convention has been adopted by some countries but not the United Kingdom. In UK law, this area of law is therefore governed by the 1971 Act and certain principles of common law which apply when the statutory rules are inapplicable.

Not all countries follow the UK's lead and apply the Hague-Visby Rules. Some European states do so, such as Belgium, France, the Netherlands and Sweden. Other important trading nations apply the Hague Rules, including the United States, Germany, Australia and Spain. As we shall see, whether a country applies the Hague-Visby Rules or not is important in ascertaining whether the rules apply to a particular contract of carriage.

The main import of the 1971 Act and the Hague-Visby Rules is to imply into every contract of carriage certain duties on the part of the carrier. These duties are mandatory and operate in all cases where the statutory rules are applicable. It should be noted, however, that the common law rules continue to function in those situations which are not regulated by the statutory regime.

In essence, the Hague-Visby Rules, as applied by the 1971 Act, impose four duties on a carrier in contracts of carriage. These duties cannot be contracted out of and there is no possibility of reducing the carrier's liability where the rules apply. The rules are the measure of the balance struck between the respective rights and duties of the shipper and the carrier.

8.2   Key points

a) *The incorporation of the Hague-Visby Rules into UK law by the 1971 Act*

The Carriage of Goods by Sea Act 1971 (1971, c.19) is a short statute, with only six sections, but contains the full text of the 1968 Protocol as a schedule. This schedule is given force of law by s1(2) of the Act and consequently the rules contained in the Protocol have direct effect in UK law.

Again it must be stressed that the Act and the Rules have been held to be an 'overriding statute' which means that there is no scope for the parties to avoid the operation of the Rules either by an express exclusion clause or by selecting a proper law to regulate the rights and duties of the parties which does not apply the Rules: see *The Hollandia* [1983] 1 AC 565 and *The Benarty* [1984] 3 All ER 961.

b) *The application of the Rules to contracts of carriage*

The critical first step in the application of the Hague-Visby Rules is to decide whether or not the Rules themselves apply to a particular contract of carriage. There are three elements to consider which must be cumulatively satisfied before the Rules may be deemed to apply: (i) the nature of the voyage; (ii) the documents issued; and (iii) the type of goods.

i)   The nature of the voyage

The Rules will, prima facie, have statutory application in the following circumstances:

- for any voyage where the port of shipment is a port in the United

Kingdom (even if the port of destination is also a port in the United Kingdom);

- for any voyage between ports in different states where:
  - the bill of lading is issued in a contracting party to the Hague-Visby Rules; or
  - the carriage is from a port in a contracting state.
- where there has been an express incorporation of the Rules into the contract contained in, or evidenced by, the bill of lading; and
- where the contract of carriage contained in, or evidenced by, the bill of lading provides that the express choice of law is that of a state which gives effect to the Rules.

The principles regulating the application of the Rules are embodied in Article X of the Rules.

ii) The documents issued

As a general principle, the Rules will only apply if a bill of lading, or similar document of title, is issued in conjunction with one of the particular types of voyages identified in section (i) above.

The reference to a 'similar document of title' is to those instruments in writing operating as documents of title in common law: see *Lickbarrow* v *Mason* (1787) 2 Term Rep 63.

Where the contract is contained in, or evidenced by, a non-negotiable receipt which is expressly intended to govern the contract as if it were a bill of lading, the Rules also apply. This is an exception to the general principle, permitted by s1(6)(b) of the Act.

iii) The type of goods

The Rules apply to the carriage of all types of goods except the following goods:

- live animals;
- deck cargo which means cargo which is stated in the contract will be carried on deck and which in fact is so carried.

A clause which gives the carrier an option or liberty to ship the goods on deck falls outside the exclusion and the cargo is not considered deck cargo for the purposes of the application of the Rules if the goods are not in fact carried on deck: see *Svenska Tractor* v *Maritime Agencies* [1953] 2 QB 295.

c) *The stage at which the Rules apply*

By Article I(e) of the Convention, 'carriage of goods' is defined in terms which cover the period from when the goods are loaded onto the vessel until they are discharged from the vessel.

The time for the loading of the goods starts from the moment that the first process in the operation of the loading of the goods onto the vessel is initiated. Hence, goods destroyed while being loaded aboard the vessel will fall within the terms of the Convention: *Pyrene & Co* v *Scindia Navigation Co* [1954] 2 All ER 158.

d) *The meaning of carrier*

The definition of 'carrier' in Article I(a) of the Convention includes both the owner of the ship and any charterer who enters into a contract of carriage with a shipper.

e) *The carrier's duties under the contract of carriage*

In every contract of carriage of goods to which the Rules apply, the carrier is subject to the responsibilities and rights contained in the Convention in relation to the loading, handling, stowage, carriage, custody, care and discharge of the goods: Article II.

The obligations of the carrier can be distilled into four principles: (i) the obligation to provide a seaworthy ship; (ii) the duty to properly load, stow, carry and discharge the goods; (iii) the duty to issue a bill of lading on the demand of the shipper; and (iv) the operation of the statutory estoppel.

    i)   Obligation to provide a seaworthy ship

The obligation to provide a seaworthy ship is not absolute. Instead, the carrier is required to exercise due diligence to provide a seaworthy ship: Article III, rule 1. Quite obviously, due diligence is a less onerous standard than an absolute duty.

The duty to exercise due diligence arises from the moment the Rules apply to the voyage and until the vessel sails: see *Maxine Footwear* v *Canadian Government Merchant Marine* [1959] AC 589. It does not, however, extend for the duration of the voyage. The duty is discharged, either properly or by breach, at the commencement of the contractual voyage.

It should also be noted that the duty cannot be delegated to third parties. The duty extends not only to the carrier personally but also to the acts of independent contractors within his control for which he will be liable if such contractors are negligent: see *Riverstone Meat Co* v *Lancashire Shipping Co* [1961] AC 589.

The full extent of the carrier's obligation of due diligence is set out in Article III, rule 1, which merits full reproduction at this point:

'The carrier shall be bound before and at the beginning of the voyage to exercise due diligence to:

(1) Make the ship seaworthy.

(2) Properly man, equip and supply the ship.

(3) make the holds, refrigerating and cool chambers, and all other parts of the ship in which the goods are carried, fit and safe for their reception, carriage and preservation.'

The obligation encapsulates the following requirements:

- The ship must be cargoworthy; it must be fit to receive the cargo from the time the process of loading begins and until the start of the voyage: see *The Good Friend* [1984] 2 Lloyd's Rep 586.

- The ship must be fit in its design, structure, condition and equipment to encounter the ordinary perils of the voyage.

- The ship must have competent and sufficient crew and the master must be aware of the idiosyncracies of his ship.

- A ship will be deemed unseaworthy if the cargo must be stowed in such a manner so as to endanger the safety of the vessel.

Any shipper of goods alleging a breach of the duty to exercise due diligence in the provision of a seaworthy ship must establish two factors: (i) de facto unseaworthiness; and (ii) a causal connection between the unseaworthiness and the loss or damage: see *Minister of Food* v *Reardon Smith Line* [1951] P 84.

ii) Duty to properly load, stow, carry and discharge the goods

Article III, rule 2, imposes on the carrier a duty to 'properly and carefully load, stow, carry, keep, care for and discharge the goods'.

The tasks imposed on the carrier must be 'properly carried out' which means that a recognised system must be used to load, etc, the goods. This system must also be suitable having regard to the relevant facts which the carrier knows or ought to know about a particular cargo: *Albacora* v *Westcott & Laurance Line* [1966] 2 Lloyd's Rep 53. Therefore, for example, cargoes which may taint each other should not be stowed together in close proximity.

The standard of care required is that of reasonable skill and care in using an established and sound system for loading, etc, the goods. Again the carrier cannot avoid liability for breach of this duty by delegating responsibility for such matters to a third party in the event that the third party is negligent in discharging the duty.

The standard of care itself relates to handling of the goods. If the cargo is, therefore, loaded and stowed in such a way that it is damaged then there is bad stowage if the carrier did not act reasonably by using a sound system.

The obligation to discharge the goods means a discharge to the consignee or his agent: see *Sze Hai Tong Bank* v *Rambler Cycle Co* [1959] 2 Lloyd's Rep 114.

The burden of proof is initially on the cargo owner to show that the goods have been shipped in the condition set out in the bill of lading and then to show that they have not been delivered or that they have been delivered in a damaged state: *The Torenia* [1983] 2 Lloyd's Rep 210.

In the event that a shipper supervises the loading and stowing of the cargo, and that cargo is damaged by virtue of the loading process, the shipper is estopped from denying that he approved of the loading and stowing and he cannot claim that the carrier was in breach of the duty to carefully load and stow the goods: *Ismail* v *Polish Ocean Line* [1976] 1 All ER 902.

The duty to properly and carefully load the goods is subject to 17 exceptions which the carrier can rely on to avoid liability: Article IV, rule 2(a)–(q). As a result, the carrier will not be held responsible for loss or damage resulting from the following perils:

- The acts, neglect or default of the master, mariner, pilot or the servants of the carrier in the navigation or management of the ship.

  The acts of neglect or default which are covered by this peril are those which endanger the vessel not merely those which affect the preservation of the cargo. For example, in *The Washington* [1976] 2 Lloyd's Rep 453, the master decided to maintain his course and speed despite reports of bad weather. This behaviour was held to be negligent, but was not an act of neglect or default for which exemption could be claimed under this head as it did not endanger the vessel, only the cargo.

- Fire, unless caused by the actual fault of the carrier.

  The exemption for fire damage is only available to the carrier if he can show that it occurred without his actual fault. If a fire takes place as a result of the act of an independent contractor, servant or agent, the carrier may be liable unless he can show that he exercised due diligence in discharging this duty and the independent contractor also exercised adequate diligence.

- Perils, dangers and accidents of the sea or other navigable waters.

  Not every manifestation of bad weather constitutes a peril of the sea within this exception. For example, in *The Tilia Gorthorn* [1985] 1 Lloyd's Rep 552, a Force 10 gale did not constitute a peril of the sea as it was within the contemplation of the parties and therefore the carrier was unable to rely on this exception to exclude liability when the deck cargo was washed overboard.

- Acts of God.

  An act of God is any act which occurs naturally and without any element of human intervention: *Nugent* v *Smith* (1876) 1 CPD 423.

- Acts of war.

- Acts of public enemies.

- Arrest or restraint of princes, rulers or people or seizure under legal process.

- Quarantine restrictions.

- Acts or omissions of the shipper or owner of the goods, his agent or representative.

- Strikes, lockouts, stoppage or restraint of labour from whatever cause whether partial or general.

- Riot and civil commotions.

- Saving, or attempting to save, life or property at sea.

- Wastage in bulk or weight or any other loss or damage arising from inherent defect, quality or vice in the goods.

  Inherent vice can be relied on where the damage to the cargo results from the internal condition of the goods rather than their external circumstances. Inherent vice includes, for example, oxidisation or rusting of metals, expansion of orange juice, spontaneous combustion of hemp, internal moisture levels of certain cargoes, discoloration of foodstuffs, etc: see *Berk* v *Style* [1956] 1 QB 180.

- Insufficiency of packing.

  Whether the packing is sufficient is a question of fact in every case which may be resolved by reference to trade practice. If the goods have always been packed in a particular way and have not suffered damage before this may raise a presumption of fact in favour of the adequacy of the packing: *The Lucky Wave* [1985] 1 Lloyd's Rep 80.

- Insufficiency or inadequacy of marks.

- Latent defects not discoverable by due diligence.

- Any other causes arising without the actual fault or privacy of the carrier, or without the fault or neglect of the agents or servants of the carrier.

  Although this paragraph refers to 'any other cause', it is to be interpreted as applying only to causes which have not already been excluded in other paragraphs. But, in this case, the burden of proof is on the person claiming the benefit of this exception to show that neither the actual fault of the carrier nor the fault or neglect of the agents or servants of the carrier contributed to the loss or damage.

iii) Duty to issue a bill of lading on the demand of the shipper

Article III, rule 3 provides that, after receiving the goods into his charge, the carrier or the master or agent of the carrier must, on the demand of the shipper, issue to the shipper a bill of lading showing among other things:

- the loading marks necessary for the identification of the goods as the same are furnished in writing by the shipper before the loading of the goods commences, provided such marks are shown or otherwise stamped clearly on the goods;

- either the number of packages or pieces, or the quantity, or weight as the case may be as furnished in writing by the shipper; and

- the apparent order and condition of the goods.

A carrier is not obliged to issue a bill of lading which contains information which he cannot see or verify. In addition, no carrier, master or agent of the carrier is bound to state or show in a bill of lading any marks, number, quantity or weight which he has reasonable ground for suspecting does not represent the goods actually received or which he has no reasonable means of checking.

If the shipper so demands, the bill of lading must also be a 'shipped bill' showing the goods to be actually on board rather than merely received for shipment: Article III, rule 7.

iv) Statutory estoppel

Article III, rule 4 sets up a statutory estoppel by stating that:

'A bill of lading shall be prima facie evidence of the receipt by the carrier of the goods as therein described ... However, proof to the contrary shall not be admissible when the bill of lading has been transferred to a third party acting in good faith.'

It is important to note that this estoppel has the same effect as that generated by the Carriage of Goods by Sea Act 1992. It does not confer a cause of action but merely negates a defence which would otherwise be available.

f) *Contracts of indemnity*

A carrier may agree with the shipper to issue a bill of lading in terms requested by the latter against a contract of indemnity. This can occur in two situations:

i) where the carrier in aware that the terms he is representing on the bill of lading are false;

ii) where the carrier has genuine, but unproven, reservations or misgivings as to the accuracy of the terms requested by the shipper.

The courts have not shown much sympathy to the first type of indemnity on the grounds that the consideration moving from the carrier is illegal, namely the deliberate misstating of the position with the intention to deceive innocent third parties subsequently dealing with the bill: *Brown Jenkinson* v *Percy Dalton* [1957] 2 All ER 844.

The courts have been more sympathetic to the second type of indemnity and in *Naviera Mogor* v *Société Metallurgique de Normandie* [1987] 1 Lloyd's Rep 456, the Court of Appeal held that contracts of indemnity could be implemented depending on the particular facts and the terms of the underlying contractual relationships.

g) *Maximum levels of liability*

If the Hague-Visby Rules apply, their effect is to impose on the carrier a maximum level of liability in the event of loss or damage for which he is made liable to the cargo owner. Of course, the cargo owner does not always recover this maximum limit in every case and the value recovered will depend on the value of the goods at the place of arrival. Hence Article IV, rule 5(b) provides:

'The total amount recoverable shall be calculated by reference to the value of such goods at the place and time at which the goods are discharged from the ship in accordance with the contract, or should have been so discharged.'

If the goods are actually worth more than the upper limit prescribed under the rules, the shipper cannot recover more unless one of the exceptions apply. If the goods are worth less, then the cargo owner will recover their value in accordance with Article IV, rule 5.

The measure of the maximum liability of the carrier is established in accordance with Article IV, rule 5(a), which states:

'neither the carrier nor the ship owner shall in any event be or become liable for any loss or damage to or in connection with the goods in an amount exceeding the equivalent of 666.67 units of account per package *or* two units of account per kilo, of gross weight of the goods lost or damage, whichever is the higher.'

By virtue of s1(5) of the Act, the Secretary of State is empowered to publish statutory instruments to confirm the sterling equivalent of the units of account specified above: see the Carriage by Sea (Sterling Equivalent) Order 1993 .

It should be noted that, even if the contract of carriage is governed by English law, the courts may be prepared to award judgment in currencies other than pounds sterling. For example, in *Société Francaise Bunge SA* v *Belcan NV, The Federal Huron* [1985] 3 All ER 378, the court awarded damages to the plaintiffs in US dollars.

The rules expressly provide that there are two situations in which the limits set down in Article IV, rule 5, do not apply:

i) where the nature and value of the goods have been declared by the shipper before shipment and inserted into the bill of lading: Article IV, rule 5(a); and

ii) where it is proved that the damage resulted from an act or omission of the carrier is done with the intent to cause damage or recklessly and with the knowledge that damage would probably result: Article IV, rule 5(e).

h) *Time limits for actions against the carrier*

Article III, rule 6, provides that, unless notice of loss or damage and the general nature of the loss or damage is given in writing to the carrier at the time of the removal of the goods from the custody of the carrier or, if the loss is not apparent, within three days of such removal, the removal of the goods will be prima facie evidence of the delivery of the goods by the carrier as described in the bill of lading.

The carrier and the shipowner will, in any event, be discharged from all liability in respect of the goods unless the action is raised within one year of the delivery of the goods or of the date on which they should have been delivered. This period may be extended if the parties by mutual agreement agree to do so after the cause of action has arisen.

An action for indemnity against a third party may, however, be brought after the one year period if brought within the general limitation period applied by the court seized of the case.

i) *Common law liability of the carrier*

The vast majority of contracts of carriage will be regulated by the Hague-Visby Rules which superseded the common law rules. But where the Hague-Visby Rules do not apply, the rights and obligations of the parties continue to be determined by the common law.

The common law imposes certain duties on a carrier of goods for reward. These duties may be qualified by exclusion and limitation clauses inserted by the carrier, but the use of such clauses will be restricted by the general rules of statutory law which limit the use of such clauses.

The common law imposes four basic obligations on the part of the carrier. These are as follows:

i) The carrier must deliver the goods in the same condition as when they were shipped. This duty cannot be delegated but liability is excluded for four perils:

- acts of God;

- acts of the Queen's enemies;

- loss or damage resulting from the inherent vice of the goods;

- loss resulting from jettison where the goods are thrown overboard to save the vessel.

In addition, it must also be shown that the damage to the goods, or their loss, was the result of the carrier's negligence.

ii) The carrier has an absolute duty to provide a seaworthy ship for the carriage of the goods. This duty is absolute. Therefore, even if the defect in the vessel is latent, the ship is de facto unseaworthy and, if the unseaworthiness is the cause of the loss or damage, the carrier remains liable despite the existence of other concurrent causes: see *Monarch v Karlshamns Oljefabriker* [1949] AC 196.

iii) The carrier undertakes to proceed with the voyage without unjustifiable deviation. If there is unjustifiable deviation the carrier is liable for any subsequent loss unless he can rely on any of the common law exclusions and can show that the loss or damage would have occurred notwithstanding the deviation.

iv) The carrier must complete the voyage with reasonable dispatch. If there is undue delay, the carrier is liable in damages for any loss caused by the delay unless the loss falls within one of the excepted perils and the carrier can demonstrate that he has not been negligent: see, for example, *The Athanasia Comninos* [1990] 1 Lloyd's Rep 277.

8.3 Recent cases and statutes

The Waltrand [1991] 1 Lloyd's Rep 389:– an award for summary judgement for damages caused by breach of the duty to exercise due diligence in making the ship seaworthy.

Transworld Oil (USA) Inc v *Minos Compania Naviera SA, The Leni* [1992] 2 Lloyd's Rep 48: application of the periods of limitation to claims under the Hague-Visby Rules.

Balli Trading Ltd v *Afalona Shipping Co Ltd, The Coral* [1993] 1 Lloyd's Rep 1: a case concerning the application of Article III, rule 2, and the duty of the carrier to properly stow the goods of the shipper.

Mediterranean Freight Services Ltd v *BP Oil International Ltd, The Fiona* [1993] 1 Lloyd's Rep 257: a shipper is not strictly required to inform a carrier of any dangers inherent in a cargo of which the carrier was unaware and could not reasonably be expected to become aware. However, if the shipper did not convey such a warning in these circumstances, he might become liable to indemnify the carrier for losses arising from the shipment.

8.4 Relevant materials

D Glass, *Introduction to the Carriage of Goods* (1989).

Chorley & Gilles, *Shipping Law* (8th edition, 1987).

J F Wilson, *Introduction to the Carriage of Goods by Sea* (1993).

L D'Arcy, *Law of the Carriage of Goods by Land, Sea and Air* (1992).

J Crabtree, *International Sale of Goods* (1991), pp161–186.

8.5 Analysis of questions

The application of the Hague-Visby Rules is at the heart of the law of the carriage of goods by sea. It is therefore no surprise that this area of the syllabus frequently arises in examinations in international trade. The concepts are difficult to apply, particularly to factual problems. However, it would be fatal if an attempt was made to tackle an examination in international trade law without first acquiring a thorough knowledge of this topic.

8.6   Questions

Question 1

a) The rules relating to carriers' liability contained in the Carriage of Goods by Sea Act 1971 have been described as part of a 'mandatory overriding statute'. What do you understand by this term as it applies to the 1971 Act and the Hague-Visby Rules?

b) Lillian contracted with Sophia Ltd, a firm of shipowners, for the carriage of 1,000 tonnes of beauty cream from France to the United Kingdom, to be delivered at Southampton. A bill of lading is issued by the master of *The Vanity* on behalf of the ship owners.

Lillian physically delivered the goods to the quayside. The goods were packed into cardboard cartons of 100 tonnes each. Sophia had hired a firm of stevedores to load the goods aboard the vessel. While the goods are being loaded aboard, under Lillian's supervision, a cable snaps and one consignment falls into the sea where it quickly dissipates. An argument ensues between Lillian, the stevedores and the crew as to who was responsible for the cable snapping.

It transpires that the bill of lading contained a 'Himalaya Clause' which enables independent contractors to avail themselves of the exemptions and financial limitations available to the carrier. The stevedore company argues that this protects them against claims by Lillian against them.

Lillian subsequently transfers the bill of lading to Theodore but the bill states that the consignment is 1,000 tonnes of beauty cream.

Eighteen months after these events both Lillian and Theodore seek your advice in relation to their respective claims against the carrier and against the stevedore company.

Question prepared by the Editor
April 1994

General comment

A two-part question on the subject of the mandatory application of the Hague-Visby Rules. Both parts are straightforward and constitute a gentle introductiion to this otherwise complicated subject.

Skeleton solution

a) Mandatory application.

Inability to contract out.

Choice of law clause: Article VIII Hague-Visby Rules

Article III, rule 8.

b) Breaches: Article III, rule 1

Article III, rule 2

Claim against carrier: Article III, rule 6, contract or tort.

Exemptions for carrier IV r2(a)–(q).

Claim time barred? Mutual extension by parties?

Article IV, rule 5, package or unit liability.

Suggested solution

a) The Carriage of Goods by Sea Act 1971 came into force in 1977. It incorporates the Hague-Visby Rules, a body of rules which were devised to unify the rights, obligations and liabilities of the carrier. These Rules do not apply to all contracts of carriage by sea from the United Kingdom. Sections 1(3) and 1(4), 1(6)(a) and 1(6)(b) specify the situations in which they will apply. These sections are supplemented by Article X of the Rules themselves. Insofar as the Rules do apply according to the provisions of these sections, they must apply. The wording of s1(2) makes it clear by the use of the word 'shall' that their application in such circumstances is mandatory and not discretionary. Since the Rules are an international convention to which a number of countries are signatories, their mandatory application is understandable. There would be little utility in acceding to an international convention to regulate the liability of the overseas carrier if he were free to avoid its application by choosing a different body of Rules to regulate his obligations to the shipper.

The situations in which the Rules do not apply have been made clear by the Act. They do not apply to goods shipped by a charterer, in the absence of express incorporation or to deck cargo stated on the Bill to be so carried, or live animals. In such cases either the parties have greater parity of bargaining power, so that regulation by convention has less justification, or the goods to be carried require special conditions, care and attention by the carrier, thus making it preferable that he should be able to agree the terms of carriage individually with the shipper rather than be faced with a standard of terms proposed by the Rules: Article VI.

Prior to the application of the Rules, the carrier's duties to the shipper were governed by the common law under which the carrier would often attempt to create for himself a position of restricted liability or total exemption. The effect of the Rules is to provide a minimum ceiling level below which the carrier cannot reduce his liability but beyond which he will not be liable in the absence of specific agreement to the contrary on shipment. The actual amount recovered by the shipper will be calculated by reference to value at the place of arrival: Article IV, rule 5. To ensure that the duties imposed by the Rules cannot be lowered, and the financial limits cannot be altered, Article III, rule 8 renders void any clause, covenant or agreement to this effect. It thus ensures that not only is the application of the Rules as a whole mandatory, but its individual provisions cannot be undermined by contrary agreement.

The mandatory nature of the Rules is evident not only from the wording of s1(2) and Article III, rule 8 but is apparent from each Article of the Rules dealing with the carrier's duties, all of which employ the word 'shall' to denote the mandatory nature of the duty: Article III, rule 1, Article III, rule 2, Article III, rule 3, Article IV, rule 1, Article IV, rule 5.

Thus the wording of s1(2) of the Act together with the wording of the individual Rules serves to emphasise that the Rules are to be given the coercive force of law. This means that:

'they are to be given supremacy over every other provision of the bill of lading. If there is anything else in the bill of lading which is inconsistent with the Rules or which derogates from the effect of them, it is to be rejected. There is to be no contracting out of the Rules. Notwithstanding any clause in the bill of lading to the contrary. The provisions of the Rules are to be paramount ...': per Lord Denning MR: *The Hollandia* (1983).

There would, however, appear to be a direct conflict between on the one hand the apparent supremacy of the Rules and on the other the freedom of the parties to choose a law which is to govern their contractual obligations. With very few exceptions the parties to a contract have always had the freedom to make a virtually unfettered choice of the law to govern the creation, performance and discharge of that contract: *Vita Foods* v *Unus Shipping* (1939). If therefore the parties to a contract select, as a governing or proper law, one which does not insist upon the application of the Hague-Visby Rules, would that choice be rendered null and void by the provisions of Article III, rule 8? If the answer to this is affirmative, then it might be argued that there is a more important principle than the mandatory application of the Rules; that of maintaining the principle of freedom of contract. This argument was decisively rejected by the Court of Appeal in *The Hollandia*.

There is a greater public policy issue to be considered than that of freedom of contract which demands that goods to be carried by sea should be subject to a body of uniform rules fixing rights, liabilities and financial limitations. These should not be affected by the place of jurisdiction or the law to be applied there. The Rules should apply to all contracts of international carriage to which they were meant to apply.

There are, however, important limitations to be borne in mind in the application of this principle. The principle ought to be applied in pursuance of serving the true intention of the Rules. Their true intention is to impose standard duties under Articles III, rule 1 and III, rule 2 and minimum/maximum liability under Article IV, rule 5. Insofar as Article III, rule 8 prohibits clauses limiting liability, it is acting to ensure the application of the above articles.

It is, however, clear from the Rules that it was always intended that they should co-exist with common law limitations which may be expressly chosen by the carrier to limit his liability – Article VIII. In *The Benarty* (1984) the carrier sought to rely on a provision of the Indonesian Commercial Code which would provide him with a tonnage limitation and, consistent with this choice, Indonesian law, which does not apply the Hague-Visby Rules. The Court of Appeal upheld the choice. It is, however, submitted that this decision does not provide the carrier with the ammunition successfully to avoid the application of the Rules. The carrier had chosen a tonnage limitation. Such a limitation does not exist in the Hague-Visby Rules which deals only with package or unit limitation on liability. He had given an undertaking on affidavit not to attempt to rely on any other provision of the Indonesian Code that was more favourable to him than the Rules.

All of these factors led the Court of Appeal to say that the choice of a foreign law ousting the Rules is not ex facie void and ineffective and there may be other factors to consider. In this case comity demanded that a national of a country should be able to pick his own law to govern his contract especially where the provision on which he particularly sought to rely was one with which the Rules did not deal, and which in consequence could not be rendered null and void by Article III, rule 8 because it did not fall within its terms as a matter of statutory interpretation.

In conclusion, it is submitted that *The Benarty* is a case which is special on its facts according to the clause chosen and the intention of the parties but it is unlikely that such a choice by English nationals would be upheld. Otherwise the validity of s1(2) would be eroded to such an extent that it would become redundant, as would the Rules themselves. If any clause actually fell within the wording of Article III, rule 8, the court might refuse recognition on that basis. Alternatively it could refuse recognition on the grounds that the choice infringed the public policy of the forum.

b) *Lillian*

Article III, rule 2 requires the carrier to properly load, handle, stow, etc. and discharge the goods carried. This duty is personal to him. It cannot therefore be discharged by the appointment of stevedores and crew who are certified to be competent. The standard imposed by Article III, rule 2 is that the carrier must act properly and carefully. 'Properly' being in accordance with a sound system: *Albacora* v *Westcott & Laurance Line* (1966); 'carefully' being with reasonable skill and care such as that which would be exercised to satisfy the common duty of care. Neither would appear to be satisfied and it would appear that the carrier is in breach of this Article. In addition the carrier would appear to be in breach of Article III, rule 2(b) requiring him properly to man, equip and supply the ship. Once again the standard is that of due diligence and it can be assumed from the facts given that no such care was taken in the provision of the crew.

If the carrier were to be pursued personally for breaches of these obligations it may be possible for him to claim reliance on individual exemptions afforded by Article IV, rule 2; perhaps Article IV, rule 2(a) 'insufficient packing', or Article IV, rule 2(q) 'any other cause' might be utilised. This cannot be determined without further information and will not be discussed since it is outside the scope of the advice sought and the claim against him would appear to be statute barred.

It appears that Lillian was herself exercising a degree of supervision over the unloading. The carrier may well have sought to rely on Article IV, rule 2(i) in consequence, claiming that the damage was due to an act or omission on Lillian's part: *Ismail* v *Polish Ocean Line* (1976). This would in any event be unlikely to succeed. Lillian's protestations make it clear that she objected to the methods used and an estoppel would not arise against her. Moreover, the carrier would be able to rely on this exemption successfully only if he established the requisite degree of causation between the act or omission of Lillian and the loss. That would require him to show that the method of unloading was the proximate cause of loss and would not have been utilised but for Lillian. This cannot be done. It is not the method of unloading which is the proximate cause of loss but the incidental behaviour of those involved in the process.

If a claim is to be brought against the crew instead of the carrier himself, they too will be able to rely on the exclusions available under Article IV, rule 2(a) – (q) and Article IV, rule 5 providing a financial limit on liability. This is explicitly permitted by Article IV bis. However, Article IV bis is subject to a proviso in Article IV, bis rule 4 which states that no reliance can be placed by the servant or agent on the provisions of Article IV if he acts intentionally, or recklessly and with knowledge that damage would probably result. This would have to be proved by Lillian on a balance of probabilities.

Assuming that the crew are shown to have acted in such a way, Lillian will be able to recover more than that permitted by the financial limits in the Rules and the crew will not enjoy the benefit of the exemptions in Article IV, rule 2. They will, however, remain subject to the duties imposed by the remainder of the Rules.

If the crew did not act deliberately or recklessly, then they may be able to rely on Article IV, rule 2 (a) – (q), in particular Article IV, rule 2(i) and IV, rule 2(n) although success for the former is unlikely and there is no evidence of the latter. Their liability will be fixed by Article IV, rule 5(a) and an upper ceiling of 666.67 units of account per package, or two units of account per kilo, whichever is higher. The actual amount recoverable will be calculated by reference to the value of the goods at the place and time of discharge: Article IV, rule 5(b). If their acts are deliberate or reckless then the limitation cannot be relied upon: Article IV, rule 5(l).

The contract between the consignor and the carrier would appear to contain a Himalaya Clause. This enables independent contractors to avail themselves of the exemptions and financial limitations available to the carrier himself: *The Eurymedon* (1974). It is necessary since Article IV *bis* does not apply to independent contractors: *The New York Star* (1981). The clause creates privity of contract between the independent contractor and the carrier. His consideration for this contract lies in his discharge of the goods at the unloading port. It might be argued here that the discharge was so inadequate that the goods became unmerchantable and therefore consideration has totally failed.

The success of this argument would depend upon the facts, of which more information would be needed. Its result, if successful, would be to allow the consignee to sue for amounts in excess of those stipulated by Article IV, rule 5.

It seems unlikely that any of the exemptions in Article IV, rule 2 could be successfully raised but in the absence of proof of deliberate or reckless conduct the financial limits will continue to apply. The financial limits will apply whether Lillian sues in contract or in tort: Article IV, *bis* rule 1. The aggregate amounts recovered cannot exceed the limits provided by the Rules: Article IV, *bis* rule 3.

Theodore

Theodore can sue in contract only if he is the consignee of a bill of lading by reason of the consignment of which he took property in the goods: s1 Carriage of Goods by Sea Act 1992. This is unclear from the facts. It may be property passed before or after transfer of the bill or the goods are unascertained before appropriation on discharge. If he had paid the freight an implied contract on which he could sue would have been created: *Brandt* v *Liverpool, Brazil and River Plate Steam Navigation Co* (1924). This seems unlikely since the goods are shipped on cif terms requiring the seller to pay the freight.

Therefore, his only course of action would appear to be to sue in tort. This depends upon showing that there is sufficient proximity or neighbourhood between himself and the carrier to justify the existence of a duty of care: *Schiffhart & Kolen* v *Chelsea Maritime* (1982). Whilst Theodore would have risk on shipment, that is unlikely to be sufficient if he has not also some propriety or possessory right in the cargo at the time of damage: *Leigh & Sillivan* v *Aliakmon* (1986). In any event, insofar as his loss consists of pure economic loss not consequential on physical damage it will be irrecoverable. Despite the decision by the House of Lords in *Junior Books* v *Veitchi* (1982) there is a more important public policy requiring that the carrier's liability be capable of being clearly assessed: *Candlewood* v *Mitsui* (1985).

Time bar

The action against the carrier is statute barred. It is likely that the action against the stevedoring firm and/or the crew is also statute barred. Article III, rule 6 provides the carrier with a limitation of one year, replacing the normal statutory limitation period. This runs from the date of delivery and would require that either the writ be issued or arbitration proceedings be started within 12 months: *The Merak* (1965). Article III, rule 6 applies to the carrier and the ship, thereby preventing actions in personam or in rem outside the statutory period. It would also, however, be invoked by the independent contractors and the crew: *Godina* v *Patrick Operations* (1984).

Therefore it would appear that unless Lillian can show deliberate or reckless conduct taking away the benefit of the exemptions, the claim must fail as statute barred, unless there has been an agreed extension of this period: Article III, rule 6: *Lokumel & Sons* v *Lotte Shipping Co* (1985).

In any event, it will be necessary for Lillian to obtain leave to serve the writ out of the jurisdiction under the provisions of Ord 11 Rules of the Supreme Court (1982), showing that the case is a proper one for service out: Ord 11 r4(2). Alternatively, she may issue a writ in rem against the vessel, to be served when she is within the jurisdiction.

Finally, she may be able to claim on his insurance policy if it is assignable as the cif contract requires.

The insurance company would then be subrogated to his rights against those responsible for the damage: s79 Marine Insurance Act 1906.

Question 2

Apple ships two containers of computers from England on a vessel bound for Portland, USA. The bill of lading issued for the cargo states that 'two containers said to contain computers' were loaded aboard in apparent good order and condition.

The ship is short of hands and in order to put to sea the shipowners hire a First Officer after examining his credentials. It turns out that the First Officer has a drinking problem and at the first port of call is found unconscious from alcohol. The loading of the vessel at the first port is attended to by the ship's cook who takes on insufficient bunkers for the next leg of the journey.

Immediately after leaving the first port, the ship hits a rock, which is chartered, and the vessel is holed. It transpires that the First Officer, in a drunken stupor, set an erroneous course. One of the containers is damaged in the collision but the ship is able to return safety to the first port of call.

After repairs have been effected, the ship sets sail again but runs short of fuel on the next part of the voyage and has to put into a port 25 miles off the normal route for bunkers.

Eventually the ship arrives at Portland four weeks late. On unloading, the second container is damaged by stevedores, but a clause in the bill of lading exempts the shipowner from liability for negligence of stevedores.

On inspection, around half the computers have been smashed. Apple had resold all the computers under a contract with strict time limits as to delivery. These time limits had expired when the ship arrived at port.

Advise Apple of their rights.

Question prepared by the Editor
April 1994

General comment

This is a slightly more complicated hypothetical problem requiring the application of the Rules of the 1971 Act to a voyage which is in several stages. Although different rules apply, the answer remains in Article III of the Hague-Visby Rules.

Skeleton solution

Article III, rule (1)(b).

Two possible instances of deviation: setting an incorrect course and going 25 miles off the normal route.

Liability of stevedores.

Suggested solution

The carrier

As the bill of lading is issued in England it is assumed that the Hague-Visby rules will apply to the contract of carriage, s1 CGSA 1971.

Apple must be advised on the following:

1   the liability of the carrier;

2   the liability of the stevedores.

It is clear law that the holder of a bill of lading can demand goods from the carrier in the stated 'good order and condition' and if they are found damaged on arrival then the presumption is that the damage occurred while the goods were in the carrier's care, *Peter der Grosse* (1875). The carrier would therefore seek to rely on the exemptions afforded by the Hague-Visby rules.

Apple would be advised to allege that the carrier failed to properly 'man the ship', Article III, rule (1)(b), by appointing a drunken first officer. The carrier will say that under the Hague-Visby rules he discharged his duty of due diligence by accepting the crew's qualifications as they were presented to him, and that he was entitled to do so, *Adamastos Shipping Co Ltd* v *Anglo-Saxon Petroleum Co Ltd* (1959). Apple may counter this by citing *The Farrandoc* (1967), which suggests that merely looking at certificates is not enough to discharge the duty.

Apple should also allege that the ship was unseaworthy on leaving the first port of call; the carrier will contend that the duty of seaworthiness arises only at the beginning of the voyage and not, as at common law, at the commencement of each stage: *The Cheybassa* (1967).

Apple will be advised to allege that the carrier deviated and such deviation renders him liable to fulfil the duties of the common carrier; that is, he must deliver the goods in a condition identical to that in which they were shipped. If not the carrier will be liable for all damage caused to the goods. The contract of carriage will cease and the exemptions and limitations of the Hague-Visby Rules will not avail.

There are, in this problem, two possible instances of deviation:

a) setting an incorrect course;

b) going 25 miles off the normal route.

a) Generally a carrier is bound to follow the customary route so the carrier must show that the actual route was a normal or reasonable route. If so, then striking a rock may be covered by the exemption in Article IV, rule (2)(a) – neglect in navigation.

b) 25 miles off normal route. If a ship runs short of fuel it generally points to unseaworthiness – if deviation is necessitated by the unseaworthiness of the vessel then the deviation would be justified under Article IV, rule (4) as being reasonable: *Kish* v *Taylor* (1912).

153

However, *Monarch* v *Karlshamms* (1949) states that deviation is not justified for such a reason if the shipowners know the vessel was unseaworthy.

If deviation can be proved, then Apple can proceed against the carrier for full damages, as he will be under the onerous duty of a common carrier. If deviation is not shown, then the Hague-Visby rules provide for package limitation: the carrier's liability is limited to an amount per package carried.

In the case of containers the bill of lading must state the number of packages within the container, Article IV, rule (5). If not, the limit is based on the container itself; that is the container is the package for the purposes of calculation. It appears that this rule will apply here so the liability would be limited to the two containers and not the packages therein.

The stevedores

Generally the stevedores may themselves claim benefit of any exemptions in the contract of carriage, but on the conditions laid down in *Scruttons* v *Midland Silicones* (1962). *The Eurymedon* (1974) manifested the growing inclination of the courts to allow stevedores to claim the benefit of the available exemptions. *The New York Star* (1981) held that each case had to examine the precise relationship of carrier and stevedore, but commercial practice would generally favour the stevedores.

The clause in this question, however, would not satisfy the *Scruttons* requirements, so at common law it is difficult to see how the stevedores could avail of any of the contract exemptions. Further, under the Hague-Visby rules, Article IV, bis rule (2) would allow them to claim the benefit only if they are agents who are not independent contractors. Apple is therefore to be advised to proceed against the stevedores as well as the carrier.

Question 3

Tom sells a consignment of rat poison to Jerry, fob London, Jerry to nominate the vessel for the carriage of goods and Tom to obtain a non-negotiable bill of lading from the carrier. The goods are in fact shipped on a vessel chartered by Jerry from Fred, a national of Cartoonland.

Fred duly issues a bill of lading to Tom naming Tom as consignor and Jerry as consignee. The bill is marked 'non-negotiable' and has been signed by the ship's master. A clause in the bill refers all disputes to arbitration in London. The bill also states that 5,000 tonnes of rat poison have been shipped.

Before the poison is loaded aboard, Jerry agrees to have the holds of the vessel cleaned at his expense. The cargo eventually is shipped to the port of destination in good condition, but when the goods are landed only 4,500 tonnes of poison are present. In addition, Fred discovers that the ship's holds have been corroded as a result of the detergent used to clean the holds.

Advise Fred as to his possible defences against the claims for the missing cargo, his remedies in respect of the damage to the vessel and the appropriate fora for both actions.

Question prepared by the Editor
April 1994

General comment

A question in a similar vein to Question 2, but this time requiring the application of the common law rules. An additional complication is added by the role of the bill of lading in the transaction.

Skeleton solution

The non-application of the 1971 Act: the failure of the bill of lading to satisfy s1(3) of the Act.

Authority in common law for the Master to sign the bill.

The rule that a charterparty prevails over the terms of a bill of lading.

Application of the rules to decide the forum for the arbitration.

Suggested solution

Fred would not be precluded by the issue of the bill of lading stating that 5,000 tonnes of rat poison had been shipped from adducing evidence that only 4,500 tonnes were in fact shipped.

In any event , the Hague-Visby Rules ('the Rules') do not apply to the carriage of the cargo of rat poison.

Although the voyage is one to which the Rules prima facie apply (Article X of the Rules and s1(3) of the Carriage of Goods by Sea Act 1971 ("COGSA")), the document issued does not satisfy the requirements in s1(6) COGSA or Article X(c) of the Rules. The document is a straight consigned bill of lading which is not a document of title at common law.

It does not expressly incorporate the Rules as required by s1(6)(b) COGSA so as to give the Rules statutory force when a non-negotiable receipt is used. The arbitration clause referring disputes to London is not a choice of law clause. However, it may be arguable that since the courts in England treat the Rules as an overriding statute, a London arbitration clause would satisfy the requirement in s1(6) of express incorporation of the Rules. This argument has not been tested in the courts. In *The Vechstroon* (1982) a liberal approach was taken to the interpretation of the subsection by eliminating the requirement that the incorporation clause should state that the Rules should govern "as if the receipt were a bill of lading". There was, however, an express incorporation clause in that case which indicates that the present argument does more violence to the statute and may not be acceptable to the courts.

The Carriage of Goods by Sea Act 1992 similarly does not apply since the document is not a common law bill of lading being marked 'non-negotiable'. In any event s3 of the Carriage of Goods by Sea Act 1992 only confers a right of action against the master or other person who actually signs the bill of lading, and therefore would not involve Fred himself.

At common law the Master does not have actual or ostensible authority to sign a bill of lading for goods which are not in fact shipped: see *Grant* v *Norway* (1851); *The Saudi*

Crown (1986). There can therefore be no common law estoppel on the basis of reliance by Jerry on the Master's representation in the bill of lading that 5,000 tons were shipped.

Alternatively, if Fred cannot adduce evidence to show that only 4,500 tons of sulphur were in fact shipped, he will have to rely on one of the four common law exceptions to the duties of a carrier by sea for reward if he is to defend the claim for lost cargo. There is no evidence that any of the exceptions applies. They are: act of God; act of the Queen's enemies; inherent vice; jettison.

The contract of carriage is governed by the charterparty made with Jerry, the purchaser of the rat poison. The bill of lading in this case has no contractual function.

Fred is entitled to receive the ship after the termination of the charterparty in the same condition as that in which it was hired. This is a non-delegable duty. Fred would therefore be able to claim damages from Jerry for breach of the charterparty. Jerry would not be able to defend the claim by arguing that the damage was actually caused by Tom.

Alternatively, Fred might be able to sue Tom for negligence. Since he was the owner of the vessel at the time the damage occurred, he would be the appropriate party for such a claim in tort: *Leigh & Sillivan* v *Aliakmon Shipping, The Aliakmon* (1986). It would seem that he was both a foreseeable and proximate party to succeed in the action.

At no time did the bill of lading contain the contract of carriage. This was governed by the charterparty. Hence the arbitration clause in the bill has no contractual effect, and terms to the contrary could be adduced as to the true nature of the charterparty.

If the charterparty were silent, it seems that there are arguments either way as to whether London or Cartoonland is the correct forum.

In favour of London are the facts that all the evidence relevant to exactly what was shipped and the witnesses are in England.

In favour of Cartoonland is the fact that the proper law of a charterparty is often presumed to be the law of the flag of the ship in the absence of express terms.

However unless evidence is adduced to the contrary, Cartoonland law would be assumed to be the same as English law. It would seem that the balance of convenience is with the English courts. Fred should therefore be advised to issue a writ and serve it on Jerry, who appears to have a place of business in England. It would then be for Jerry to apply for a stay of the English proceedings if he considered some other forum to be more appropriate.

As regards the damage to the vessel, again the action is based on the charterparty, and the same arguments as above apply. It would seem therefore that England is the more convenient forum.

Question 4

Gulf Oil agrees to purchase 100,000 tonnes of crude oil from Texaco cif London. The cargo is shipped abroad *The Bad Luck* on 15 July 1994 where it is mixed with 15,000 tonnes of oil belonging to Shell (UK). No other oil has been loaded aboard the vessel. A bill of lading is issued to Texaco and the Hague-Visby Rules are expressly incorporated into the bill.

Six days later, *The Bad Luck* arrives at Madrid in order to deliver the cargo belonging to Shell. Due to the negligence of the carrier, 18,000 tonnes are delivered to Shell's order and only 97,000 tonnes of oil remain aboard.

The vessel immediately leaves after the oil has been discharged and thereafter Texaco indorses the bill of lading in favour of Gulf. Gulf presents the bill of lading to the vessel's master and obtains delivery of the oil when the vessel arrives in London.

Advise Gulf as to whether or not it can sue the owners of *The Bad Luck* in either tort or contract for the shortage in delivery.

Question prepared by the Editor
April 1994

General comment

A question requiring the student to demonstrate the application of the law of commercial credits to a factual situation with the additional complexities of issues of negligence.

Skeleton solution

The role of the bill of lading in the transaction.

Article III(2) Hague-Visby Rules.

Immunities and limitation of liability under the Hague-Visby Rules.

Period of limitation.

Liability in tort.

Suggested solution

Since the contract is for the sale of crude oil cif London, Texaco negotiates the contract of carriage for transportation aboard *The Bad Luck*. The bill of lading is therefore issued to Texaco, which is subsequently endorsed to Gulf Oil. As between carrier and indorsee, the bill of lading represents the contract of carriage even although as between the carrier and original shipper it is merely evidence of the contract. Therefore, Gulf Oil must look to the bill of lading in order to establish its contractual rights.

Due to the negligence of the carrier, the cargo of oil is delivered short by 3,000 tons. The bill of lading incorporates the Hague-Visby Rules and according to Article III, rule (2) of these rules, the carrier must 'properly and carefully load, handle, stow, carry, keep, care for and discharge' the goods. Whether the carrier has fulfilled this duty is a question of fact. 'Properly' in this context is not simply synonymous with careful, but means in accordance with a sound system designed to facilitate safe transportation: *G H Renton & Co* v *Palmyra Trading Corp of Panama* (1957).

In the present case, the shortage of 3,000 tons of oil is substantial evidence of a failure to comply with the obligation to properly carry the goods. Further, admission or proof that the cargo was originally shipped in good order and condition is prima facie evidence of a breach of the contract of carriage by the shipowner. Since the master of *The Bad Luck* issued a clean bill of lading to Texaco's order for 100,000 tons of crude, the onus is on the shipowner to show that the damage was due to one of the clauses specifying exemption from liability in the Hague-Visby Rules.

The carrier will be unable to rely on the immunities contained in the Hague-Visby Rules since the loss was due to the negligence of his employees. However, these rules specify limits of liability. The shipowner is liable only for a maximum of 10,000 units of account per package or kilo of gross weight of the goods lost. The total amount recoverable must be calculated by reference to the value of the goods at the place and time at which they were discharged from the ship in accordance with the contract, or should have been so discharged. In the case of oil, the value must be fixed according to the commodity exchange price, or, if there is no such price, according to the current market price.

Although the same rules also limit the amount of damages that may be awarded against the carrier in the event of loss of the goods, the limitation does not apply if it can be established that the damage resulted from an act or omission of the carrier done with either the intent to cause damage or recklessly.

In order to avoid the application of the limitation provision, Gulf Oil would have to show that the loss of part of the cargo was due to the recklessness of the carrier.

Article III, rule (6) of the Rules sets a limit of one year for the raising of actions, calculated from the time that the goods were, or should have been delivered. This period may be extended if the parties to the action so agree. However, it would be prudent for Gulf Oil to raise its action for non-delivery of the goods immediately.

It has not yet been definitively established whether or not a third party to a contract of carriage can raise an action in tort to claim damages for losses attributable to the negligence of the carrier. The courts have, in the past, been reluctant to apply a duty of reasonable care on the part of a carrier to a purchaser in a cif contract. However, since the question expressly attributes the loss of the goods to the negligence of the carrier, the issue of vicarious liability does arise and probably should be tested in the courts.

It should be further noted that the limits of liability established by the Hague Rules apply in any action against the carrier in respect of loss or damage covered by a contract of carriage, regardless of whether the action is founded in contract or tort.

Question 5

Winnie arranges with the owners of *The Pooh Bear* for the carriage of a consignment of steel coils from Steeltown (USA) to Ferville (France) and a bill of lading is issued to Winnie who is resident in the UK. The bill is expressly stated to be subject to English law.

On its previous voyage, *The Pooh Bear* carried a cargo of caustic salts. The vessel had arrived in Steeltown on 5 May 1994 and discharged the salts five days later. The holds were flushed in an attempt to cleanse them. The steel was then loaded aboard the vessel on the 11th and 12th of the same month and the vessel sailed the following day.

On the voyage, *The Pooh Bear* ran into a storm and sea water entered the holds because the cargo holds had been left open.

When the cargo was unloaded, it was found to be badly corroded. The possible causes of the corrosion were: (a) the failure to adequately clean the holds; (b) the failure to close the hatches; and (c) the failure of the crew to pump out the bilges.

Winnie decides to sue the shipowners in the English courts for damages. She seeks your advice in the possibility of success. What do you advise?

Question prepared by the Editor
April 1994

General comment

Another common subject for examination, this question involves the topic of the liability of a carrier under a bill of lading. The main difficulty is in deciding which set of principles apply, the common law principles or the Hague-Visby Rules. But once this matter has been resolved, the question is relatively straightforward.

Skeleton solution

Application of the Hague-Visby Rules.

Article III, rules (1) and (2).

Duty of care: due diligence.

Limitations on the right of action: limits on compensation and time limits for raising actions.

Suggested solution

The contract for carriage was agreed between Winnie and the shipowners for transport of steel coils from Steeltown to Ferville. The bill of lading issued to Winnie was to be governed by English law. English law is therefore the applicable law for the interpretation of the contract of carriage.

The fact that English law is the express law of the contract is sufficient to incorporate the Hague-Visby rules into the contract. The Hague-Visby rules are given effect in English law by the Carriage of Goods by Sea Act 1971 and, under Article X(c) of the rules, the rules apply if the contract contained in, or evidenced by, the bill of lading provides that the rules, or legislative provisions giving effect to the rules, are to govern the contract.

However, had the contract merely referred to the exercise of jurisdiction by the British court, in which case the courts would have had to infer the proper law of the contract, it is unlikely that the rules would have applied because the United States is not a party to the Convention containing these rules: see *The Komninos S* (1991).

It should be noted that, if the rules apply, a carrier cannot contract out of the application of the Hague-Visby rules in order to avoid liability. Such a putative term would be immediately null and void.

The Hague-Visby rules impose a number of obligations on a carrier as regards the carriage of cargo. Article III, rule (1) of the rules requires that the carrier ensures that, prior to the commencement of the voyage, the ship is seaworthy, properly manned and that the holds are safe for the carriage of goods.

Similarly, under the same provision, the carrier is obliged to ensure that the goods are properly loaded, handled, stowed and preserved through the course of the voyage. This duty extends to the acts of his employees during the course of the voyage.

The standard of care in the performance of both these duties is the requirement of exercising due diligence. In other words, the carrier must act in a negligent manner in order to attract liability. This contrasts with the common law position where the obligation to provide a seaworthy ship is absolute.

It is an implied condition of providing a seaworthy ship that the cargo will be protected against damage during the voyage. In other words, if the cargo hold is in such a condition at the time of loading that the cargo itself will be damaged or destroyed, the ship is deemed unseaworthy. The carrier is required to use reasonable diligence to ensure that the cargo will be secure in the hold.

In this particular case, the cargo was damaged due, inter alia, to the failure to adequately clean the holds of the previous cargo. The previous cargo was a substance which, it is reasonable to assume, would damage the steel load in the event that both came into contact with each other. The steps that the shipowners took to cleanse the holds were clearly insufficient to remove residues of the salt. The holds were flushed with fresh water after the salt was discharged. But no further measures were taken.

Obviously these measures were insufficient because the steel corroded as a result of the coming into contact with the residues of the salt. There is therefore a prima facie case of negligence on the part of the shipowners which would allow Winnie to claim damages for failure to comply with the obligation to provide a seaworthy vessel.

The corrosion of the steel cargo was also caused by the failure to close the hatches, compounded by the failure to pump out the bilges during the storm. Under Article III, rule (2) a shipowner is liable for the negligent acts of his crew as regards keeping and caring for the goods: see *Pyrene & Co* v *Scindia Navigation Co* (1954).

The fact that the hatches to the cargo hold were left open during the storm indicates that the crew were negligent in ensuring that the cargo was properly secure. Seepage of water into the cargo hold would most likely damage any type of cargo being stored there. Further, failing to pump out water that had entered the hold because the covers had not been secured must have substantially contributed to the damage sustained by the goods.

Article IV of the rules provides a number of exceptions to the duty to exercise due diligence, but in the circumstances of this case it is unlikely that any of these could be relied upon. For example, the shipowner is not liable for damage caused by the negligent acts of harbour masters, the perils of the sea or inherent defects in the goods being carried.

There are two major limitations to Winnie's right to claim damages against the shipowners. The first stems from the maximum limits of shipowners' liability established by Article IV, rule (5). The rules for calculating liabilities are complex, but essentially depend on the number of packages, the nature of the cargo and express declarations of value prior to shipping. In normal circumstances, the compensation payable will be considerably less than that which could be claimed in an action for damages.

There are two exceptions to this rule. First, the nature and the value of the goods can be declared at the beginning of the voyage and in the bill of lading, which has the effect of increasing the amount of compensation that may be claimed. Second, if it can be shown that the damage was done through the intentional or reckless acts of the carrier, no limitation on liability applies.

The other limitation on Winnie's right to claim is that Article III, rule (6) gives carriers an absolute defence to any claim in respect of goods damaged or destroyed during transit unless the action is commenced within one year of the delivery of the goods or their loss if the whole consignment has been destroyed. Winnie would therefore have to raise the action prior to the expiry of a one-year period after the goods arrived in Ferville.

9 MARINE INSURANCE I – CONTRACTS AND POLICIES

9.1   Introduction

It is common practice for the parties to an international sales contract to arrange for the goods to be insured against loss or damage caused during the voyage. By arranging for the goods to be insured, the parties pass the risk of loss or damage to a professional risk underwriter. In return for a premium, the underwriter agrees to compensate the assured for any loss or damage to the goods.

In this chapter, we shall examine the general principles regulating the formation of the insurance contract and, in particular, the duty of the parties to exercise utmost good faith in making representations as well as the different types of policy commonly used for the purposes of insuring goods during voyages. In the next two chapters, we shall elaborate in greater detail on the types of cover available and the legal principles governing both loss and indemnity.

9.2   Key points

a) *The contract of insurance*

According to s1 of the Marine Insurance Act 1906 (MIA 1906):

'Marine insurance is a contract whereby the insurer undertakes to indemnify the assured, in a manner and to an extent thereby agreed, against marine losses, that is to say, losses incident to a marine adventure'.

To understand how a contract of marine insurance is formed, it is necessary to briefly consider the mechanisms of obtaining a policy. Normally, the following steps are taken:

i) The person wishing to insure the goods (known as the proposer) approaches a broker who will note certain details such as the value of the goods, their condition, the name of the owner of the goods, the present location of the goods, the means of transportation for the goods and the relationship of the sales contract to other contracts. In addition, the type of insurance requested and the risks to be covered will be noted. The broker is deemed to be the agent of the proposer for the purpose of obtaining the necessary cover.

ii) The broker will approach a number of underwriters with this information in an attempt to find the cheapest and most cost-effective policy. He will present the underwriters with the information gathered from the proposer.

iii) The underwriters will signify their acceptance of the risk of the destruction of the goods during the voyage by signing their names on the slip which is simply a piece of paper with details of the proposal. An underwriter can accept all the risk, or a proportion of the risk in which case other underwriters will cover the remaining portion of the risk.

iv) Once 100 per cent of the risk has been covered, the broker will prepare a policy and will notify the proposer that cover has been effected. The proposer now becomes known as the assured. The final policy will be forwarded to the assured.

v) The broker will request the premium from the assured and will pass this on to the underwriters after deducting his commission.

In fact, it is the slip that is the complete and final contract between the parties, fixing the terms of the insurance and premium, even though a policy may not have been issued: *Ionides* v *Pacific Fire and Marine Insurance* (1871) LR 6 QB 674.

Once the slip is complete and before the policy is issued, a cover note may be sent to the assured. This is a memorandum to the effect that insurance has been arranged and the note generally assumes one of two forms:

i) An open cover note – this is sent to an assured in circumstances where, although the broker has arranged insurance, relevant details are still required from the assured.

ii) A closed cover note – this is sent to the assured in circumstances where the broker was in full possession of all the details of the insurance and nothing remains to be clarified or communicated by the assured.

Eventually a policy of marine insurance will be issued. This need not assume any particular form, but ss23–26 of the MIA 1906 details the matters which should be specified in the policy including:

i) the name of the assured or the person who effects the insurance on his behalf;

ii) the signature of the insurer or the insurers; and

iii) designation of the subject-matter with a degree of reasonable certainty.

The broker is not, however, required to issue the policy until the premium has been tendered. It is the duty of the assured to pay the premium at the time the policy is issued (s52 MIA 1906).

b) *The relationship between the assured and the insurer*

The relationship between the proposer/assured and the insurer is one of uberrimae fidei, or of utmost good faith. In the event that utmost good faith is not observed by either party the contract may be avoided by the innocent party (s17 MIA 1906). Generally it is the insurer who will seek to avoid the obligations under the contract by citing the lack of good faith on the part of the assured. The obligation of good faith exists before, and continues after, the conclusion of the contract: *Black King Shipping* v *Massie* [1985] 1 Lloyd's Rep 437.

There are several aspects to the duty of uberrimae fidei. These may be summarised as follows:

i) Disclosure of material circumstances(ss18 and 19)

The assured must disclose to the insurer every 'material circumstance' which is known or ought to have been known by him in the ordinary course of business, and failure to do so will allow the insurer to avoid the contract. A 'circumstance' includes any communications made to, or information received by, the assured (s18(5)).

There are certain circumstances which, by statute, need not be disclosed such as:

• Any circumstance which diminishes the risk.

• Any circumstance which is known or presumed to be known to the insurer. The insurer is presumed to know matters of common notoriety or knowledge and matters which an insurer in the ordinary course of business ought to know.

• Any circumstance for which information is waived by the insurer.

• Any circumstance which is superfluous by reason of. any express or implied warranty.

Under s18(3)(b) of the Act, an underwriter will only be deemed to know certain facts if he has specialist knowledge of that particular type of trade: see *Anglo-African Merchants Ltd* v *Bayley* [1970] 1 QB 311.

The duty to make disclosure applies not only to the assured but also to his or her broker. Section 19 of the MIA 1908 states 'where insurance is effected for the assured by an agent, the agent must disclose to the insurer ... every material circumstances which is known to himself'.

ii) Materiality of circumstances

An insurer will only be discharged from his liabilities under the contract if an undisclosed circumstance is material. This means that a circumstance must be such as to influence the judgment of a prudent insurer in deciding whether or not to accept the risk and in fixing the premium: s18(2). The test of whether or not a circumstance is material is an objective one: *Container*

Transport International v *Oceanus Mutual Underwriting* [1984] 1 Lloyd's Rep 476.

Examples of material circumstances have, in the past, included the following:

- Overvaluation of the cargo: *Ionides* v *Pender* (1874) LR 9 QB 531.

- The existence of other policies of insurance covering the same goods.

- The unsuitability or incompetence of the master of the vessel used in the voyage.

- Failure to disclose a criminal conviction on a charge pertinent to the risk being insured: *Alden* v *Raven, The Kylie* [1983] 2 Lloyd's Rep 444.

The duty to disclose material circumstances applies before and after the contract has been concluded.

iii) Accuracy of material representations

In addition to the obligation to ensure that all material circumstances are disclosed, the assured is also under a duty to make sure that all material representations made by him or his agent to the insurer are correct and accurate: s20(1). Again, a representation is deemed material if it would influence the judgment of a prudent underwriter in fixing the premium or determining whether or not to take the risk. The penalty for inaccurate representations is avoidance of liability by the insurer.

Representations fall into two categories: (1) representations of matters of fact; and (2) representations of matters of expectation or belief.

1) Representations of matters of fact

Representations of matters of fact can be subdivided into representations of existing facts and representations of future facts. Both types of representation are positively affirming the existence of a particular set of factual circumstances and therefore it is irrelevant whether or not the facts exist at present or at some time in the future.

A representation of a matter of fact must be substantially true. Section 20(4) of the Act provides that:

'A representation as to a matter of fact is true if it be substantially correct, that is to say if the difference between what is represented and what is actually correct would not be considered material by a prudent insurer.'

Although representations as to future matters of fact normally involve an element of uncertainty, a representation relating to future events over which the assured has control, if not substantially satisfied at the time when it was claimed it would occur, may invalidate the policy: *Edwards* v *Footner* (1808) 8 East 126.

2) Representations of matters of expectation or belief

To ascertain whether or not a statement made is one of fact or one of expectation or belief it is necessary to examine all the circumstances in which it was made, and the degree of power or control which the assured has over the subject-matter of the representation.

Unlike representations of matters of fact, representations of matters of expectations or belief need not be substantially true but must be made in good faith: s20(5). In other words, it must be a belief that a reasonable person would honestly entertain.

iv) Fraudulent misrepresentations

A representation is fraudulent when it is made in the knowledge that it is untrue or has been made recklessly.

In the event that an assured makes a representation which is not only untrue but also fraudulent he is prevented from arguing that a prudent underwriter would not have regarded the representation as material.

v) Avoidance of the policy

Where an assured has failed to disclose a material circumstance or there has been a material misrepresentation, the policy of insurance is avoidable at the instance of the insurer and he has the option of deciding whether to affirm or repudiate the contract.

If the insurer elects to avoid the policy, this election is effective ab initio and the policy is set aside from the very beginning. The assured must therefore repay any sums which have been paid to him in respect of losses incurred under the policy and the insurer must return the assured's premium: s84(1). Entitlement to the return of the premium does not arise where there has been fraud or illegality on the part of the assured.

If the insurer decides to affirm the policy, he remains liable on the policy despite the non-disclosure or misrepresentation. Affirmation may be express or implied by conduct, but can only take place when the insurer is in possession of all the facts.

c) *Insurable interest*

It is an essential prerequisite of a contract of marine insurance that the proposer/assured has an interest in the subject-matter of the insurance so that, in the event that the goods are lost or damaged, he or she can be indemnified for the effect the loss or damage has on his or her interest. If he or she does not have an interest, there will be no financial loss in the event that the goods are lost or damaged. This interest is known as an 'insurable interest'.

Under s5 of the Act, every person has an insurance interest for this purpose if they have an interest in a marine adventure. A person is interested in a marine adventure if he or she:

'stands in any legal or equitable relation to the adventure or to any insurable property at risk therein, in consequence of which he (or she) may benefit by the safety or due arrival of the insurable property or may be prejudiced by its loss, or by damage thereto, or by detention thereof, or may incur liability in respect thereof.'

Insurable interest is not restricted to mere ownership but may also take one of the following forms:

   i)   risk in the property;

   ii) partial interest;

   iii) defeasible or contingent interest;

   iv) advance freight;

   v)   insurance charges;

   vi) wages to be paid to the crew or any individual member of the crew.

As we shall see, the Institute Cargo Clauses A, B and C, which will be examined in detail in the next chapter, expressly state that an assured must have an insurable interest in the subject-matter insured at the time of loss.

It is important to note that an assured must be interested in the subject-matter insured at the time of loss; it is irrelevant that there was no interest at the time the insurance was effected.

Where an assured has no insurable interest and enters into an insurance contract with no expectation of acquiring such an interest, the policy is void under s4 of the Act, as it is deemed to be a gaming or wagering contract.

d) *Types of policy*

In general terms, insurance policies may be categorised into three groups: (i) voyage policies; (ii) time policies; and (iii) mixed policies. The distinctions between these types of policy are important.

   i)   Voyage policies

   A policy of insurance obtained to cover the transportation of goods from one place to another is known as a voyage policy. The port of departure and the port of destination must both be designated in the policy.

   Since the voyage is the critical factor in the operation of the policy, deviation of the vessel during the course of the voyage from the designated route may, in certain circumstances, discharge the insurer of liability. Broadly speaking, the insurer will be discharged from liability if a change of course by the vessel occurs which is deemed manifest or the voyage is not prosecuted with reasonable dispatch and any delay becomes unreasonable in the circumstances; see, for example, *Kallis* v *Success Insurance* [1985] 2 Lloyd's Rep 8.

Both deviation and delay are justified under such a policy only if they fall within the terms of s49 of the Act which lists the following grounds:

- where authorised by any special term in the policy;
- where caused by circumstances beyond the control of the master and his employer;
- where reasonably necessary in order to comply with an express or implied warranty;
- where reasonably necessary for the safety of the ship or the subject-matter insured;
- for the purpose of saving human life or aiding a ship in distress where human life is in danger;
- where reasonably necessary to obtain medical aid or surgical aid for a person aboard a ship;
- where caused by the barratrous conduct of the master or crew.

In the event that one of these excuses justify deviation or delay, the ship must resume her course and prosecute her voyage with reasonable dispatch or once again the insurer will be discharged. However, it is important to note that the insurer will remain liable up to the date of the breach and for any events covered which occur prior to the date on which his liability is discharged by reason of unjustified deviation or delay.

There is also implied into such policies a warranty that the vessel on which the goods will be carried is seaworthy: s33(3) MIA 1906. This implied warranty exists at the commencement of the risk and to each stage of the voyage where the policy covers voyages to be performed in stages.

ii) Time policies

A time policy offers insurance cover over the goods for a specified and defined period of time. Although the Act refers to a 'definite period of time' this requirement is not infringed if the insurance policy contains a clause which allows the insurance to continue in the event of a justifiable delay in the course of the voyage: *The Eurysthenes* [1976] 3 All ER 243.

Although technically there is no implied warranty of seaworthiness as with a voyage policy, s39(5) of the Act declares that:

'In a time policy, there is no implied warranty that the ship shall be seaworthy at any stage of the adventure, but where, with the privity of the assured the ship is sent to sea in an unseaworthy state, the insurer is not liable for any loss attributable to unseaworthiness.'

Although at first sight this may seem to amount to an implied duty of seaworthiness, in fact it is a provision limiting the liability of the insurer rather than an implied warranty on the part of the insurer.

iii) Mixed policies

> Quite simply, mixed policies are a combination of voyage and time policies. The most common mixed policy is a policy covering the transportation of goods from one location to another between specified dates.

e) *The value of the interest*

All policies of marine insurance are either valued or unvalued: s27. A valued policy is one which specifies the agreed value of the subject-matter insured under the policy. Under such a policy it is not open to the insurer to contend that the goods are not worth their policy value or to reopen the valuation for certain items: *Loders & Nucolene* v *Bank of New Zealand* (1929) 33 Ll LR 70. Where there is total loss under a valued policy then the measure of indemnity is the value of the goods fixed by the policy.

The valuation in such a policy can only be set aside where there is fraud or where there has been material non-disclosure where these circumstances lead to an over-valuation of the interest of the assured.

An unvalued policy does not specify the value of the subject-matter insured but, subject to the limits of the sum insured, leaves this to be ascertained in a manner specified in the Act. Section 16 provides that, in the case of insurance on goods or merchandise 'the insurable value is the prime cost of the property insured plus the expenses of and incidental to shipping and the charges of insurance in the whole'.

f) *Assignment of the policy*

In the absence of a term in a policy which expressly prohibits assignment, the benefit of a marine insurance policy is assignable: s50(1). The effect of such an assignment is to pass beneficial interest in the policy to the assignee which enables him or her to sue on the policy in his or her own name.

Thus, a cif seller may assign the insurance policy when he tenders correct documents, allowing the assignee to sue for any damage to the goods which has occurred in transit.

Providing the assignment is valid, it makes no difference that the assignment takes place at a time when the goods have already been lost providing, of course, that the assignee has an insurable interest at that time.

While a valid assignment operates to transfer to the assignee all the rights which were held by the assignor, it also has the effect of making the assignee subject to all the defences which were available against the assignor: *Pickersgill* v *London & Provincial Marine Insurance Co* [1912] 3 KB 614.

9.3 Recent cases and statutes

Pan Atlantic Insurance Co v *Pine Top Insurance Co* [1993] 1 Lloyd's Rep 496: a case concerning representations made by a broker on behalf of his client and whether or not these were fair and material representations for the purposes of establishing whether or not the policy was voidable.

Apostolos Konstantine Ventouris v *Trevor Rex Mountain, The Italia Express (No 2)*
[1992] 2 Lloyd's Rep 281: the plaintiffs insured a vessel under a marine insurance
policy which fixed the value of the vessel under valued policy. The underwriters
disputed that the vessel was a total loss and the dispute became protracted. In their
pleadings the plaintiffs claimed for the value of the vessel under the policy and
damages. The court rejected the claim for damages on the grounds that ss67–68 of the
MIA 1906 conclusively fixed the value of the claim as stated in the policy.

9.4   Relevant materials

D O'May & J Hill, *O'May on Marine Insurance* (1993).

A Arnould, *Marine Insurance* (1981)

9.5   Analysis of questions

It is important to grasp the legal principles applicable to the formation of the contract
of insurance before proceeding to consider matters such as the types of policies as well
as loss and indemnity. In the following questions, issues such as the duty of good
faith and material representations are highlighted as important areas for further
consideration. In addition, the final question deals with a novel point of law raised by
a recent case.

The types of questions set in this chapter are either problem-type questions or essay-
type questions. It should be noted that this topic is ideal for setting essay-type
questions where the student is required to provide a narrative answer to a particular
statement.

9.6   Questions

Question 1

'A contract of Marine Insurance is a contract based upon the utmost good faith and if
the utmost good faith be not observed by either party, the contract may be avoided by
the other party': s17 Marine Insurance Act 1906.

What are the implications of this duty of good faith and how has it been developed in
the jurisprudence of the English courts?

Question prepared by the Editor
April 1994

General comment

An essay-type question requiring a narrative answer.

Skeleton solution

Duty of good faith.

Duty to disclose material circumstances.

Standard applied: judgment of a prudent insurer.

Suggested solution

Section 17 of the Marine Insurance Act 1906 imposes a duty on parties to a marine insurance contract to demonstrate the utmost good faith. In such contracts of uberrimae fidei, the parties have a rigorous duty of disclosure. Under s18 of the 1906 Act, upon entering a contract of marine insurance, the assured is required to disclose the existence of any facts or circumstances which might affect the obligations of the contract. The assured is not only obliged to disclose 'every material circumstance which is known to the assured' but is also 'deemed to know every circumstance which, in the ordinary course of business, ought to be known to him'. Non-disclosure may be fraudulent or innocent. In any case, the result is the same – the contract is voidable at the option of the insurer.

The test set under the Act for the determining of a 'material circumstance' is whether such a circumstance would influence the judgment of a prudent insurer in fixing the premium or determining whether or not to assume the risk. Whether or not a particular circumstance, which has not been disclosed, is material or not is a question of fact. Under the Act certain circumstances need not be disclosed:

a) any circumstance which diminishes the risk;

b) any circumstance which is known or presumed by the insurer;

c) any circumstance which has been waived by the insurer; and

d) any circumstance which is superfluous to disclose because of an express or implied warranty.

Where insurance is procured by an agent on behalf of a principal, the agent is also subject to a duty of disclosure. In particular, the agent must disclose every material circumstance which is known to himself. An agent is deemed to know every circumstance which in the ordinary course of business ought to be known by, or communicated to, him. An agent is also obliged to disclose every material circumstance which the assured is bound to disclose.

Recent jurisprudence from the English courts has developed the duty of good faith as established under the 1906 Act. In particular, the test of a 'prudent' underwriter has been developed by the court. Also, the scope of the obligation to disclose has been extended to cover not only disclosure prior to the negotiation of the insurance contract but also during the period of performance of the contract.

Originally the English courts took the view that 'the Court's task in deciding whether or not the defendant insurer can avoid the policy for non-disclosure must be to determine as a question of fact whether, by applying the standard of the judgment of a prudent insurer, the insurer in question would have been influenced in fixing the premium or determining whether to take the risk if he had been informed of the undisclosed circumstances before entering into the contract'; per Kerr J, in *Berger and Light Diffusers Pty Ltd* v *Pollock* (1973). In *Container Transport International* v *Oceanus Mutual Underwriting* (1984), Parker LJ adopted a less rigorous standard. Any circumstance which increases the risk is deemed to influence the judgment of a prudent

171

insurer. An element of subjectivity was introduced to an otherwise objective test. Evidence could be led to establish that the risk resulting from a particular material circumstance would lead a prudent underwriter to increase the premium or decline to enter the contract. However, Lord Parker acknowledged that there is no absolute standard upon which a judgment can be based in ascertaining the actions of a prudent insurer.

The duty to disclose material circumstances during the performance of the contract of insurance was also considered by the English courts in *The Litsion Pride* (1985). Section 19 of the 1906 Act clearly requires the disclosure of material circumstances prior to the contract, but makes no mention of the continuation of such a duty throughout the performance of the contract. In *The Litsion Pride* case, a contract of insurance was negotiated for a vessel for the carriage of crude oil, but the vessel entered a war zone without disclosing this fact to the insurers. The vessel was damaged and a claim was entered under the insurance policy. The insuring company refused to pay on the basis of the omissions attributed to the shipowners. The court upheld the agreements of the insurance company and decided that the duty on the assured to disclose material circumstances continues throughout the whole insurance period.

Question 2

Slimbo, an exporter, wishes to insure his goods for £10,000 on a voyage from London to New York. He instructs Basil, a broker, to arrange insurance against total loss.

Basil knows that underwriters are reluctant to enter contracts to insure cargo against total loss unless they can themselves reinsure their risk under such contracts by entering contracts of reinsurance with reinsurers. So, if he cannot arrange reinsurance, he will earn no commission. Basil therefore approaches several reinsurers, one of whom is Ron. He asks Ron if he will agree to reinsure the liability of underwriters for £10,000. It is usual in cases of marine insurance for brokers to conclude agreements with more insurers (whether original underwriters or reinsurers) than they need to, with the result that the insurers' liability under contracts they enter is reduced to lower amounts than they originally agree. Basil tells Ron that he therefore expects he will only turn out to be liable for about 40 per cent of the risk (ie £4,000), so Ron agrees to sign a reinsurance contract for £10,000.

Basil then approaches Unwin, an underwriter, and tells him that, if he (Unwin) will insure Slimbo's cargo, Basil will enter his (Unwin's) name on the reinsurance contract with Ron. Unwin therefore contracts to insure Slimbo's cargo. Basil will enter his (Unwin's) name on the reinsurance contract with Ron. Unwin therefore contracts to insure Slimbo's cargo for £10,000, and Basil enters Unwin's name on the reinsurance contract. However, Basil does not make arrangements with any other insurers.

Slimbo pays a premium for the contract with Unwin, from which Basil receives a commission, and Unwin pays a premium for the contract with Ron, from which Basil receives a further commission.

Slimbo's cargo is so damaged that Slimbo claims there is a total loss. Unwin is not sure, so he asks Basil to acquire an expert assessor's report on the condition of the cargo. Basil obtains the report, which he and Unwin refuse to show to Slimbo.

Advise Basil, Unwin and Ron in the following circumstances.

Slimbo demands to see the report and to be paid for the loss by Unwin. Basil tells Ron that, if Slimbo recovers from Unwin, Unwin will claim the sum from Ron. Ron says that his arrangement with Basil was on the basis that, if he were liable to an underwriter, it would only be for £4,000.

University of London LLB Examination
(for External Students) Commercial Law 1987 Q4

General comment

The key to any question which sets out complicated facts is to make a list of the things which have happened and then to go through them one at a time, stating the legal effect of them (ie list all the things Basil has done). If approached in this way, this question can be attempted, although it is far from easy even once the issues have been spotted. Probably the hardest part is dealing with the possible misrepresentation made to Ron and its consequences.

Skeleton solution

Implied authority of an insurance agent.

Representations as to the future as misrepresentations.

Contract of re-insurance voidable?

Are the commissions received by Basil in breach of his duties?

Liability of Unwin to Slimbo.

Suggested solution

Basil was appointed by Slimbo to arrange for his (Slimbo's) goods to be insured for their voyage from London to New York. Nothing is known about Basil's instructions, save that he had to insure the goods to Slimbo's benefit for £10,000. It will be assumed that no further instructions were received by Basil.

An agent who is authorised to make a particular transaction has implied authority to make that transaction in any way which is normal in the trade concerned. As far as Slimbo was concerned, however, all that Basil had authority to do was to insure the goods. If the insurer wished to be covered by reinsurance then that was a separate matter and any contract of reinsurance would not be made as agent of Slimbo but as agent of the insurer.

The contract of insurance was made with Unwin. On the information given Basil had authority to make that contract on Slimbo's behalf, so it is effective and can be enforced by Slimbo against Unwin.

The contract made with Ron to re-insure the goods was made by Basil at a time when no one had authorised him to make such a contract. When it was made Basil represented that Ron's liability was likely to be £4,000. This turned out not to be correct, but was only a misrepresentation which made the contract voidable if at the time Basil made it he did not intend to carry out his stated intention because it was a representation as to future facts. There is no information one way or the other whether Basil intended to make other reinsurance contracts.

Basil did not name the intended underwriter whose risks Ron was to re-insure, nor did he say that there was only going to be one underwriter. Indeed, it appears that the practice is that more than one underwriter is often involved as the primary insurer. Normally a contract can only be ratified if the agent made it on behalf of an identifiable principal and then only that identifiable principal may ratify (*Keighley Maxsted & Co v Durant* (1901)). There is however a way out of the problem here. Unwin paid a premium which, presumably, was accepted by Ron; on this basis Ron will be estopped from denying the validity of Unwin's ratification.

The contract of reinsurance, however, will be voidable at Ron's option if, firstly, Basil made a misrepresentation and, secondly, the ratification by Unwin was not only of the contract but also of the misrepresentation. It has already been established that there is insufficient information to say whether there was an actionable misrepresentation here. If there was no such misrepresentation then Ron will have no ground for attempting to avoid the contract, nor will he have any action against Basil on any ground. But if Basil had made an actionable misrepresentation then the ratification of the contract would be an acceptance by Unwin of responsibility for the way in which it was negotiated, because the back-dated authority to make a contract includes authority to make representations in the course of negotiations. Ron would therefore be entitled to rescind the contract and claim damages from Unwin.

Alternatively, Ron may be able to take action against Basil on the basis of a collateral contract. This would require Ron to establish that Basil was promising that if Ron made the contract of reinsurance then Basil would ensure that other contracts of reinsurance were made. It is always difficult to establish a collateral contract and, it is submitted, no such contract could be proved here because it is not sufficiently clear that Basil intended the representation as a promise.

The two commissions received by Basil are not in breach of his duties to Slimbo and Unwin because there is no conflict between his duty to perform a specific task for each of them and his receipt of the two commissions. The position would, of course, be different if Unwin had paid him a commission on the contract with Slimbo but he did not, he paid a commission on the contract with Ron and that is something which is not of concern to Slimbo. In fact we are not told on what basis the commission was paid, whether by virtue of prior agreement or for a past consideration. In either event it would be irrecoverable save for breach of duty, as to which see below.

When Basil obtained the report he did so as agent of Unwin. Although he owed Slimbo a duty not to disclose information obtained in the course of his agency with him (*Faccenda Chicken Ltd* v *Fowler* (1986)), the report appears not to have involved Basil in any breach of confidentiality. Indeed, if Basil were to show the report to Slimbo then he would be in breach of his duty of confidentiality to Unwin.

Basil's position, therefore, is that he had authority to make the contract with Unwin on behalf of Slimbo and is entitled to retain the commission paid by Slimbo. His action in making the contract with Ron was ratified by Unwin and, prima facie, the commission which was paid by Unwin cannot be recovered. But, if Basil made a misrepresentation then he would have acted in breach of his duties to Unwin. The breach occurred in that on ratification Basil is deemed to have had authority throughout and, therefore, to have been under the duty of an agent to obey his instructions and to act bona fide in the interests of his principal (*Bonsor* v *Musicians' Union* (1955)). That duty was breached because by misrepresenting the true position to Ron so Basil did not act in Unwin's interests. The loss caused to Unwin was the loss of the benefits of the contract on rescission of it by Ron. This, in turn, means that Basil cannot claim commission because on rescission of a contract the law treats it as though it had never been made and, of course, if Basil never made a contract with Ron so he cannot be said to have earned a commission.

Consequently, Unwin's position is that he is liable to Slimbo because Basil had authority to make the contract of insurance on Slimbo's behalf. Although Basil did say to Unwin that he would enter his name on the reinsurance contract and therefore implied that Unwin was protected by that reinsurance contract, this possible misrepresentation was not, it is submitted, made by Basil in his capacity as Slimbo's agent but in his capacity as Unwin's agent to make the reinsurance contract. Unwin may be entitled to reclaim the commission on the grounds given above and may find that he cannot enforce the reinsurance contract against Ron. In principle Unwin can then recover the premium because it was paid for a consideration which have wholly failed.

Ron's position depends entirely upon whether Basil made an actionable misrepresentation and, for reasons given earlier, it cannot be stated categorically that such a misrepresentation was made.

Question 3

William contracts with Andrew for the sale of 5,000 tonnes of Cypriot potatoes cif Bristol. William, the seller, arranges for the potatoes to be loaded aboard a vessel called *The Marina* at Thessoloniki, a port in Cyprus. Andrew, the purchaser, arranges for cargo insurance with a broker for the voyage from Thessoloniki to Bristol. The broker effects the insurance but erroneously the vessel referred to in the policy is *The Mariana*, and in fact no such vessel exists.

The broker also fails to inform Floyd, the underwriter with whom the cover has been arranged, that there is a rumour that the 1994 Cypriot potato harvest has been badly infested with pest. This fact has not been transmitted by Andrew to the broker quite simply because Andrew was unaware of the rumour. If Floyd had known of the rumour he would have increased the premium for the policy.

Andrew pays William for the potatoes and then sells the whole cargo to Adrian cif Bristol. Andrew indorses the bill of lading to Adrian and subsequently assigns his rights under the insurance policy against payment of the price.

Before the vessel has left the Mediterranean, Adrian instructs the ship master to make for Dublin instead of Bristol since the spot price for potatoes is at that time higher in Ireland than in the United Kingdom. Adrian also advises Floyd that this instruction has been issued.

On course to Dublin, the vessel's cook decides to go on strike and the ship's master decides to put into port at a Spanish port for a replacement cook. However, before the change of course has been effected, the second mate is struck down with acute appendicitis. The master alters course to find a replacement cook and is subsequently informed by the crew that the second mate has been struck down with the ailment.

The ship lands at the Spanish port and a new cook is found as well as a hospital for the second mate. The ship then resumes its course for Dublin. Just after setting sail, the vessel develops a leak before the water line and seawater seeps into the hold rendering 2,000 tonnes of the potatoes worthless. Repairs are made at Bordeaux which take two weeks. Thereafter the ship continues its voyage.

The potatoes are discharged in Dublin but the remaining 3,000 tonnes of potatoes are found to be mouldy.

Advise Adrian of his rights against Floyd.

Question prepared by the Editor
April 1994

General comment

The key to this question is to identify which type of insurance contract is being used and whether and defences can be raised by Andrew which could also be raised by Floyd.

Skeleton solution

Insurance defences against Andrew? Equally valid against Adrian – *assignee* (ss15, 50, 51, MIA 1906).

Misdescription of vessel: negligence by broker? Misrepresentation? Section 20.

Non disclosure by broker s19. Excuse? Matter of common notoriety? Materiality 18(2).

Change of voyage – Adrian's instruction: cl 10. Failure by broker to communicate?

Deviation, cl 8.3.

Leak – unseaworthiness? Sections 39–41 MIA 1906.

Suggested solution

We are to advise Adrian, the purchaser of a quantity of potatoes shipped on cif terms by Andrew. We are not told which law governs the contract between the parties to the insurance policy. There does not appear to have been an express choice. However, cl 19 of the Institute Cargo Clauses states that English law and practice will apply. This is clearly only so where the policy is issued through a Lloyds' broker which we are told is so.

In a normal cif contract Adrian would receive an insurance policy, an invoice and a bill of lading: *Arnold Karlberg* v *Blyth, Green, Jourdain & Co* (1916). The policy ought to cover the goods for their cif value for the whole of the journey against risks usual in the trade. We are not told on what terms the goods have been insured but a medium range cover such as ICC 'B' would no doubt suffice.

Adrian will be able to claim on the insurance for loss by a peril insured against only if the policy is properly assigned to him. A marine policy is assignable unless it contains a term expressly prohibiting assignment. It may be assigned either before or after loss: s50(1). As a result Adrian may sue thereon in his own name but he will be subject to all the defences which could have been raised against Andrew: s50(2). There is some suggestion on the facts of an assignment which may not be adequate. The mere fact that Andrew is selling the goods to Adrian does not thereby result in an assignment under the contract of insurance unless there is an express or implied agreement to that effect: s15. The mere fact of a cif sale is not sufficient to bring about an automatic assignment of the policy. Under s51 of the Act the assured (Andrew) must assign the policy before or at the same time as he parts with his interest in the insured goods. The facts suggest that assignment may only have taken place at a later stage. If this is so, whilst the right to indemnity can of course be assigned by Andrew, as can any other chose in action, the insurance interest cannot.

The misdescription of the vessel constitutes a misrepresentation. Whether the fault is with the broker or Andrew is not clear, although this is of little consequence since the broker is the agent of Andrew, the assured. Section 20 of the Act requires every material representation to be true. If it is not, the insurer may avoid the contract. It is for the insurer to show that this representation is material in that a reasonable and prudent underwriter would have been affected by it in his assessment of risk or acceptance of premium: s20(2); *Container Transport International* v *Oceanus Mutual Underwriting* (1984).

Unless *The Mariana* is a vessel which is so fundamentally different from *The Marina*, it is difficult to see how such misrepresentation would be material. Whether the representation is true for the purposes of s20 depends upon whether or not it is one of fact or one of expectation or belief. A representation of fact must be substantially correct: s20(4); one of expectation or belief need only be honestly made: s20(5). The nature of this representation would appear to depend not on the words used but the degree of control in the representor to bring it about. On that basis it is a representation of fact but it is unlikely to be material.

Formerly the Held Covered clause would have entitled the carrier to an extension of cover on payment of additional premium, in the event of misdescription of the vessel. However, this clause is no longer part of the standard ICC insurance cover. It has been replaced by the Change of Voyage Clause which is of narrower ambit and of no use in this situation.

There may of course be an express warranty as to the vessel on which the goods are to be carried: s35, breach of which would discharge the insurer from the date of breach:

s33(3). But there is not in fact a breach here as the goods are shipped on *The Mariana* anyway.

There is non disclosure of the pest affecting the crop. The breach is by the broker. If Andrew ought to have known of the pest then he ought to have communicated the fact to the broker. The broker is then obliged to communicate to the underwriter all that which he ought to know in the ordinary course of business and ought to have had communicated to him: s19(a). It matters not that the existence of the pest is only a rumour, however ill founded, since the underwriter would have considered it material. The test is, however, purely objective, not whether the underwriter in question would have been affected but whether a reasonable underwriter would have been: *Container Transport International* v *Oceanus Mutual Underwriting* (1984).

The change of destination from Bristol to Dublin constitutes a change of voyage: s45. Adrian is entitled to a mandatory extension of cover providing that he gives prompt notice of the change to the underwriters: cl 10, and will probably become liable for additional premium (assuming that Adrian is able to claim on the assigned policy and does not simply have a right to the assigned debt). Whilst the broker has been informed of the change, it is not clear whether he has communicated it to the underwriters. If he has not done so then there will be no extension of cover and any loss irrevocable in consequences would have to be the subject matter of a claim against the carrier himself or in negligence against broker.

Despite the deviation the insurance remains in force: cl 8.3. The insurance remains in force during any deviation. However the leak may be an indication of unseaworthiness. If this is so and the unseaworthiness causes the loss, the insurer will not be liable: cl 5.2. If the unseaworthiness was present at the outset then the assured is in breach of his undertaking to provide a seaworthy vessel: ss39–41; and the insurer will be discharged: s33(3), unless the assured was not at fault or privy to this unseaworthiness: cl 5.2.

Even if the insurer remains liable, the actual loss would appear to come not from the entry of the sea water but from the mould which it causes. The proximate cause of loss in such a case would, it is submitted, be the unseaworthiness and would therefore be irrecoverable: *The Tolmidis* (1983). In any event, unless it could be shown that the loss occurred before the vessel was delayed, then the insurer would claim that the loss was caused by delay and therefore excluded under cl 4.5.

Question 4

What are the major differences between open and floating insurance cover and how do both of these differ from the specific insurance of a cargo? Also, to what extent does the documentation provided to an assured under each of these different arrangements satisfy the needs of the parties under a cif contract.

Question prepared by the Editor
April 1994

General comment

This is a short essay-type question providing little undue hardship to answering.

Skeleton solution

Distinction between floating policies and open cover.

Explanation of open cover.

Cif requirements vis-à-vis insurance.

Suggested solution

Floating policies consist of a number of voyage policies issued pursuant to the payment of a single premium. They are used when the assured intends to ship a large amount of goods by shipments of differing sizes and on differing dates. The assured then declares each shipment and the available cover will be reduced by the amount of that declaration.

On each declaration the policy will attach to the goods so long as they are of the type specified and on the route specified. The declaration must be made within a reasonable time after shipment, if not the underwriter will be discharged if the omission is not bona fide. If the declaration is made after the loss or arrival of the ship the floating policy will be treated as an unvalued policy regarding that shipment, s29. The danger exists that the premium may be dissipated without the knowledge of the assured, who may find that he is not covered for subsequent losses, see *Greenock* v *Maritime Insurance* (1903).

The assured will be under a duty of disclosure throughout the operation of the policy, *The Litsion Pride* (1985). A floating policy consisting as it does of a number of separate policies satisfies the requirements for documents under a cif contract which calls for an insurance *policy*.

Open cover is not a policy at all. It is a type of permanent agreement to insure. It may be available for a year but more usually it is available for an indefinite period, subject to cancellation by either side. The open cover may even be on a world wide basis covering a range of different cargoes. The most likely routes and subject matter will usually be known at the start of the cover. Generally the underwriter will insist on a limit per bottom, which means that there will be a maximum specified for carriage by any one vessel.

The assured is still under a duty to declare each shipment. He will usually sign one of the blank insurance certificates with which he is supplied and send one to the buyer, with a copy to the broker who will receive a policy from the underwriter.

The benefit of the open policy is that there is no danger of the cover being exhausted and there is no premium to pay until the individual policies are issued. Since cif contracts generally require a policy, the certificates available under open cover are not acceptable, in theory. In practice, however, they are considered adequate.

Question 5

Pratleys Bank gave a loan of £2.5 million to Bright Ideas Ltd, the loan being secured by a charge over a consignment of motor cars on route from Tokyo to Newcastle aboard *The Sitting Duck*, a vessel registered in the UK. One of the conditions of the loan was that Bright Ideas Ltd insure the consignment of motor vehicles against a number of perils, including war risks. Accordingly, Bright Ideas Ltd took out the appropriate policy to cover all the necessary perils with the Prudent Insurance Company. The terms of the policy included a provision which warranted that *The Sitting Duck* would not enter a prohibited war zone.

The benefit of all insurance was assigned to Pratleys Bank and the insurers undertook, in a separate agreement with the bank, to advise the Bank promptly if they ceased to insure the vessel for any reason.

Not surprisingly, *The Sitting Duck* entered a prohibited war zone where it struck a submerged wreck. Both the ship and the cargo were lost. Bright Ideas Ltd gave the insurers notice of claim for loss of the cargo on the war risks insurance.

The bank also enquired with the Prudent Insurance Company as to the progress of the claim and were informed that the insurers were investigating the matter in the usual way. Subsequently, Pratleys increased the loan facility to Bright Ideas Ltd which they insist would not have occurred had they known that there was a possibility of the insurance claim being rejected.

The Prudent Insurance Company rejected the claim and the Bank have now claimed damages from the Insurance Company.

Advise the Prudent Insurance Company of their liabilities.

Question prepared by the Editor
April 1994

General comment

This is a question based on one of the recent cases in marine insurance arising from the Iran-Iraq war in the 1980s. The issues raised are relatively straightforward but, without a knowledge of the applicable case law, the question might be difficult to answer because the peculiar nature of the main legal point raised.

Skeleton solution

Liability under the insurance contract: additional premium areas and prohibited war zones.

Automatic discharge of the insurer under s33 of the Marine Insurance Act 1906.

Construction of the obligation to notify promptly.

Duty to notify the bank of the grounds of the notice of claim.

Issues of proximity and remoteness of damages.

Suggested solution

In this question, the bank secured a loan by a charge on a consignment of vehicles which, according to the terms of the loan agreement, required the borrowers to insure the cargo against war risks. Insurance was procured with the Prudent Insurance Company and the insurance company entered into a separate agreement to notify the bank in the event that they ceased to insure the consignment.

The loss of the cargo raises separate questions as to Prudent's liability, firstly to the policy holders under the terms of the policy, and secondly to the bank under the terms of the agreement requiring Prudent to notify the bank promptly in the event that they ceased to insure the cargo.

It is extremely unlikely that the war risks insurance policy taken out by Bright Ideas Ltd would insure the cargo against all loss caused by acts of war, particularly since the policy contained a warranty requiring *The Sitting Duck* to refrain from entering prohibited war zones. Rather, it is more likely that the policy provided protection against general war risks and that a further premium must be paid in the event that the ship enters an additional premium area. Loss of the insured goods in such an area would not be covered unless the additional premium had been paid in advance.

However, often certain areas are declared prohibited war zones and vessels must refrain from entering such areas at all times. These are areas of such extreme danger that it is not considered acceptable that vessels should be covered by insurance at all. Loss of the insured goods in such an area relieves the insurers of all liability for loss under the policy.

This is the position in the present case. The ship and the cargo were lost in a prohibited war zone and as such Prudent would be able to avoid liability under its policy. The fact that Bright Ideas Ltd gave the insurers notice of claim for the loss of the cargo does not alter this position. Similarly, a claim by Bright Ideas Ltd that it was ignorant of the existence of prohibited areas would not change the position.

Under s33(3) of the Marine Insurance Act 1906, discharge of the insurer from liability is automatic and not dependent on any decision by the insurer to treat the insurance contract as being at an end. Prudent is not therefore required to serve notice that the contract is an end, although under s34(3) of the act an insurer is entitled to waive a breach of warranty. In this case, it would clearly not be in Prudent's interests to do so.

The second aspect of Prudent's liability concerns its undertaking to inform the bank promptly if it ceased to insure the goods.

Once the ship entered the prohibited area, it was uninsured and the insurers were discharged from liability as from the date of breach. Accordingly, if the insurers have warranted to mortgagees that they will advise them promptly in the event that the cover ceases, they are required to notify the mortgagees as soon as they become aware of any event giving rise to the termination of the cover: *Bank of Nova Scotia* v *Hellenic Mutual War Risks Association (Bermuda) Ltd, The Good Luck* (1991).

In this case, entry into the prohibited area terminated the cover and Prudent was required to inform the bank immediately it became aware of information giving rise to termination of the cover.

Prudent would not be successful in claiming that it was entitled to a reasonable period of notice to decide whether it should waive the breach of warranty and to conduct an investigation into the facts of the matter. The breach was of a sufficient magnitude that no advantage could accrue from waiving the breach. Postponing the time for giving notice exposed the bank to a prolonged risk of the goods being uninsured without its knowledge at a time when that knowledge would be crucially important to it in making further advances.

In contrast, Bright Ideas Ltd gave Prudent notice of the loss of cargo immediately the loss occurred. Despite inquiries by the bank, this information was not disclosed and the bank made further advances on the basis that the insurance claim was likely to be successful. In fact, Prudent had knowledge that the claim was unlikely to succeed and that the bank's advances would be exposed for lack of security.

There was no practical or business difficulty in the insurers giving prompt notice to the bank of the events giving rise to the loss of the security as required under its undertaking to the bank. At the very least, Prudent should have notified the bank of the existence of evidence to suggest that the claim would be rejected. This would have allowed the bank to draw its own conclusions as to whether or not it was advisable to immediately treat Bright Ideas Ltd in default of the loan agreement because it had failed to procure adequate insurance cover.

Prudent could argue that its failure to notify the bank of the loss of cover was not the immediate cause of injury sustained in the event that further advances are irrecoverable. Similarly, there is also an argument, based on remoteness of damages, that Prudent was unaware of the extension of credit facilities and knowledge of such facilities could not be attributed to the company.

Nevertheless, it is unlikely that either of these arguments would succeed. Firstly, Prudent's failure to comply with its express contractual obligations resulted in the bank making further advances that were not properly secured and that would not have been made if the bank had been promptly notified of the loss of the vessel in a prohibited war zone. The bank's loss was caused by the breach of this undertaking and the injury was proximate.

Secondly, since the injury was sufficiently proximate, any damages suffered by the Bank would not be too remote. This is because the loss was inevitable in light of the fact that the goods against which the charge had been created had become uninsured at the time of their destruction.

Therefore, while Prudent would not be liable to Bright Ideas Ltd for the loss of the consignment of motor vehicles under the insurance policy due to the fact that the vessel entered a prohibited war zone, it cannot avoid liability to the bank for failing to promptly notify it of the prohibited entry giving rise to the termination of the cover.

It is also likely that Prudent are liable for losses sustained by the bank for the original credit and the subsequent advances. The failure to notify jeopardised the existing charges and, had the bank known of the facts of the matter, the whole matter of the renegotiation of the security would have been treated differently.

10 MARINE INSURANCE II – TYPES OF COVER

10.1 Introduction

10.2 Key points

10.3 Recent cases and materials

10.4 Relevant materials

10.5 Analysis of questions

10.6 Questions

10.1 Introduction

In the last chapter we discussed the principles surrounding the formation of marine insurance contracts and the functioning of the policy. In this chapter, the discussion moves on to consider the types of cover which are available for the carriage of cargo from one location to another. The term 'cover' simply refers to the risks which are embraced by the terms of a particular policy.

Different types of insurance cover are required by parties engaging in international sales transactions. Full comprehensive insurance may not be required for a cargo which has little value or which is transported a short distance through a safe route. Less extensive insurance may suffice depending on the circumstances of the transaction. Obviously, where the insurance cover is restricted to relatively few perils, the premium payable for the cover is less than would be due for comprehensive insurance. However, any party with an insurable interest is at liberty to select the type of cover which he or she wishes.

The selection of cover is simplified by the existence of standard policies and clauses to cover risks. These documents are widely used in the marine insurance industry. The bulk of this chapter is dedicated to consideration of these policies and clauses.

10.2 Key points

a) *The Lloyd's Marine Insurance Policy and the Institute Cargo Clauses*

Until 1982, the form of marine insurance policy in general use was the Lloyd's SG Policy which was attached as an appendix to the Marine Insurance Act 1906. In January 1982 a new marine insurance policy was introduced known as the Lloyd's Marine Policy which is used in conjunction with one of three separate types of cover (known as 'clauses').

The three different types of cover are described as Institute Cargo Clauses A, B and C respectively. These Clauses have been devised for use along with the revised policy and since 1 April 1983 use of the new policy and the Cargo Clauses has been mandatory.

b) *Institute Cargo Clause A*

Insurance on the basis of Institute Cargo Clause A covers an assured for all risks of loss or damage to the subject matter insured by virtue of clause 1 of the policy. Hence, this form of insurance is known as an 'all risks' policy.

Although the policy is deemed to be all risks, certain exclusions are in fact contained in the other clauses of the policy. For example, under clause 4, liability is excluded for:

   i)   wilful misconduct of the assured;

   ii)   ordinary leakage, loss in weight or volume, or ordinary wear and tear of the subject matter insured;

   iii)   loss, damage or expense caused by insufficient or unsuitable packing or preparation of the subject matter insured;

   iv)   loss, damage or expense proximately caused by delay, even if the delay is caused by a risk insured against;

   v)   loss, damage or expense arising from the insolvency or financial default of owners, managers, charterers or operators of the vessel; and

   vi)   loss, damage or expense arising from the use of any weapon of war employing atomic or nuclear fission and/or fusion.

The exceptions protecting the insurer from liability continue under clause 5, which provides that in no case will the insurance cover loss, damage or expense arising from: unseaworthiness of vessel or craft, unfitness of vessel, craft or conveyance used for the carriage of the subject matter insured where the assured, their servants or agents are privy to such unseaworthiness or unfitness at the time the cargo is loaded.

Clause 6 relates to perils caused by acts of war and civil strife and specifies that the insurance will not cover loss, damage or expense caused by:

   i)   war, civil war, revolution, rebellion, insurrection, civil strife, etc;

   ii)   capture, seizure, arrest, restraint or detriment and consequences thereof or any attempt thereat;

   iii)   derelict mines, torpedoes, bombs or other derelict weapons of war.

Finally, clause 7 contains the exceptions relating to strikes and civil commotions and provides that liability is excluded for loss, damage or expense caused by:

   i)   strikers or persons taking part in labour disturbances, riots or civil commotions;

    ii)   strikes, lock outs, labour disturbances, riots or civil commotions;

    iii)   any terrorist or any person acting for a political motive.

While the Institute Cargo Clause A policy is described as 'all risks' clearly the coverage of the policy is less than comprehensive.

It should be noted that Clause A cover protects for loss or damage against 'risks' only, not against events which are certain to occur. So the Clause A policy does not protect an assured for loss or damage due to 'inevitabilities'; rather the insurance cover is intended to protect against the happening of a fortuitous event: *British & Foreign Marine Insurance* v *Gaunt* [1921] 2 AC 41.

c) *Institute Cargo Clauses B and C*

Institute Cargo Clauses B and C offer less protection to the assured for loss or damage to the subject matter insured than Institute Cargo Clause A. The assured will therefore be able to obtain these types of cover at a lower premium.

Instead of covering 'all risks' except those expressly excluded, which is how Clause A cover works, Cargo Clauses B and C are designed to cover only particular perils. Therefore, in order for a cargo to be protected under Clause B or C cover, the damage to the cargo must be caused by one of the perils included within the scope of the policy.

The risks against which both Cargo Clauses B and C offer protection from loss or damage are as follows:

    i)   Loss of, or damage to, the subject matter insured, reasonably attributed to:

        •   fire or explosion;

        •   the vessel or craft being stranded, grounded, sunk or capsized;

        •   overturning or derailment of land conveyance;

        •   collision or contact of vessel/conveyance with any external object other than water;

        •   discharge of cargo at port of distress.

    ii)   Loss or damage to the subject matter caused by:

        •   general average sacrifice;

        •   jettison.

The difference between Clause B and Clause C cover is that Clause B policies cover slightly more risks. There are four notable additional risks insured under Clause B cover:

    i)   damage reasonably attributable to earthquake, volcanic eruption or lightning;

    ii)   loss or damage caused by washing overboard;

iii) entry of sea, lake or river water into the vessel craft, hold, conveyance, etc, or place of storage; and

iv) total loss of any package lost overboard or dropped whilst loading on to or unloading from vessel or craft.

d) *Additional exclusions*

Section 55(2) of the MIA 1906 specifically states that there are certain perils against which an insurer will not offer cover unless the policy provides otherwise. For the most part, the exclusions which are set out in s55(2) are duplicated in the exclusion clauses of the Clause A, B and C policies.

The following perils are excluded by statute:

i) liability for loss attributable to wilful misconduct of the assured: s55(2)(a);

ii) liability for loss proximately caused by delay, although the delay is caused by a peril insured against: s55(2)(b);

iii) liability for ordinary wear and tear and leakage: s55(2)(c);

iv) liability for ordinary breakage or loss proximately caused by rats or vermin and any injury to machinery not proximately caused by maritime perils: s55(2)(c);

v) liability for inherent vice: s55(2)(d).

Where the additional exclusions found in s55(2) are not repeated in the policy, they may be relied on by the insurer to exclude liability for loss or damage in appropriate cases.

e) *Individual analysis of the exclusion clauses in Institute Cargo Clauses A, B and C*

The various excluded risks identified in the Institute Cargo Clauses A, B and C, as well as in s55(2) of the MIA 1906, refer to circumstances which justify the exclusion of liability. Each of these will now be examined in closer detail.

i) Wilful misconduct of the assured

Loss or damage will be excluded if it is attributable to the wilful misconduct of the assured. It is unlikely that the exclusion will apply where the conduct of the assured is merely negligent.

ii) Ordinary leakage, etc

This exception covers not only damage or loss caused by incursion of water due to the age of the vessel but also in the case of water or moisture which exudes from cargoes as a result of natural sweating: *Wadsworth Lighterage & Coal* v *Sea Insurance* (1929) 35 Com Cas 1.

iii) Insufficient or unsuitable packaging

The exception applies where the loss or damage is the result of inadequate packing material, packing material which is inappropriate for the particular type of cargo, or packaging of the goods in a way not suitable because of their particular qualities.

iv) Inherent vice

For an insurer to rely on the exclusion of inherent vice, it must be shown that the loss or damage is the result of the internal condition of the subject matter insured.

So if, for example, a cargo of hemp, which is spontaneously combustible, catches fire and is destroyed an insurer would be excluded from liability providing that the fire was the result of spontaneous combustion. However, if the fire spreads to another cargo which is damaged, the insurer would continue to remain liable for the damage to the second cargo: see *Noten (TM) BV* v *Harding* [1989] 2 Lloyd's Rep 527; and *Soya GmbH Mainz Kommanditgesellschaft* v *White* [1983] 1 Lloyd's Rep 122.

v) Delay

Where the vessel is delayed for a reason other than a lawful excuse, the insurer will not be liable for any loss, damage or expense which is proximately caused by that delay. This rule applies even if the delay itself was caused by a risk insured against.

The 'lawful excuses' for delay are found in s49(1) and delay is justified in the following circumstances:

- where authorised by any special term in the policy;
- where caused by circumstances beyond the control of the master and his employer;
- where reasonably necessary in order to comply with an express or implied warranty;
- where reasonably necessary for the safety of the ship or the subject matter insured;
- for the purpose of saving human life or aiding a ship in distress where human life may be in danger;
- where reasonably necessary for the purpose of obtaining medical or surgical aid for any person on board the ship.

Even if the delay is justified, the vessel must resume its voyage with reasonable dispatch once the cause of the delay has ceased to exist.

Deviation often causes delay and it is appropriate at this point to discuss the principles applicable to deviation. Section 46 of the Act sets out these principles in the following terms:

- Where a ship without lawful excuse deviates from the voyage contemplated by the policy, the insurer is discharged from liability as from the time of deviation and it is immaterial that the ship may have regained her route before any loss occurs.

- There is a deviation from the voyage contemplated by the policy where (a) the course of the voyage is specifically designated by the policy and the vessel departs from that course; or (b) the course of the voyage is not specifically designated by the policy but the usual and customary course is departed from.

- The intention to deviate is immaterial; but there must be a deviation in fact.

Deviation, like delay, is excused if it falls within one of the listed exceptions in s49(1).

vi) Financial default of owners, etc

The insurer will be excluded from liability in circumstances where the loss or damage arises from the insolvency or financial default of the shipowners.

vii) Deliberate damage

This particular exclusion is found in Clauses B and C, not Clause A. However, the assured may protect against deliberate damage by adopting the Institute Malicious Damage Clause which, for an additional premium, covers against this peril.

viii) Unseaworthiness

An insurer excludes liability for the unseaworthiness of the vessel or its unfitness to carry goods. This is an implied restatement of the duties which are imposed in ss39 and 40 of the Act which require the vessel to be seaworthy, fit to carry the goods (in a voyage policy) and not to put to sea in an unseaworthy condition (in a time policy).

ix) War exclusion clause

Liability for damage caused as a result of armed conflict is often excluded and it should be noted that this exclusion extends to certain perils which are not the immediate consequence of armed conflict.

Special cover may, however, be obtained to cover war risks, again for an additional premium.

x) Strikes, etc, exclusion clause

This clause protects the insurer from loss or damage which is caused by strikers, persons taking part in labour disturbances and terrorists.

f) *Proximity*

Once it has been established that loss or damage has been caused by a particular peril against which the assured is insured, it is necessary to demonstrate that the peril is the proximate cause of loss. The need for proximity is stated in s55(2)(a) of the 1906 Act which provides that 'the insurer is liable for any loss proximately caused by a peril insured against'.

The burden of showing that the loss was proximately caused by a peril insured against lies with the assured who must show that, on the balance of probabilities, loss or damage was due to the peril insured against. In *The Tropaiofaros* [1960] 2 Lloyd's Rep 469, the House of Lords observed that 'the choice of the real or effective cause of loss is made by applying commonsense standards'.

When the loss is proximately caused by an insured peril, but the loss was also caused in part by negligence, the assured is still entitled to recover under the policy. This principle is elaborated in s55(2(a) of the Act which states:

'The insurer is liable for any loss even though the loss would not have happened but for the misconduct or negligence of the master or crew.'

This rule does not, of course, apply in the case of loss, damage or expense attributable to the 'wilful misconduct' of the assured: see *Century Insurance Co of Canada* v *Case Existological Laboratories* [1986] 2 Lloyd's Rep 524.

10.3 Recent cases and materials

Lamb Head Shipping Co Ltd v *Jennings, The Marel* [1992] 1 Lloyd's Rep 402: the onus is on assured to establish that the loss of the subjects was caused by a peril covered by the terms of the insurance policy. Unless the assured can establish this fact, the insurer is not obliged to pay under a policy even if the assured has successfully proved that the loss was not caused by those perils which lie outside the cover.

10.4 Relevant materials

P Whitherby, *Reference Book of Marine Insurance Clauses* (1984).

R H Brown, *Analysis of Marine Insurance Clauses* (1985).

N Leloir, 'The Lloyd's Marine Policy and the Institute Cargo Clauses' (1985) *Journal of Business Law* 228.

10.5 Analysis of questions

Answering questions on this topic is generally a test of ability to memorise the detail contained in the various Institute Cargo Clauses. Once this has been mastered, it is a relatively straightforward process to apply the applicable rules and exceptions to the questions posed.

The following questions deal mainly with hypothetical factual situations where cover has been obtained either under Cargo Clause A or B. Questions concerning cover under Cargo Clause C have not been included in any detail due to the similarity between Clause B and C cover.

10.6   Questions

Question 1

Pierre, a farmer in Lyons (France) sold 12,000 tonnes of peaches to Del cif London. The peaches were to be dispatched in six separate consignments in July/August 1993 and each shipment was insured by Del in Institute Cargo Clause A terms for the carriage of each consignment of the goods from Lyons to London.

The first consignment was seriously damaged when engine oil seeped into the goods in transit from Pierre's warehouse to the port at Lyons.

The second shipment was stored in open-topped containers at the quayside in Lyons and were exposed top sunlight which caused the peaches to spoil. When the goods arrived in England, they were found to be unfit for human consumption but an English company offered to purchase the consignment to make peach juice at 25 per cent of the original contract price.

The third consignment was loaded aboard a vessel which collided during a hurricane in the English Channel and became a total loss.

The fourth shipment was successfully transported to London but the off-loading of the goods was delayed by a strike at London docks. The lorries carrying the goods did not arrive at Del's warehouse in Bath until September. However, the warehouse in Bath into which the goods were to be stored has been repossessed by the landlord because Del, who is in financial trouble, failed to pay the rent. Only two of the ten lorries carrying the goods were unloaded at the warehouse. The goods in four of the lorries were redirected to another of Del's warehouse and those in the remaining four vehicles sold to Ernest in Manchester. While these goods were being transported to Manchester, the lorries were involved in a serious accident and the peaches substantially damaged. In the following week, both warehouses were destroyed by a deliberate arson attack and the goods stored were lost.

The fifth cargo arrived in London but contained only 1,500 tonnes of peaches instead of the 2,000 tonnes which were agreed.

Finally, the sixth consignment was hijacked on route to London by an organisation devoted to famine relief and diverted to Africa.

Del gave notice of claim to the underwriters for all six consignments. Advise the underwriters as to their legal position.

Question prepared by the Editor
April 1994

General comment

Do not be overly confused by the facts of this problem as presented. If the six separate scenarios can be dealt with independently, the question is much simplified. Each separate scenario requires a decision on whether the facts constitute an exception or are covered by the 'all risks' nature of the policy.

Skeleton solution

Situation 1 – warehouse to warehouse cover.

Situation 2 – Insufficiency of packing.

Situation 3 – No exclusion.

Situation 4 – Exclusion for labour disputes.

Situation 5 – No indication of the peril.

Situation 6 – Hijacking of the vessel.

Suggested solution

Pierre would have taken out the insurance as he is the cif seller. Whatever defences the underwriters would have been able to raise against any claim by Pierre on the policies, would be available against Del. Each shipment is covered by an Institute Cargo Clause A policy. In any claim the burden of proof is on the assured to prove that the loss/damage was caused by a peril insured against.

First shipment

A claim may be made if it can be shown that the loss/damage was *caused* by a peril insured against. Policy A is an all risks policy so oil damage would be an included risk. The question arises, however, whether the loss/damage occurred within the ambit of the policy. Clause 8, incorporated in all ICC policies, is the 'warehouse to warehouse' clause. Which means that the subject matter will be covered in transit from the seller's warehouse to the port of shipment. It is submitted that on the present facts the goods will be covered if they were packed for shipment.

Second shipment

This damage is clearly within the ambit of clause 8 (above) and is covered by the all risks policy. Prima facie the underwriter would not be able to rely on the exclusions contained in clause 4 unless clause 4.3 applies – relating to insufficiency of packing. It would only apply if the packing was done by Pierre or his servants. This is a question of fact. If the loss is covered then it must be resolved whether the loss is total or partial, again a question of fact.

If it is total the basis of assessment (depending on whether the policy is valued or unvalued) is governed by s68 of the Marine Insurance Act 1906. On paying out for a total loss the underwriter would be subrogated to the rights of the assured under s79 of the same Act. This means that he would be able to maintain any action the buyer would have had. It is important to distinguish between the underwriters' rights on paying out for a partial or total loss. If total he takes over the interest of the assured s79(1) if partial he assumes no such interest, s79(2). These subsections seem to be subject to the principle that the underwriter may not recover more than he has paid out. The question which arises therefore is if s79(1) applies and the underwriter takes over the assured's interest in the subject matter, may he then recover more than the indemnity by selling the goods? The authorities are undecided.

Third shipment

The loss caused by the hurricane is covered by Clause A. No exclusions in clause 4 would appear to apply. Generally ss39 and 40 require the ship to be seaworthy and if not the underwriter is discharged from the date of breach. Clause 5.1 of the A policy indicates that the underwriter will still be liable if the assured or his servants are not privy to such unseaworthiness. The measure of indemnity will be assessed according to s68(1) if the policy is valued or ss16(3) and 68(2) if unvalued.

Fourth shipment

Exclusion of losses caused by financial difficulties are confined to those suffered by the owners etc, of the vessel, clause 4.6. Loss damage or expense caused by labour disputes are excluded by clause 7.1. So the underwriters would not be liable for any expense caused by the delay. As regards the rest of the events described, it is necessary to make a thorough examination of clause 8. The clause terminates 'on delivery at the consignees or final warehouse or place of storage at the named destination', 8.1.1 'on delivery to any other warehouse or place of storage, whether prior to or at the destination which the assured elects to use either for storage other than in the ordinary course of transit or for allocation or distribution', 8.1.2. It is a question of fact as to whether the goods would be covered to the second Bath warehouse – is it the final warehouse? The formulation *'on delivery'* indicates that the loss caused by the fire would not be covered, as the fire took place subsequent to delivery.

Regarding the lorries going to Manchester clause 8.1.3 would set 60 days as an overall maximum period of coverage. However, it is submitted that the goods are not covered as they are forwarded to a destination other than the named destination and this forwarding has not been forced on the assured by circumstances beyond his control: *The Caspiana* (1957).

Fifth shipment

500 tonnes have been lost. There is no indication as to what the cause of this loss is. If the loss has been caused by a peril insured against and no exclusion clause is available to the underwriter then he will clearly have to pay a partial loss. The basis of assessment for the indemnity will be governed by s71(1) if the policy is valued or s71(2) if the policy is unvalued.

Sixth shipment

The cause of loss here is the hijack. If hijacking is piracy then it is covered by policy A clause 6.3. If this argument is accepted then the underwriters must pay a total loss, valued policy basis s68(1) unvalued s68(2). If the likelihood of hijack was known to the assured the failure to inform the underwriters may amount to material non disclosure which would discharge the underwriters from liability.

Question 2

The Cheap Clothing Company agreed to purchase a large consignment of leather handbags from Goochie, a Turkish leather goods manufacturer. The terms are fob Istanbul (Turkey). The Cheap Clothing Company arranged to have the goods insured with the Fly-By-Night Insurance Company on Institute Cargo Clause A terms which included a warehouse to warehouse clause.

The handbags were wrapped in thick paper bags and placed inside strong durable cardboard cartons for the voyage. Each of these cartons contained 120 handbags. The cartons were transported to the docks in covered vehicles and at the dockside they were packed into closed-top containers.

On arrival of the goods in England, the bags were stained and mouldy. It transpires that the proximate cause of the damage was moisture escaping from the bags and cartons and condensing on the inside of their containers. The condensation dropped onto the cartons, seeped into the cartons and stained the bags.

The particular type of leather from which the bags were manufactured is particularly susceptible to the absorption of moisture. It is also subsequently discovered that the cartons had remained unsealed for two days at the factory in Turkey before being transported to the port for exportation.

The Fly-by-Night Insurance Company has refused to pay out on the policy and the Cheap Clothing Company has sought your advice on two points:

a) the chances of success in a claim against the Fly-by-Night Insurance Company; and

b) the possibility of success against Goochie.

Question prepared by the Editor
April 1994

General comment

This is a two-part question requiring the identification of the remedies available against two parties involved in the performance of the contract. Success against the insurance company depends on the construction of the policy, while success against the seller will be determined by the principles applicable to contracts for the sale of goods.

Skeleton solution

i)   Coverage provided in a Cargo Clause A policy.

Exceptions on the grounds of wilful misconduct and ordinary wear and tear.

Inherent vice.

Insufficient or inadequate packaging.

ii) Risk in the goods in a fob contract.

Sale of Goods Act.

Duty to mitigate loss.

Suggested solution

In this question, we are asked to advise the Cheap Clothing Company as to their chance of success in pursuing a claim against: (i) the Fly-by-Night Insurance Company under the contract of insurance; and (ii) Goochie, the manufacturer of the goods on the grounds that the goods were defective.

194

i) The goods were sold fob Istanbul and therefore the obligation to procure insurance lies with the Cheap Clothing Company as the purchasers. The insurance contract was entered into with the Fly-by-Night Insurance Company on Institute Cargo Clause A terms. The policy included a warehouse-to-warehouse clause.

The Institute Cargo Clause A policy is the most comprehensive form of Institute insurance and covers all risks of loss or of damage to the insured subject-matter subject to certain limited exclusions.

The first excluded category is loss, damage or expense attributable to the wilful misconduct of the assured. In this case, the assured is the Cheap Clothing Company, who took out the policy, and not the carrier responsible for the transportation of the goods. From the facts presented, there appears to be no basis for claiming that the damage was caused by wilful misconduct on the part of the Cheap Clothing Company who did not enter into possession of the goods until they were finally delivered in England.

The second exclusion from the terms of Clause A relates to damage caused by ordinary leakage, ordinary loss in weight or volume, or ordinary wear and tear of the subject matter of the insurance contract. None of these factors appears to account for the damage to the goods and the Fly-by-Night Insurance Company cannot rely on this provision as a defence to non-payment under the policy.

The third ground for avoiding liability relates to loss, damage or expense caused by insufficiency or unsuitability of the packing materials or preparation of the subject-matter that has been insured. The sufficiency or suitability of the packaging materials depends on both the nature of the goods and the customary practice in a particular trade.

Where goods are particularly susceptible to damage from external elements such as air or water, naturally the packaging must provide a greater degree of protection than for goods that are resistant to such elements. Similarly, where goods have been packaged in such a manner that they cannot withstand the usual conditions to be expected on a particular voyage, the insurers are entitled to reject any claim for damage that might subsequently occur: see *Berk* v *Style* (1956).

At the same time, if goods are customarily packaged in certain manner to ensure their protection, packaging failing to meet this standard may be held to be insufficient.

In this particular case, the goods were placed in thick paper bags and placed in cardboard cartons before being transported to the docks for consignment. There is no reason to believe that the packaging was insufficient.

While the bags were made out of a material susceptible to damage from water, adequate precautions were taken to prevent the bags becoming wet. The dampness originated from escaping moisture from the bags and cartons. This is therefore no basis for claiming that the packaging was insufficient.

Finally, a fourth exclusion under the policy is where the damage or loss occurs as a result of an inherent vice, or the particular nature, of the goods insured.

There are a number of reasons for believing that the goods contained an inherent vice. The moisture trapped in the bags which subsequently escaped and which finally resulted in the damage to the goods, was the direct cause of the damage. This originated from the goods themselves, albeit because they were exposed to abnormal conditions before consignment and immediately after manufacture.

In addition, the goods themselves, due to the condition in which they were shipped, were inherently defective insofar as they were the immediate cause of their own discolouring.

It is on this last ground that the Fly-by-Night Insurance Company may be able to avoid liability under the policy if an action is brought against them by the Cheap Clothing Company.

ii) Goochie is both the manufacturer of the goods and the seller. The goods themselves were ruined by escaping moisture which condensed inside the container in which they were being transported. The moisture entered the goods because the cartons in which they were stored were left unsealed for two days at the factory in Turkey. However, the actual damage to the goods occurred during transit.

The contract was expressed to be fob Istanbul. In a fob arrangement, risk of accidental loss in the goods passes when they are shipped in the absence of an express or implied stipulation in the sales contract to the contrary. Therefore, the risk of the accidental loss of the goods passed from Goochie to the Cheap Clothing Company when they crossed the ship's rail at Istanbul.

However, it is unlikely that a court would be willing to listen to an argument based on the contention that the goods were accidentally destroyed. The immediate cause of condition was deterioration during transit brought about by the exposure of the goods to humid conditions immediately after manufacture. The primary question is not therefore whether the goods were accidentally damaged, but whether the goods that finally arrived in England were of merchantable quality.

In all fob contracts there is an implied term that the goods shall be of merchantable quality, not only when they are being loaded but also upon arrival at their final destination. According to s14(2) of the Sale of Goods Act, goods are considered to be of merchantable quality if they are fit for the purpose for which goods of that kind are commonly bought as is reasonable to expect, taking into account the description applied to them, the price and all other relevant circumstances.

Clearly the goods supplied by Goochie are not of merchantable quality. The bags are wet, stained, mouldy and discoloured and cannot be resold as a finished product unless they are discounted. It is also unlikely that the bags could be dried and repaired given the degree of damage that has occurred to them.

In the circumstances, the Cheap Clothing Company may exercise the right to reject the goods because Goochie has not supplied goods of a merchantable quality. Since

196

this duty is a implied condition to the contrary, the Cheap Clothing Company is also entitled to sue for recovery of the price and for damages.

If the Cheap Clothing Company wish to reject the goods, they should be advised that they must reject all the goods. They are not entitled to accept part of the consignment and to reject other parts. Acceptance of part of the goods will deprive the Cheap Clothing Company of its right of rejection.

Also, the Cheap Clothing Company should be advised that they have an duty to mitigate their losses. Any loss that could be reasonably avoided cannot be claimed in damages. The standard of this duty is to act reasonably. Thus, the Cheap Clothing Company is required to take all reasonable steps to minimise losses.

In this particular case, the goods cannot be sold as handbags because the damage that occurred to them rendered them unfit for this purpose. However, if a reasonable alternative purpose can be found for the consignment, this course of action must be followed if it will mitigate loss.

Question 3

Boris agreed to sell Christie 30,000 rare bird's eggs cif Moscow (Russia) at 70p per egg. The parties agreed that the goods should be insured on Institute Cargo Clause A terms. Separate insurance terms were arranged for three shipments, one each in April, May and June.

The underwriters put their initials on the slip presented by Boris' broker and Boris tendered to insurance certificate for the three consignments together with the shipping documents to Christie who in return paid against them.

The goods have now been inspected and the following defects discovered:

a) The eggs in the first consignment have been spoiled because they were packed into a container with defective refrigeration equipment when they were being transported to the port. Christie's employees were aware of the damage to the goods several days before the goods actually reached Christie's warehouse.

b) The second consignment was lost overboard during a storm. Christie believes that this was caused by the incompetence of the crew which failed to adequately secure the cargo on deck. It subsequently transpires that Boris' loading broker was aware that the carrier had hired a totally inexperienced crew for the voyage.

c) The final consignment was stolen by Free Bird, an animal rights protection group, whilst the goods were awaiting collection at the port of discharge. The organisation will only return the goods on payment of a £5,000 ransom and if a full page advert is placed in Birdwatcher's Weekly.

The underwriters are refusing to pay Christie's claim arguing, inter alia, that the premium was never paid.

What is your advice to the underwriters?

Question prepared by the Editor
April 1994

General comment

The question should be approached by separating the three issues raised for each consignment. Thereafter the question becomes quite simple.

Skeleton solution

Consignment 1: Insufficiency of packaging.

Consignment 2: Negligence of the crew.

Consignment 3: Acts of a terrorist organisation.

Suggested solution

By s52 of the Marine Insurance Act 1906, the issue of the policy and the payment of the premium are concurrent conditions. However where an insurance broker is used as in the instant case, he is directly liable to the insurer for the payment of the premium. By a fiction therefore if a broker is used and a policy is issued, then as between the underwriter and the assured, the premium is deemed paid, even where the policy does not contain an acknowledgment that the premium has been paid.

In the instant case the underwriter cannot defend the claim by arguing that the premium has not been paid. That is an issue between the underwriter and the broker.

The underwriters could defend the claim as a whole on the basis that Christie only has an insurance certificate which is not admissible in court to prove the existence of the contract of insurance: Marine Insurance Act 1906 s2.

Assuming that the argument above is circumvented by Christie, the underwriter must seek to avoid the various losses.

a) The loss seems to have been caused by the insufficiency of the container to carry the eggs. The exception in clause 4.3 of the policy does not apply in the present case. The packing in the container occurred after the attachment of the insurance.

   The type of loss in question however is not clear. Something has been delivered, although it is no doubt not fit for human consumption. It seems on this basis that the loss is a constructive total loss.

   The delay between the date when the insurance terminated (when the goods reached the final warehouse at Christie's premises) and the discovery that the eggs were not fit and the cause thereof has several connotations.

   First it might be that the eggs only went off during the period of delay after the insurance had ceased. If so, the underwriter could escape liability. This of course would be difficult for the underwriter to prove.

   Second, it is assumed that Christie has accepted the eggs in the underlying contract of sale. If his acceptance is due to the delay and he lost the right to reject in ss34 and 35 of the SGA, he might be in breach of the duty of the assured clause 16. This does not prevent the underwriter from paying out under the policy if there is no other exclusion, but it enables the underwriter to claim damages from the assured for any damages or loss resulting from the assured's breach of his duty. This could cover the whole of the insured value of the goods in this case, since if the duty had been fulfilled, there would have been no claim on the policy.

It would seem that if there still is a product, there is not an actual total loss, but a constructive total loss. There does not seem to be scope for arguing that there is only a partial loss, as the eggs would commercially be a different thing. Constructive total loss requires Christie to serve a notice of abandonment on the underwriter. There is no proof that he has done so. Failure would mean that the loss is treated as being partial only. It does not seem that this would have much effect in the present case, as there is no risk of partial loss being superseded by a total loss which is not covered.

b) Loss in heavy weather is a risk covered by the A Clauses: clause 1. Obviously there is an actual total loss, and in this case, it seems that Christie has fulfilled the duty of the assured clause.

There is no exception in the A clause for the deliberate acts of third parties.

It seems however that the policy may be avoided in respect of this consignment on the basis of non-disclosure.

It is arguable however whether the employment of the inept crew is a material fact. If the fact in question does not constitute the basis for an exception of liability it cannot be a material factor for the underwriter. The negligence of the crew is not an exception within the A clause.

Nevertheless, the underwriter is entitled to argue that there is an exception if the assured or his agent is privy to the unseaworthiness of the vessel. The provision of an inadequate crew would render the ship unseaworthy. It seems that the fact would in the instant case be material. It has not been disclosed.

The knowledge of an agent is imputed to his principal when the agent is of a type expected to or responsible for informing the principal of the matter in question. It would seem that a loading broker would be in such a position, provided that he is an agent and not in fact an independent contractor. If the loading broker is similar to an insurance broker, he would be an agent.

The effect of non-disclosure of a material fact is to give the underwriter the option either to affirm or to avoid the contract. Once the underwriter has full knowledge of the non-disclosure and its nature, he then has a reasonable time in which to make his election. What is a reasonable time is a question of fact: see *Liberian Insurance Agency* v *Moss* (1977).

The underwriter should therefore seek more information about the circumstances. If there has been material non-disclosure the underwriter would be advised to avoid the policy. There would be no liability to pay out and no need to reimburse the assured for the value of the premium since this has not been paid.

c) Since Clause A is an all-risk policy it would be enough for the assured to show that the loss was proximately caused by some event covered by that general expression.

199

However there is an exclusion for loss damage or expense caused by any terrorist or any person acting from a political motive in clause 7.3. It is of course arguable whether Free Bird is a politically motivated body or whether its concerns are for the welfare of animals only. The application of the exclusion is therefore in doubt.

The loss in question cannot be classed as a commercial total loss. The cost of the recovery of the eggs is minimal compared with their commercial value. There is no scope for Christie to argue that there is no hope of ever retrieving the eggs. It is clearly within his power.

The loss therefore is partial, and the most which the underwriters would have to pay would be the cost to Christie of the £5000 or that of the advertisement.

Any loss damage or expense caused to Christie by the delay would not be covered by the policy by reason of exclusion clause 4.5.

Question 4

Arthur enters into two separate contracts. The first is with Hans for the sale of 1,000 tonnes of corned beef from Argentina cif Hamburg at a price of $100 per tonne. The second is with Serge for 1,000 tonnes of wool cfr Leningrad at a price of $50 per tonne. Both consignments are loaded aboard the same vessel, a ship which has recently had her certificate of seaworthiness withdrawn.

The corned beef is loaded on the deck, the usual manner of carrying such goods. Arthur arranges unvalued insurance for these goods on Institute Cargo Clause B terms but does not notify the underwriters that the cargo will be carried in this manner.

Serge arranges insurance for the consignment of wool, also unvalued, on Institute Cargo Clause C terms. In addition, Deutsche Bank which holds shares in Serge's company and which has made loans to the company also takes out insurance against the non-arrival of the goods.

The ship runs into a storm and a number of on-deck containers are lost. Subsequently the vessel suffers from engine failure due to defective fuel pumps. These pumps were defective when the vessel left Buenos Aires. The vessel is rendered powerless and drifts towards rocks. The ship's master jettisons the remaining on-deck containers in the belief, in fact erroneously held, that the vessel is in danger of running aground.

After the cargo has been jettisoned, the engines pick up and the vessel proceeds to Hamburg to take on bunkers. The ship then collides on the way from Hamburg to Leningrad and sinks.

Serge is advised that the wool, which has been stored in water-tight containers, is recoverable and will probably be in good condition. The cost of the recovery is estimated at around $600,000.

Advise Hans, Serge and the Deutsche Bank of their rights in a claim against the underwriters.

Question prepared by the Editor
April 1994

General comment

This is a factually complicated question which requires that the separate issues are isolated to allow the application of the terms of Cargo Clauses Band C.

Skeleton solution

Hans

Necessary to consider any rights against carrier – insurance company will be subrogated.

Voyage policy – if so implied warranties ss39–41 – breach will discharge clause 5.2 – but waiver by insurer, clause 5.2.

Non disclosure by Arthur – s18 – withdrawal of class, deck stowage, also operates against assignee – s51.

Matter of common knowledge – s18(3).

Actual total loss – cause of loss – peril of sea, washing overboard, general average.

Serge

Same problems about breach of s39/clause 5.2.

Constructive total loss? – value exceed by recovery costs – s61.

Is loss caused by peril insured against and whilst insurance is operative – insurance in force only for normal course of transit – clause 8.1.

Deutsche Bank

No insurance interest in cargo – unless has been pledge of documents or charge over goods – thus contingent interest.

Otherwise shares in company insufficient: *McAura* v *Northern Assurance.*

Suggested solution

Hans

It is the obligation of Arthur to take out insurance covering the goods for their contractual journey on terms usual in the trade. For this purpose it can be assumed that the unvalued and medium range cover provided by Institute Cargo Clauses B is adequate as a matter of trade practice.

Hans must be able to claim on any such policy by virtue of its assignment to her. This assignment must take place before Arhtur has parted with his interest in the goods at the time of tender of cif documents against payment of the cash price.

It would appear that two problems arise in the above respects.

First, there has been an inadequate cif tender. Ordinarily an invoice, bill of lading and insurance policy are required: *Karlberg* v *Blythe* (1916). Hans has received only a bill and a certificate of insurance. Such a tender may of course have been specifically agreed between the parties. This is especially so since the price is being paid in US

Dollars. If the insurance was taken out in the United States where certificates are frequently used instead of policies and offer all the advantages of a policy, then it may well be that Hans is in an equally good position despite the fact that he holds a certificate which technically he could have rejected. We shall assume this is not so. The cif tender was therefore defective. Hans ought to have rejected the incomplete documentation: *Kwei Tek Chao* v *British Traders and Shippers* (1954). It would have been obvious from the face of the document that she was given a certificate and not a policy, therefore she has lost the right to reject the insurance certificate at this stage: *Panchaud Frères* v *Etablissements General Grain Co* (1970).

Second, Hans now has an insurance document on which he is unable to claim. He might be able to persuade Arthur to assign to him the right to be indemnified under the policy. If he succeeds in this he will of course be subject to all those defences which the insurance company could have raised against Arthur the assignor himself.

Before considering whether there are any possible defences which could be raised by the insurer, it is necessary to consider whether Hans is in a position to reject the goods themselves so that he has no need to make any claim on the policy. This, of course, is a right of rejection which is quite distinct from the right to reject documents: *Kwei Tek Chao* v *British Traders & Shippers Limited* (1954).

It would appear that, of the containers carrying the beef, two are consciously jettisoned by the master and lost overboard.

As for the lost containers, even though they may have been lost before Hans paid against documents, and thereby obtained property, he would have had risk from the time of shipment, and therefore had to pay against correct documents even if the goods were already lost, tender of the documents being constructive tender of the goods: *Karlberg* v *Blythe* (1916). Since the bill of lading was probably clean then it would seem that the remedy in respect of the lost containers is against the carrier if there cannot be a claim on the insurance. If a claim on the insurance can be successfully maintained then the insurance company will be subrogated to this right of claim against the carrier: s79 Marine Insurance Act 1906.

The fact of stowage on deck may in itself be a breach of contract by Arthur. Section 32(2) of the Sale of Goods Act 1979 states that a seller must make such a contract with the carrier as may be reasonable regarding the nature of the goods and if they are damaged in transit then the buyer may decline to treat the delivery to the seller as delivery to himself, or hold the seller liable in damages. Since the beef is containerised and it is usual to carry containers on deck, the likely success of this argument seems slim. In any event, even if deck stowage were not permitted, the fact of deck stowage would no doubt have been noted on the bill which has been accepted and paid against by Hans, without reservation.

There are several possible defences to payment which could be raised by the underwriters:

a) If this is a voyage policy, the vessel must be seaworthy: ss39–41 Marine Insurance Act 1906. The warranty of seaworthiness is promissory: s33. If not complied with the insurer will be discharged: s33(3). He is, however, obliged to give a mandatory waiver under clause 5.2 ICC 'B', if the assured and his servants were not privy to the unseaworthiness. Privity would be either positive knowledge or wilful refusal to accept facts by the shipowners themselves: *The Eurymedon* (1938). It is submitted it would also be sufficient for Arthur to have such knowledge prior to shipment/sailing; as to which more information is needed. It would therefore be necessary to know how recently the vessel has had her class withdrawn; the implication of that withdrawal – which may not in fact affect her seaworthiness; Arthur's state of knowledge. In any event the vessel may be unseaworthy because of her defective fuel pumps.

b) If withdrawal of class does amount to unseaworthiness, Arthur will not be in breach of s18 Marine Insurance Act 1906 in failing to disclose it since s18(3)(d) states that it is not necessary for there to be disclosure of facts which are the subject of express warranties. If, however, this is not a voyage policy and the above warranties do not apply: s39(5), then Arthur will be in breach of s18 in failing to disclose the withdrawal of class if he knew or ought to have known of it in the ordinary course of business. The insurer will be able to avoid the contract if he can show the materiality of such non disclosure: s18(2). This would be quite easy. Clearly, no prudent insurer would give cover for goods which he knew were to be carried on a ship not fit to carry them: *Container Transport International* v *Oceanus Mutual Underwriting* (1984).

c) There may also be a non disclosure under s18 regarding deck stowage. That would, however, only be so if Arthur knew of deck stowage before or at the time of conclusion of the contract of insurance: s21. However, even beyond that point he might be lacking in good faith in failing to communicate the fact: s17.

Assuming that none of the above could be utilised by the insurer to discharge him or enable him to avoid the policy, has the loss been caused by a peril insured against? ICC 'B' covers 'washing overboard' only where it occurs during loading to or unloading from the vessel. Therefore, the loss of the containers would appear to be irrecoverable.

It may be that the carrier himself was at fault as the containers were not adequately lashed, but this will be a question of fact and trade practice: *The Tilia Gorthorn* (1985).

There is no suggestion of this loss being a general average sacrifice for the protection of other cargo since it was not consciously and voluntarily made.

There is no doubt that the carrier is in breach of his common law obligation to provide a seaworthy ship. However it would not appear that the unseaworthiness was the proximate cause of this loss of the beef. Rather it is more likely to be inadequate stowage.

In conclusion it is unlikely that the loss of the containers would be covered by the insurance and Hans would be obliged to pursue a remedy against the carrier direct under the contract contained in his bill of lading.

Whilst the vessel is drifting the master jettisons the remaining containers. The mere fact that there is deviation at the time of loss would not affect the right to claim on the policy (clause 8.3). Grounding is a peril insured against under clause 112 of ICC 'B'. A general average act to avoid loss by such a peril would be reasonably made: clause 2. However, s66(2) of the 1906 Act would require a general average sacrifice to be both voluntarily and reasonably incurred in order to justify a rateable contribution from all other parties whose goods were saved in consequence: s66(6). Since this act is not reasonable, it is not general average, nor apparently does it actually result in a saving of the goods anyway: *Ralli* v *Troop* (1894).

Serge

Serge is able to insure goods which he is buying on cfr terms even though at the time he is not the owners of such goods. He has an insurable interest in the wool since he has risk on shipment and a binding contract to become the owners: *Inglis* v *Stock* (1885).

The same defences regarding unseaworthiness and non disclosure of that fact apply in relation to any claim by Serge.

There would appear to have been a deviation in taking on bunkers at Rotterdam. This does not affect the operation of the insurance which continues during any deviation: clause 8.3. There has, however, also been a delay. Whilst the insurance remains in force during the delay, it must be beyond the control of the assured: clause 8.3, and the insurer will not be liable for any loss occasioned by the delay: clause 4.5. These provisions would not appear to have any implications for Serge since at the time of the loss in question the vessel has returned to the normal course of transit. There would appear to be a loss by collision, which is covered by ICC 'C'. It does not matter that the collision is caused by the negligence of the master or crew: s55 Marine Insurance Act 1906, providing that it is not the result of wilful misconduct by the Assured or his alter ego: clause 4.1, or the wrongful act of any person or persons: clause 4.2.

There would appear to be a constructive total loss of the wool since the cost of recovering the goods would appear to exceed their value on arrival. Serge must therefore give notice of abandonment if he wishes to claim for the loss as though it were an actual total loss: s62. In addition, he must act to preserve any rights against the carrier responsible for the damage: clause 16.2, so that these may be pursued by the insurer.

Deutsche Bank

Deutsche Bank cannot insure against the non arrival of the wool. It has no insurable interest. The fact that it owns shares in Serge's company or is a creditor of Serge's company is not sufficient unless Deutsche Bank have some kind of lien or security over the timber. It stands in no legal or equitable relation thereto and has no right to be indemnified. Nor would it be owed a duty of care in tort by the carrier, for the same reason.

11 MARINE INSURANCE III – LOSS, INDEMNITY AND DURATION OF THE POLICY

11.1   Introduction

In this final chapter on the subject of marine insurance, the types of loss will be considered together with the methods for calculating the measure of indemnity which an insurer must pay to an insured if the subject matter insured is lost or damaged. In addition, the right of an insurer to acquire the rights and claims of an assured after indemnification will also be considered.

Then the important subject of general average loss will be reviewed before proceeding to discuss, as a final matter, the duration and scope of marine insurance policies.

11.2   Key points

a) *Categories of loss*

A marine insurance policy, whether on Cargo Clause A, B or C terms, provides an assured with indemnity for three kinds of damage – total loss, partial loss and damage to the insured goods. Such a policy will also indemnify for loss which has occurred as a consequence of a general average act.

b) *Total loss*

In the absence of express stipulations in the policy to the contrary, insurance against total loss will cover actual total loss as well as constructive total loss.

  i) Actual total loss

  Actual total loss can be subdivided into three categories:

  • Destruction of the subject matter insured.

205

- Damage to the subject matter to such an extent that it ceases to be an article of the kind insured. The MIA 1906 requires that the goods must no longer be in specie when they arrive for this condition to be fulfilled; they must have lost their essential form: see, for example, *Asfar & Co* v *Blundell* [1896] 1 QB 123.

- Irretrievable deprivation of the subject matter insured. For this requirement to be satisfied there must be no means available to the assured to restore the goods.

One additional and special category of actual loss is to be found in s58 of the MIA 1906 which provides:

'Where the ship concerned in the adventure is missing and after the lapse of a reasonable time no news of her has been received, an actual total loss may be presumed.'

In the case of an actual total loss no notice of abandonment need be given to the underwriter. The assured needs only to claim on the policy in the event of actual total loss.

ii) Constructive total loss

Section 60 of the MIA 1906 governs constructive total loss which occurs where the goods, although not totally lost or destroyed, are effectively lost because the expense incurred in recovering, repairing or forwarding them would be prohibitive. The statutory definition contained in s60(1) reads as follows:

'[T]here is constructive total loss where the subject matter insured is reasonably abandoned on account of its actual total loss appearing to be unavoidable, or because it could not be preserved from actual total loss without an expenditure which would exceed its value when the expenditure had been incurred.'

Examples of constructive total loss include:

- Where an assured is deprived of the possession of his ship or goods by a peril insured against and, either it is unlikely that he can recover the ship or the goods or the cost of recovering the ship or goods would exceed their value when recovered.

- In the case of damage to a ship, where it is so damaged by a peril that the cost of repairing the damage would exceed its value once repairs had been effected.

- In the case of damage to goods, where the cost of repairing the damage and forwarding the goods to their destination would exceed their value on arrival.

Where an assured has suffered a constructive total loss, there is an option of two alternative bases of claim. He or she can either (1) abandon the subject matter to the insurer and treat the loss as though it was an actual total loss; or (2) treat the loss as a partial loss and claim the appropriate measure of indemnity for partial loss: s61 MIA 1906.

If the goods are abandoned, the insurer takes over the assured's interest in the subject matter and all incidental proprietary rights. The insurer may then attempt to mitigate the loss by attempting to recover the subject matter or by selling the interest to someone else who can attempt recovery.

iii) Notice of abandonment

The requirement of a valid abandonment is a prerequisite to a claim for constructive total loss. Abandonment is intimated to an insurer by means of a notice of abandonment which must be given with reasonable diligence after receipt of reliable information about the loss: s62(3).

Once the notice of abandonment has been accepted by the insurer, he is entitled to take over the interest of the assured in whatever way he considers appropriate.

c) *Partial loss*

Any loss other than total loss is a partial loss: s56(1) MIA 1906. According to s56(5) of the Act:

'Where goods reach their destination in specie, but by reason of obliteration of marks or otherwise, they are incapable of identification, the loss, if any, is partial, and not total.'

Partial loss is a residual category of loss. It encompasses all losses which cannot be brought within the definition of actual total loss or constructive total loss.

d) *Conversion from partial loss to total loss*

In the event that an assured suffers a partial loss which circumstances later convert into an actual total loss, in order to make a valid claim, the conversion from one type of loss to the other must come about as a result of an unbroken sequence of events: *Fooks* v *Smith* (1924) 30 Com Cas 143.

This principle applies whether or not the actual total loss occurred before or after the expiry of the policy provided that the initial cause of the loss arose during the term of the policy.

e) *Damage to the goods insured*

Where the goods are neither totally lost or partially lost, but merely adversely affected in some way or another, then the injury sustained by the goods is considered to be damage. A claim for compensation for the damage sustained to the goods is the appropriate procedure for an assured to follow.

f) *Measure of indemnity*

The extent to which an assured is entitled to be indemnified in respect of his or her loss is referred to as the 'measure of indemnity'. The means of calculating the measure of indemnity for which the insurer is liable varies according to whether the loss constitutes total loss, partial loss or mere damage to the goods.

i) Total loss

The measure of indemnity where the loss is total varies according to whether the policy is valued or unvalued.

The sum which an assured can recover under a valued policy, where there is total loss, is the value fixed on the policy: s68(1). On the other hand, where the policy is unvalued, the measure of indemnity is the insurable value of the subject matter insured: s68(2).

ii) Partial loss

Where there is a partial loss of goods, merchandise or other movables, the measure of indemnity is determined as follows:

- In a valued policy, it is that proportion of the sum fixed under the policy which the part of the interest lost bears to the insurable value of the goods as a whole.

- In an unvalued policy, the measure of indemnity is calculated in accordance with s16(3) which provides that 'in insurance on goods or merchandise, the insurable value is the part lost of the property insured, plus the expenses of and incidental to shipping and the charges of insurance on the whole'.

iii) Damaged goods

Where the goods are neither totally lost or partially lost but only damaged, the measure of indemnity which the assured can recover is computed in accordance with s71 of the MIA 1906.

Once again the statute distinguishes between a valued and an unvalued policy but the formula for calculating the measure of indemnity is substantially the same. Section 71(3) states:

'Where the whole or any part of the merchandise has been damaged at its destination then the measure of indemnity is such proportion of the sum fixed by the policy in the case of a valued policy, or the insurable value in the case of an unvalued policy, as the difference between the gross sound and damaged values at the price of arrival bears to the gross sound value.'

Gross value means 'the wholesale price, if there be no such price the estimated value, with, in either case, freight, landing charges and duty paid beforehand': s71(4).

g) *General average loss*

The MIA 1906 defines general average loss as 'a loss caused by or directly consequential on a general average act including general average expenditure as well as general average sacrifice': s66(1). A general average act is one where 'any extraordinary sacrifice is made or expenditure is voluntarily and reasonably incurred': s66(2).

A general average act occurs when, in circumstances of imminent danger, the master of the vessel makes a deliberate sacrifice of goods in order to preserve the overall safety of the vessel and the act is in the best interests of the ship and crew, its cargo and freight. It remains an open question whether or not the act must actually result in the saving of the goods: *Pirie* v *Middle Dock* (1881) 44 LT 426.

Where a cargo-owner finds that he has suffered a general average loss, for example, by his goods being jettisoned, he or she may seek a general average contribution from other cargo-owners whose goods were saved by the act in question.

A party who suffers a general average loss may, if he so chooses, opt to recover the loss from his insurer. Institute Cargo Clauses A, B and C provide an assured with protection for a general average loss. However, an assured may not recover for any general average loss which was not incurred for the purpose of avoiding a peril insured against: s66(6).

Where a cargo-owner elects to claim against an insurer, the insurer is subrogated the rights of the assured against the other parties and may recover the contributions owed by them.

h) *Subrogation*

Subrogation has been defined concisely in the following terms:

'The substitution of one person or thing for another, so that the same rights and duties which attached to the original person or thing attach to the substituted one. If one person is subrogated to another, he is said to "stand in the other's shoes", ie an insurer is subrogated to the rights of the insured on paying his claim': *Osborn's Concise Law Dictionary.*

An insurer's right of subrogation in the case of a total loss is to be found in s79(1) of the MIA:

'Where the insurer pays for a total loss either of the whole, or in the case of goods of any apportionable part, of the subject matter insured, he thereupon becomes entitled to take over the interest of the assured in whatever may remain of the subject matter so paid for and he is thereby subrogated to all the rights and remedies of the assured in and in respect of that subject matter as from the time of the casualty causing the loss.'

An insurer's right of subrogation is more limited in circumstances where there is only a partial loss. Section 79(2) sets out the right of subrogation in such circumstances as follows:

'Where an insurer pays for a partial loss, he acquires no title to the subject matter insured or such part of it as may remain, but he is thereupon subrogated to all rights and remedies of the assured in and in respect of the subject matter insured as from the time of the casualty causing the loss, in so far as the assured has been indemnified according to this Act, by payment for the loss.'

The fundamental difference between the right of subrogation in cases of total loss as opposed to partial loss is that, in the former case, in addition to the right of subrogation the insurer actually takes over the interest of the assured in the remains of the subject matter, whereas in the latter case he merely has the right to pursue claims against third parties without obtaining a co-existing interest in the goods.

In the event that an insurer recovers more than the measure of the indemnity paid to an assured, whether or not the insurer is required to pay the additional amount to the assured depends on whether the loss is total or partial.

If the loss is total, under s79(1) the right of subrogation is not expressed to be limited to the extent of the indemnity already paid out by the insurer. However, it is not yet settled law whether or not the insurer is obliged to account to the insured for sums successfully recovered in excess of the sums paid out as indemnity. Conflicting dicta exist on this point: compare *Glen Line* v *Attorney-General* (1930) 36 Com Case 1 and *North of England Steamship* v *Armstrong* (1879) LR 5 QB 244.

On the other hand, if the loss is partial, s79(2) clearly provides that the right of subrogation is limited to the amount payable to the assured and, if a greater sum is recovered, the insurer must remit the excess amount to the assured.

i) *Duration of the policy*

In a voyage policy, risk attaches while the goods are being transferred from one port to another, whereas in a time policy risk attaches for a specified period of time. Before the A, B and C Clauses were introduced, in a voyage policy if the insurer wished the policy to extend to the transportation of the goods from the warehouse to the vessel, the cover had to be expressly extended to cater for this transportation.

Now Clause 8.1 of the policies, which deals with the duration of the cover, reads as follows:

'Insurance attaches from the time the goods leave the warehouse or place of storage at the place named herein for the commencement of the transit, continues during the ordinary course of transit and terminates either:

1) on delivery to the consignee's or other final warehouse or place of storage at the destination named herein;

2) on delivery to any other warehouse or place of storage whether prior to or at the destination named herein, which the assured elects to use either:

   a) for storage other than in the ordinary course of transit;

   b) for allocation or distribution; or

3) on the expiry of 60 days after completion of discharge overside of the goods hereby insured from the overseas vessel at the final port of discharge.

whichever shall first occur.'

This clause is known as the 'transit clause' and is common to each of the ICC A, B and C policies. Therefore, now, even if the assured has taken out a voyage policy, risk will attach from the time of departure from the inland warehouse unless the risk is expressly stated to attach at some later stage: see *Silver Dolphin Products* v *Parcels & General Assurance* [1984] 2 Lloyd's Rep 404.

11.3   Recent cases and statutes

Apostolos Konstantine Ventouris v *Trevor Rex Mountain, The Italia Express (No 2)* [1992] 2 Lloyd's Rep 281: the agreed value clause in a marine insurance policy is equivalent to a liquidated damages provision and a plaintiff's claim in the event of a total loss of the subject matter insured cannot include a claim for damages even if the insurer does not promptly pay out under the policy.

11.4   Relevant materials

J K Goodacre, *Marine Insurance Claims* (second edition, 1981), pp168–786.

M E V Denny, *Freight Insurance* (1980).

E R H Ivamy, *Marine Insurance* (third edition, 1979), pp371–492.

11.5   Analysis of questions

In the questions that follow, many of the legal issues raised are relatively straightforward and should not present much difficulty. One question from each of the major themes of this chapter is included namely, total loss, partial loss, quantification of loss and the duration of the liability of underwriters.

11.6   Questions

Question 1

The African Queen was detained in a port in the Persian Gulf from 1980 until 1988 during the war between Iran and Iraq. During this period, her crew stayed aboard the vessel and the vessel was able to leave port. The decision of the shipmaster to stay in port came about because of the possibility of aircraft attack or striking a mine during the voyage should the vessel run the Straits of Hormoz. Throughout this period of detention, the Iraqi government also issued edicts prohibiting the passage of merchant ships in its internal waters, part of which extend out to the median point of the Straits.

The vessel itself had been chartered at the time of her detention and the charterparty specified that hire was to remain payable until re-delivery of the vessel was made. The charterparty also contained a provision which stated that the hire would end in the event of the actual loss, or constructive total loss, of the vessel.

At the end of the conflict in 1988, it was discovered that the vessel had been corroded to such a degree that she was only good for scrap. At the same time, the company which had chartered the vessel was liquidated.

John, the owner of *The African Queen*, is a Greek national domiciled in Athens. He had insured *The African Queen* with the Manana Insurance Company, an Argentinean insurance company with its main office in Buenos Aires. The insurance contract, which was governed by English law, extended the cover for the vessel to loss or damage caused by perils or war or hostilities, but not for damage caused by restraint of princes.

John claims that the vessel is now a constructive total loss but the insurance company refused to pay under the policy. Can John sue the insurance company in England and, if so, what are his prospects of success?

Question prepared by the Editor
April 1994

General comment

A question involving constructive total loss. The student must be familiar with the legal requirements for establishing constructive total loss together with related questions of insurance law. However, on the whole the question is relatively straightforward and has potential for allowing the student to score well.

Skeleton solution

Concept of constructive loss: (a) the replacement cost of the vessel; (b) proximate injury caused by the peril.

Loss must be attributed to actual attack.

Restraint of princes.

The need for a notice of abandonment.

Jurisdiction of the courts over the matter.

Suggested solution

Constructive total loss occurs when an assured is deprived of the subject-matter on account of a peril which has been assured against and, either it is unlikely that he can recover the goods or alternatively that the cost of recovering the vessel would exceed its value when recovered; see s60(2) Marine Insurance Act 1906. Therefore, in order to prove constructive total loss, John would have to establish: (a) that the costs of saving the vessel are more that its value; and (b) that the loss was caused by a peril covered by the insurance policy.

It is in John's interests to establish that the vessel was a total loss immediately following its detention, and not as a result of it having been scrapped. The time charterers went bankrupt in 1988 and therefore John would be unable to pursue a claim for unpaid hire. Had the charterers remained solvent, then John might have been able to claim hire prior to the scrapping of the vessel.

The vessel in question was detained for eight years due to the hostilities between Iran and Iraq but even after the end of hostilities, the vessel was unable to sail due to its condition. Thereafter it was scrapped. There is support for the proposition that the vessel has been a constructive loss since its detention in 1980 because such loss has, in the past, been permitted by the English courts in the event of a voyage being frustrated; see *British and Foreign Marine Insurance Co* v *Samuel Sanday & Co* (1921). Total loss may be effected not only by the destruction of the vessel, but also by the total permanent incapacity of the ship to perform the voyage.

In addition, the loss must be caused by a peril covered by the policy. *The African Queen* was at all relevant times insured against loss or damage caused by perils of war or hostilities, but not against loss or damage caused by restraint of princes. John would therefore have to establish that the facts which occurred between 1980 and 1988 constituted perils of war. Although during this period the vessel was capable of sailing with prudent navigation and a small crew, the risk of hostile air attack was considered too substantial to allow her to venture out of port.

It may be difficult, however, to establish that the detention of the vessel was the immediate cause of its loss. Warlike or hostile operations were not conducted against the vessel. The events which contributed to its eventual scrapping arose from the failure to maintain the vessel. Where the insured vessel is damaged by the direct action of hostile forces, or by attempts to avoid that action, the causal connection is relatively clear. But in the present case, it is difficult for John to demonstrate that the detention of the vessel arose through the hostilities between Iran and Iraq because the decision to detain *The African Queen* was attributable to a fear of an attack rather than an actual attack.

During this period, the Iraqi government prohibited the movement of merchant shipping on Iraqi waterways. If the vessel had been insured against restraint of princes, it is likely that the Manana Insurance Company would be liable to pay out on the policy because there would be a direct link between the loss of the vessel and an insured peril, namely the prohibition of movement by the Iraqi government.

Such restraint need not necessarily involve the use of actual physical force. Any authoritative prohibition on the part of a governing power is sufficient. Nor need the order be directed against any particular vessel or country. In such circumstances, John could claim that the order in itself effectively caused the constructive loss of the vessel.

In order to show that the loss was proximately caused by the restraint of princes, John must show that on a balance of probabilities, the loss was due to the peril. Proximate cause was discussed in *Canada Rice Mills* v *Union Marine and General Insurance* (1941), where the House of Lords stated that the choice of the real or effective cause was made by applying common sense standards.

In his attempts to establish constructive total loss, John also faces the hurdle of his failure to notify the Manana Insurance Company of his intention to abandon the vessel. When an assured decides to abandon the vessel, he or she must normally give notice of this abandonment to the insurer with reasonable diligence; see Marine

Insurance Act 1906 s62. Notice of abandonment may be given in writing or by word of mouth, but must be given in terms which indicate the clear intention of the assured to abandon his insured interest in the subject matter. The purpose of the notice is to provide the insurer with an opportunity to act to save the assured subjects.

It is not possible for John to give notice of abandonment retrospectively in order to claim from the period at which the detention commenced because constructive total loss only begins at the time that the notice of abandonment is given.

If John was able to establish total constructive loss, it is unlikely that the English courts would reject the action on the ground that John is a Greek national and the Manana Insurance Company an Argentinian insurance company which has its main office in Buenos Aires. The contract of insurance was made subject to English law which raises a presumption that the English courts have jurisdiction over the matter. Parties are generally free to choose whichever law they wish to govern the contract providing their choice is bona fide and not illegal or contrary to public policy: see *Regazzoni* v *Sethia* (1958).

However, assuming that John is successful in his action, it will clearly be difficult to enforce decree since it is unlikely that the Manana Insurance Company has assets within the jurisdiction of the English courts.

Question 2

Adrian sells Lillian 5,000 tonnes of potatoes at £10 per tonne fob a UK port October-December 1993. Adrian agrees to arrange shipping space on Lillian's behalf for carriage of the goods to Oslo and that he will advance freight of £2 per tonne on Lillian's account.

Adrian also sells 5,000 tonnes of turnips to Olaf cif Stockholm. The insurance contract is made through Adrian's broker who is informed that the goods will be shipped aboard the same vessel carrying the potatoes to Lillian. The broker is aware that turnips, when stored next to potatoes, deteriorate due to the absorption of moisture which emanates from stored potatoes. Adrian, who is unaware of this fact, arranges insurance on Institute Cargo Clause A terms at a cost of £0.50 per tonne.

Before the turnips are shipped on board the vessel, 50 tonnes are stolen from the consignment. A further 200 tonnes are badly bruised while being stowed. The 200 tonnes which are bruised are sold when the vessel arrived at Stockholm for animal feed at a total price of £750. The remainder of the consignment deteriorates as a result of being stored next to the potatoes.

During the voyage, Lillian is told that 2,500 tonnes of potatoes have been shipped and arranges voyage insurance on Institute Cargo Clause C terms for this consignment believing that the remainder of the consignment is to be sent later.

There is a fire aboard the vessel and 2,500 tonnes of the potatoes are damaged. These are sold at another port of call for a total of £5,000. Had transhipment been available at this port to carry the goods to Stockholm, this part of the consignment would have fetched £10,000. The remaining 2,500 tonnes of potatoes do arrive safely but are worth only £8 per tonne because, as a smaller consignment, they are less marketable.

Both Lillian and Olaf intimate claims to the underwriters in respect of their losses. Advise the underwriters on the prospects of resisting the claims and limiting their liability.

Question prepared by the Editor
April 1994

General comment

This question provides a contrast between the operation of the Institute of Cargo Clauses A and C. However, there are a number of additional complications to add spice to the answer.

Skeleton solution

Adrian – insurable interest, cause of the injury is an insured peril, duty to minimise loss.

Olaf – failure to disclose by the broker, insured peril of theft, damage by stevedore and rain also insured perils.

Suggested solution

Adrian

Adrian's contract with Lillian on fob terms contains the 'extra' provision that Adrian will act as shipper - paying £2 in advance freight on Lillian's account – (an insurable interest). Adrian must inform Lillian of the shipment in sufficient time for her to effect insurance of the goods during transit, otherwise, the risk will remain with the shipper, Adrian: s32(3) Sale of Goods Act.

It is a fundamental requirement of any insurance that the assured must have an insurable interest at the time of the loss, s6 Marine Insurance Act; clause 11.11.1, of the Institute Cargo Clauses (A, B and C). The assured may recover for a loss incurred before the conclusion of the contract, unless the assured was aware of the loss: clause 11.11.2 ICCs.

The damage to the 2,500 tonnes was caused by fire, a peril insured against: clause 1.1.1 policy C. The proximate cause of the damage would have to be shown to be the fire in order for the assured to recover. Lillian would wish to claim on her policy. We are not told if the policy is valued or unvalued.

If valued, the amount she would wish to claim would be the agreed value of the goods – or in the case of partial loss, she would wish to claim for the portion that the loss bears to the value as a whole: s71 Marine Insurance Act 1906.

If the policy is unvalued s16 defines the insurable value – prime cost of goods plus shipping and insurance expenses. The value of the lost part is set out in s16(3) – insurable value of part loss plus the expenses of shipping and insurance on the whole. The loss will be calculated on the ratio that the loss bears to the whole cargo.

Section 78 of the MIA and clause 16 of the 'C' policy states that the assured is under a duty to minimise the loss, so Lillian should have forwarded the goods to Oslo. The policies incorporate a forwarding charges (clause 12) which means that the underwriters will be liable for any forwarding charges where the insured voyage stops at a port short of its destination, because of a peril insured against.

The question arises as to whether Lillian ought to have incurred expenditure sending the goods on to where she could have got a better price; the duty is to act reasonably to minimise, and if she has done so she can recover expenses incurred in minimising that loss (of general average, salvage etc): *Integrated Container Service v British Traders Insurance* (1984). Presumably the assured will not recover if the loss could have been minimised or at least recover the amount the minimised loss would have totalled.

Olaf

Olaf would have an insurable interest in the contract goods as a buyer under a cif contract. The underwriters would be interested to know if the broker's failure to disclose would be a reason to avoid the insurance contract, as the information the broker has would be a circumstance likely to affect the judgment of the prudent insurer in fixing the premium: s18. The circumstances are those which are known or ought to have been known to the assured – and includes matters in the ordinary course of business. The courts would have to decide if Adrian, as proposer under the policy, ought to have known about the mysterious propensity of turnips.

Policy 'A' covers theft and it should be recoverable. The location of the goods at the time of the theft would be covered by the policy as all policies now incorporate a warehouse to warehouse clause.

The 200 damaged by the stevedores would be recoverable unless the damage was caused by improper packing: Exclusion 4.3. The rain, the cause of the subsequent damage, is covered by the policy, and is recoverable if it is proved that rain was the proximate cause of the loss. However, if the proximate cause was the inherent vice of the goods – propensity to deteriorate – then the loss will not be recoverable as it is excluded under 4.4. The assured must show that on the balance of probabilities, the proximate cause of the loss was a peril insured against.

Olaf will claim for partial loss subject to his duty to minimise and that loss will be calculated as above.

The underwriters cannot avoid the contract; they will be subrogated to any remedies the assured may have had against, in this example, the carrier and the stevedores.

Question 3

The Chocolate Society is a small Midlands company specialising in the manufacture of sweets. It enters into three separate sales contracts as follows:

a) With Dawn for the sale of 1,000 tonnes of marzipan at £100 per tonne fob Liverpool. Dawn subsequently sells the marzipan to a buyer cif Pretoria and she insures the goods for the voyage from Liverpool to Pretoria at an agreed value of £100,000.

b) With Valentino for the sale of 2,000 tonnes of Turkish Delight at £75 per tonne fob Southampton. Valentino also arranges insurance for the onward shipment of the goods to Pretoria for an agreed value of £200,000.

c) With Graham for the sale of 2,500 tonnes of milk chocolate at £50 per tonne fob London and again Graham insures the goods for onward shipment to another buyer also in Pretoria at a premium of £0.50 per tonne.

All the insurance cover arranged by each of these parties is on Institute Cargo Clause A terms. All three purchasers nominate the same vessel at a freight rate of £5 per tonne.

Due to a strike at Liverpool, the marzipan is delivered by the Chocolate Society to Southampton where it is loaded beside the Turkish Delight. The vessel then proceeds to London where it is discovered that the market price for milk chocolate has risen to £75 per tonne. 2,000 tonnes of chocolate are loaded aboard but the master informs Graham that the vessel is now fully loaded. Graham insists on the full cargo being loaded which in fact happens.

The vessel runs into heavy weather and the vessel is in danger of capsizing because it is overloaded. The ship's master puts into Casablanca where all the cargo is discharged and the following events occur.

The marzipan is loaded onto the quayside where it melts in the hot weather. Dawn wishes to abandon the goods for the purposes of the insurance policy.

The Turkish Delight is loaded into containers which previously contained oil. A large part of the consignment is spoiled.

Finally, the chocolate is left in the hold which is not refrigerated and four-fifths of the cargo ruined.

Advise Dawn, Valentino and Graham on their valuation of their claims against the insurance underwriters.

Question prepared by the Editor
April 1994

General comment

A question allowing a comparison to be drawn among the different ways of computing loss, depending on whether the loss is total or partial and whether the policy is valued or unvalued.

Skeleton solution

Dawn – constructive total loss, notice of abandonment, rule in s13 MIA 1906.

Valentino – partial loss, gross sound value, proportion of gross sound value.

Graham – partial loss, unvalued policy.

Suggested solution

We are asked to advise Dawn, Valentino and Graham as to the correct quantum of claims they may have under their insurances.

Dawn

We are informed that Dawn wishes to abandon, which means that she proposes to treat her loss as a constructive total loss: s52(2) Marine Insurance Act 1906. The measure of indemnity, if the underwriters accept her notice of abandonment, is the sum fixed by the policy, £100,000.

Failure to give notice would enable the assured to treat the loss only as a partial loss: ss61 and 62. Notice must be given quickly either orally or in writing and is a condition precedent for a claim for a constructive total loss (cf clause 13 A, B, C policies). The notice must clearly indicate the assured's intention. The telex is probably enough as it evidences an intention which can be accepted or rejected by the underwriters. If the loss were not treated as a total loss the liability of the underwriters would be assessed on the basis of s71(3) which states:

'Where the whole or any part of the merchandise has been damaged at its destination then the measure of indemnity is such proportion of the sum fixed by the policy in the case of a valued policy, or of the insurable value in the case of an unvalued policy, as the difference between the gross sound and damaged values at the price of arrival bears to the gross sound value.'

According to s71(4):

' "gross value" means the wholesale price if there be no such price the estimated value, with, in either case, freight, landing charges, and duty paid beforehand ...'

Valentino

The Turkish Delight has been insured at an agreed value £200,000 but the cargo has been damaged or partially lost if the soiling amounts to damage (the basis set down in s71(3)).

Gross sound value – gross damaged value at the place of arrival.

Gross value is defined in s71(4)

ie 2,000 x 125	=	250,000
plus expenses	=	10,000
		260,000
minus damaged value	*130,000*	
		130,000

Measure of Indemnity

$$\frac{130,000}{260,000} \text{ x insured value} = £200,000$$

Claim will be for £100,000

If, however, the loss amounts to a total loss of part of the cargo then Valentino's claim would be based on s71(1) as the portion of the agreed value which the insurable value of the part lost bears to the insurable value of the whole. The insurable value is calculated on the basis in s16(3). It is not possible to quantify the claim on this basis here as the premiums are not known.

Graham

Graham has an unvalued policy. Therefore to recover his partial loss the insurable value must be calculated according to s16(3), ie:

the insurable value is the part lost of the property insured plus the expenses of and incidental to shipping and the charges of insurance on the whole.

£2,500	x £50	= prime cost
£2,500	x £5	= expenses
£2,500	x £0.50	= insurance charges

= £138,750 – as 4/5 was lost the measure of indemnity should be £111,000.

The underwriters would be advised that as each insurance was effected on the basis of a voyage policy, there is an implied warranty that the ship shall be seaworthy for the voyage: ss39(1) and 40(2). This requirement applies at the start of the voyage. Seaworthiness falls to be defined: s39(4) – ie the ship is able to withstand the ordinary perils of the voyage.

Dawn and Valentino's claims cannot be avoided on this basis as the ship was seaworthy on leaving England but it is suggested that the underwriters can avoid the contract with Graham even if it can be proved that the seaworthiness did not cause the loss. Graham's lack of knowledge would be irrelevant; but his knowledge of the overloading would be a material particular which ought to have been disclosed to the underwriter: ss18 and 19.

If the ship had not been overloaded she still may have been unseaworthy as she could not withstand the ordinary perils of the voyage, nor was she fit to carry cargo.

A, B and C policies contain a clause – clause 5 – which says that the breach of implied warranty can be waived, unless the assured was privy at the time of loading.

Question 4

Hank, in the United States, sold a consignment of grain to Lech, in Poland, the terms of which were cif Riga October 1993. Insurance was arranged with three syndicates in

London known as Syndicates X, Y and Z on Institute Cargo Clause B terms with cover five weeks before shipment. At first the underwriters were reluctant to extend cover but on 14 October, Syndicate X agreed to cover part of the risk and on 16 October, Syndicate Y followed with Syndicate Z eventually signing up on 20 October. Each Syndicate agreed to share different portions of the risk, being 20 per cent, 40 per cent and 60 per cent respectively.

In fact the goods were shipped from Hank's warehouse in Omaha on 7 October and after a two week period of storage at New Haven docks, arrived at Gdansk on the 7th of the following month. They were then shipped to Riga the following week.

It appears that the grain was contaminated with radioactivity from a discharge from a nuclear power station at New Haven while the consignment was sitting at the dockside. Even before the grain arrived at New Haven, a substantial portion had been spoiled by the negligent acts of the workers at the shipment depot. Hank was made aware of this fact by the freight forwarders but failed to disclose this to the insurers.

After the vessel was loaded, the freight forwarders noted that the hatch covers of the vessel were defective and not wind and water tight. Again this fact was never initiated to the underwriters. The cargo subsequently became saturated by sea water.

Finally, during the course of the voyage, the vessel collided with another ship outside Gdansk. The cargo was salvaged but no-one arranged for the drying out of the grain in order to minimise the losses which had occurred.

Advise the three syndicates of their liabilities under the policy.

Question prepared by the Editor
April 1994

General comment

When cover begins and ends is an important matter in assessing the liabilities of an insurer. Liability can be avoided if the damage occurs after the cover expires or before the commencement of the policy. This question is intended to provide some guidance on these points.

Skeleton solution

Institute Cargo B Clause includes warehouse-to-warehouse term.

Contract of utmost faith: need to disclose all material circumstances.

Cover of the perils: radioactivity, wetting, defective hatch covers, and contamination with water.

Suggested solution

Under s17 of the Marine Insurance Act 1906, contracts of marine insurance are subject to the requirement of uberrimae fidei (utmost good faith). Parties to such a contract are subject to onerous duties of disclosure and, in particular, an assured is required to disclose the existence of any facts or circumstances which might bear upon the contract: *Container Transport International* v *Oceanus Mutual Underwriting*

Association (1984). In fact, the assured is not only obliged to disclose every 'material circumstance' known to him, but is also deemed to know every material circumstance which 'in the ordinary course of business ought to be known to him' (s18). This obligation is subject only to limited exceptions.

The cargo of grain left Omaha on 7 October, presumably in a merchantable quality. However, prior to shipment, the depot in which the grain had been stored uncovered was affected by a leakage of radioactivity. Section 18(3)(b) of the 1906 Act does not require an assured to disclose the existence of circumstances which are matters of common notoriety or knowledge. It could therefore be argued that the assured was not required to disclose the existence of the radioactive leakage before accepting insurance due to the worldwide publicity which such an event would likely receive in the media.

Further, although the Institute Cargo B clauses exclude damage caused by radioactive fallout, this is confined to the situation where such fallout was caused by nuclear or atomic weapons. Consequently, it is unlikely that the insurance policy agreed between the exporters and the Syndicates would be voidable due to this eventuality.

The next event to befall the consignment was the wetting of the cargo and the loss of part of the cargo due to the negligent actions of the workers at the shipment depot. The problem does not specify the exact date of this event. If the insurance cover had been negotiated with Y and Z Syndicates before part of the consignment was lost, the underwriters cannot avoid liability under the contract of insurance. However, if the accident occurred before insurance was obtained, this would have been a fact which the exporters would have been required to disclose to the insurers and would render the contract voidable at the instance of the insurers.

The duty of disclosure has been considerably expanded by a number of recent decisions from English courts. In particular, in *The Litsion Pride* (1985), the Court of Appeal held that the duty of disclose continued throughout the performance of the contract. However, if the insurance contracts were negotiated prior to these events, it is unlikely that the exporters would be required to disclose the accident since it did not create a material circumstance which would have a bearing on the subsequent performance of the contract.

After the insurance cover had been provided, the freight forwarder noticed that the hatch covers of the vessel carrying the consignment were defective. Since a freight forwarder cannot be said to be an agent of the exporters, this fact does not adversely affect the position of the exporters.

The fact that the cargo was contaminated with water is a factor which is only relevant in the determination of liability for the insurers under the insurance contract.

The Institute Cargo B Clauses cover a number of risks including loss or damage caused to the insured subject-matter as a result of collision with any external object other than water, as well as the overturning or derailment of a land conveyance. Therefore, prima facie, the insurers are liable under the insurance policies negotiated with the exporters. However, a number of perils are also expressly excluded under the Institute Cargo B Clauses including:

1. loss, damage or expense attributable to the wilful misconduct of the assured; and

2. loss, damage or expense caused by insufficiency or unsuitability of packing or preparation of the subject-matter.

If the exporters can prove that the losses which were incurred could not be attributable to these factors, the insurers could not escape liability for the losses sustained.

However, the exporters also failed to organise the drying out of the cargo after the collision of the vessel and after notification of this event by the master of the vessel. Section 78(4) of the Marine Insurance Act 1906 creates a duty on the assured and his agents to take such measures as may be reasonable for the purposes of averting or minimising losses. Further, clause 16 of the Institute Cargo Clauses also requires the assured and their servants and agents to 'take such measures as may be reasonable for the purpose of averting or minimising loss'. It might therefore be difficult for the exporters to recover damages in respect of losses which were incurred as a result of their failure to protect the cargo.

12 CONFLICT OF LAWS

12.1   Introduction

12.2   Key points

12.3   Recent cases and statutes

12.4   Relevant materials

12.5   Analysis of questions

12.6   Questions

12.1   Introduction

International trade, by its very nature, involves persons and property situated outside the jurisdiction of the English courts. For example, if a purchaser situated in Liverpool buys goods manufactured in Argentina from a Brazilian seller and the goods are to be transported from Buenos Aires in a vessel registered in Panama, the connection of the English courts in the event of a dispute between the parties might seem remote. Nevertheless, the English courts often have to unravel just such complex legal situations.

Conflict of laws essentially concerns the rules which are applied when an English court must address the legal issues raised by foreign elements in an international transaction. Where such a foreign elements are involved, the court must ask itself three questions. First, can the court exercise jurisdiction over the parties to the dispute? Second, which law should be applied by the court to the facts presented before it? Third, what account should the court take of foreign judgments rendered earlier in connection with the dispute?

If these three questions are taken in order, we can see that there are three separate dimensions to conflict of laws. These three dimensions can be conveniently grouped under three headings: (a) the jurisdiction of the English courts; (b) the choice of law applicable in a dispute; and (c) the enforcement and application of foreign judgments. A distinction between these separate issues must be borne in mind at all times in order to make sense of this intricate part of the syllabus.

12.2   Key points

a) *The exercise of jurisdiction by the English courts at common law*

The issue of the jurisdiction of the English courts has been confused by the existence of two separate regimes, one a creation of the common law, the other a creation of statute. The Civil Jurisdiction and Judgments Act 1982 radically changed the law relating to jurisdiction but only in relation to defendants domiciled in Member States of the European Union. Where the statutory provisions are inapplicable, the common law rules continue to apply.

In common law, English courts exercise jurisdiction over any person on whom a valid writ has been served within England. As the court observed in *John Russell & Co Ltd* v *Cayzer, Irvine & Co Ltd* [1916] 2 AC 298, 'whoever is served with the King's writ and can be compelled consequently to submit to the decree made is a person over which the courts have jurisdiction'.

There is no requirement that the issue in dispute should relate to a matter of English law. Similarly, it is not a prerequisite that either of the parties to the proceedings should be resident or domiciled in England. The only requirement regarding residence is that the defendant must be physically located in England when the writ is served: see *Maharanee of Baroda* v *Wildenstein* [1972] 2 QB 283.

Where a defendant is not physically resident inside the jurisdiction of the English courts special rules apply in two sets of circumstances, namely: (i) where a plaintiff has applied to the court for leave to serve the writ outside the jurisdiction; and (ii) where the parties voluntarily submit to the jurisdiction of the English courts.

i) Leave to serve a writ on persons abroad

Where a defendant is not present in England and has not submitted to the jurisdiction of the court, an application may be made to the court for leave to serve the writ outside the jurisdiction of the court: RSC Ord 11, r1.

The grant of leave to serve a writ outside the jurisdiction of the court is discretionary and is a power which is exercised by the courts 'with extreme caution and with full regard in every case to the circumstances': *Cordova Land Co Ltd* v *Victor Brothers Inc* [1966] 1 WLR 793.

RSC Ord 11 states 14 circumstances on which leave may be granted. For present purposes, the most significant of these are the following:

- Where a defendant is domiciled within the jurisdiction of the English courts, leave may be granted: RSC Ord 11, r1(1)(a).

- An injunction is sought ordering the defendant to do, or to refrain from doing, some act within the jurisdiction: RSC Ord 11, r1(1)(b).

- A person is considered by the court to be 'a necessary and proper party' in an action against a person duly served within or out of the jurisdiction: RSC Ord 11, r1(1)(c).

- A claim is brought to enforce, rescind, dissolve, annul or otherwise affect a contract, or to recover damages, or obtain other relief in respect of the breach of a contract: RSC Ord 11, r1(1)(d).

- A contract has been breached within the jurisdiction of the court. It is irrelevant whether the contract was made within or outside the jurisdiction: RSC Ord 11, r1(1)(e).

- A claim is founded on a tort and the damage was sustained, or resulted from an act committed within the jurisdiction: RSC Ord 11, r1(1)(f).

- An action is brought to enforce any judgment or arbitration award: RSC Ord 11, r1(1)(m).

ii) Jurisdiction over defendants who submit to the jurisdiction of the court

Defendants who would not otherwise be subject to the jurisdiction of the English courts may voluntarily submit to the jurisdiction. This may occur in four situations:

- When a contract has a provision which expressly or impliedly contains the consent of the parties to submission to the jurisdiction of the English courts.

- Where an action is raised by a plaintiff against a defendant, the plaintiff is deemed to submit to any counterclaims instituted by the defendant in response: RSC Ord 15, r2.

- Where a defendant instructs his solicitor to accept service on his behalf, he or she is deemed to submit to the jurisdiction of the court: RSC Ord 10, r1(4).

- Where the defendant appears in order to contest the action, this will be considered submission to the jurisdiction of the court: RSC Ord 10, r1(5). However, there is no such presumption when the defendant appears for the sole purpose of contesting the jurisdiction of the court.

b) *Stays of action and forum conveniens under the common law*

The fact that an English court may exercise jurisdiction does not necessarily imply that it must exercise that power. A court may decide to stay an action raised because there is a more appropriate forum where the case should be heard.

In *MacShannon* v *Rockware Glass Limited* [1978] AC 795, Lord Diplock laid down the modern position on stay of proceedings in the following terms:

'In order to justify a stay two conditions must be satisfied, one positive and one negative: (a) the defendant must satisfy the court that there is another forum to whose jurisdiction he is amenable in which justice can be done between the parties at substantially less inconvenience or expense, and (b) the stay must not deprive the plaintiff of a legitimate personal or juridical advantage which would be available to him if he invoked the jurisdiction of the English court ...'; see also *The Abidin Daver* [1984] 1 All ER 470.

c) *Jurisdiction within the European Union – the Civil Jurisdiction and Judgments Act 1982*

The common law principles of jurisdiction have been substantially supplemented by the Civil Jurisdiction and Judgments Act 1982 which gives effect in the UK to the Brussels Convention on Jurisdiction and Enforcement of Judgments in Civil and

Commercial Matters 1968. The Convention is an agreement negotiated among the Member States of the European Union.

The original Convention has been amended on two occasions. The first amendment occurred as a consequence of the Lugano Convention of 1988 which extended the terms of the 1968 Convention to the states of the European Free Trade Association (EFTA). The second amendment took place on the signing of the San Sebastian Convention of 1989. This Convention made certain adjustments to the 1968 Convention to allow Spain and Portugal to accede to the system.

d) *The scheme and rules of the Convention as applied by the Civil Jurisdiction and Judgments Act 1982*

The Convention uses the concept of domicile to link individuals to specific legal systems to decide the issue of jurisdiction. Hence, a court first applies its own internal law to decide if a person is domiciled within that jurisdiction.

The 1982 Act creates rules of English law to assist in determining whether an individual is domiciled in the UK. Section 41(2) states that a person is domiciled in the UK 'if and only if ... he is resident in the United Kingdom; and the nature and circumstances of his residence indicate that he has a substantial connection with the United Kingdom'. Under s41(6) of the Act a presumption of 'substantial connection' arises where a person has been resident in the UK for an immediately preceding period of three months.

The central rule regulating jurisdiction under the Convention, as stated in Article 2, is that:

'Subject to the provisions of this Convention, persons domiciled in a Contracting State shall, whatever their nationality, be sued in the courts of that state ...'.

Therefore, an individual must be sued in the court of his or her domicile as this term is defined in the national laws of the European Union countries which are parties to the Convention.

There are two separate types of exceptions which deviate from this general principle: (i) cases of special jurisdiction; and (ii) cases of exclusive jurisdiction.

i) Special jurisdiction rules

Article 5 of the Convention specifies certain situations in which a court, other than that of the defendant's domicile, is entitled to exercise jurisdiction. For present purposes, the most significant are as follows:

- Contract – in matters relating to a contract, the courts for the place of performance of the obligation in question have concurrent jurisdiction: Article 5(1).

- Tort – where proceedings relate to tort, delict or quasi-delict, the courts of the place where the harmful event occurred have jurisdiction in addition to those of the defendant's domicile: Article 5(3).

- Branches and agencies – in the case of a dispute arising out of the operation of a branch or agency, the courts of the place in which the branch or agency is situated have jurisdiction to hear the dispute: Article 5(5).

- Salvage claims – special and complicated rules have been established to deal with the unique problems created in Admiralty litigation; see *The Deichland* [1990] 1 QB 361: Article 5(7).

A person domiciled in a contracting state may also be sued (1) where he is one of a number of defendants, in the courts of the place where any one of them is domiciled; (2) as a third party in an action on a warranty or guarantee; and (3) on a counterclaim arising from the same contract or facts on which the original claim was based in the court in which the original claim is pending.

ii) Exclusive jurisdiction rules

Article 16 of the Convention stipulates that, irrespective of the issue of domicile, certain courts retain exclusive jurisdiction over particular matters. Few of these are relevant for present purposes, but it should be noted that exclusive jurisdiction is reserved in the case of the enforcement of judgments to the courts of the country in which the judgment has been rendered.

e) *Submission to the jurisdiction under the Convention*

Private parties can agree to submit to the jurisdiction of a particular court and the Convention acknowledges this freedom in Article 17. This allows the parties, if one or more is domiciled in a European Union state, to agree that the courts of a particular state are to have jurisdiction to settle any disputes which may arise in connection with a particular legal relationship. That court will have exclusive jurisdiction over the dispute.

There are a number of conditions in the Convention relating to the form of the agreement prorogating jurisdiction. The agreement must be either:

i) in writing or evidenced in writing; or

ii) in a form which accords with practices which parties have established between themselves; or

iii) in international trade or commerce, in a form which accords with a usage of which the parties are, or ought to have been, aware and which is widely known in such trade or commerce to parties to contracts of the type involved in the particular trade or commerce.

f) *Refusal of jurisdiction and staying of proceedings under the Convention*

Despite the basic principle that a defendant should be sued in the courts of his domicile, the Convention gives considerable scope to the possibility that proceedings may be raised in more than one court. In this situation, the basic rule is contained in Article 21 of the Convention.

Where proceedings involving the same cause of action and between the same parties are brought in the courts of different European Union countries, any court other than the courts first seized may, of its own motion, stay its proceedings until such time as the court first seized of the proceedings has established its jurisdiction.

In the event that the court first seized of the proceedings establishes jurisdiction, courts other than the first court are required to decline jurisdiction in favour of that court: see *Overseas Union Insurance Ltd* v *New Hampshire Insurance Co* [1992] 2 WLR 586.

g) *Proper law of contracts*

In common with the subject of jurisdiction, a two-tier system of law operates in relation to choice of law in contractual relationships. The common law principles regulating the choice of law in contracts have been largely superseded by a statutory regime introduced by the Contracts (Applicable Law) Act 1990 which itself gave effect to another European Union Convention – the Convention on the Law Applicable to Contractual Obligations 1980.

i) The common law rules for the selection of the proper law

The proper law of a contract at common law is simply the legal system which regulates the contractual relationship between the parties to the contract. From a strict legal perspective, the proper law has been defined as 'the substantive law of the country which the parties have chosen as that by which their mutually legally enforceable rights are to be ascertained': *Amin Rasheed Shipping Corp* v *Kuwait Insurance Co* [1983] 2 All ER 884.

If the parties have expressly specified in the contract a particular law to govern their agreement then, almost invariably, this choice will be upheld by the courts and will be the proper law of the contract: see *Vita Food Products Inc* v *Unus Shipping Co Ltd* [1939] AC 277.

Where the parties fail to nominate an express choice of law, the courts will attempt to identify which proper law is implied in the terms of the contract. Unfortunately this is not always an easy task and, to a large degree, depends on the facts and circumstances surrounding the negotiation of the contract.

The following factors have been taken into consideration by the courts in ascertaining the implied choice of law:

- Where the parties provide that any disputes should be submitted to arbitration in a particular country, this is a significant indication that the law of that country is the proper law by implication: see *Compagnie Tunisienne de Navigation SA* v *Compagnie d'Armement Maritime SA* [1971] AC 572.

- The language in which the contract is drafted.

- The place the contract is to be performed and the place where payment is to be made.

- The locations and places of businesses of the parties.

- The currency in which payment is to be made.

- The maturity of the legal principles in a particular legal system over the relative infancy of another. For example, the English laws of marine insurance have a special value in international trade and reference to terms in the English terminology is a strong factor in favour of the selection of English law: see *Amin Rasheed Shipping Corp* v *Kuwait Insurance Co* [1983] 2 All ER 884.

Obviously not all these factors have equal weight. It is a question of balancing the facts and circumstances of the case against each other in order to arrive at the proper law of the contract.

It is not impossible for a situation to arise in which the parties did not contemplate that a particular law should apply to their contractual relationship. In such situations, the court must assign a proper law to the contract.

In modern law, this process has been boiled down to principle that the proper law in such circumstances is 'that with which the transaction has its closest and most real connection': *Amin Rasheed Shipping Corp*, above.

Again this is a process of weighing up the wide range of factors connected to the contract and is an exercise of judgment and weighing of a multitude of factors. There is no limit to the number of factors which can be taken into consideration, provided that they have some bearing on the transaction.

ii) The 1980 Convention on the Law Applicable to Contractual Obligations

The Convention on the Law Applicable to Contractual Relations 1980 (known as the Rome Convention) has been given effect in English law by the Contracts (Applicable Law) Act 1990.

Article 1(1) of the Convention stipulates that:

'the rules of this Convention shall apply to contractual obligations in any situation involving a choice between the laws of different countries'.

The application of the Convention is not therefore restricted to situations involving a selection between the laws of two or more European Union states; they apply to any situation involving a choice between the laws of different countries, whether European Union member states or otherwise. It is the existence of a need to make a selection between competing legal systems in the course of litigation in the English courts that gives rise to the application of the Convention.

Like the common law, the Convention recognises the autonomy of contracting parties to select the legal system which will govern their contract; Article 3(1). This choice must be express and demonstrated with reasonable certainty by the terms of the contract or the circumstances of the case. The parties can select a law applicable to the whole of the contract or only to a part of it.

Where no express choice of law has been made by the parties, the contract is governed by the law of the country with which it is 'most closely connected' – Article 4(1). Article 4(2) stipulates that:

'it shall be presumed that the contract is most closely connected with the country where the party who is to effect the performance which is characteristic of the contract has, at the time of the conclusion of the contract, his habitual residence, or, in the case of a body corporate or unincorporated, its central administration.'

The presumption of closest connection is slightly modified for some types of contract including the following:

* contracts made in the course of a party's trade or profession – the country of closest connection is the country in which the principal's place of business is situated;

* contracts for the carriage of goods – the country of closest connection is the country in which the carrier has its principal place of business;

* contracts relating to immoveable property – the country of the closest connection is that of the location of the property.

Article 10 of the Convention specifies the matters which are to be governed by the applicable law. These are: interpretation, performance, the consequences of breach (including damages), the extinguishing of obligations, limitation of actions and the consequences of the nullity of a contract.

h) *Recognition and enforcement of judgments*

Where a judgment is obtained against a defendant in a foreign jurisdiction, in order to enforce the judgment, a successful plaintiff must apply to an English court to implement any foreign order in England. Foreign judgments are not automatically effective in English law and the courts are not bound to give effect to foreign court orders. It is a matter for the English courts to decide according to their own rules whether a foreign judgment should be recognised or enforced.

Once again a distinction must be made between the common law position which applies to judgments from courts outside the European Union and the position under the Civil Jurisdiction and Judgments Act 1982 which regulates intra-European Union judgments.

i) The position at common law

An English court will generally enforce a judgment of a foreign non-European Union court if that court was competent to exercise jurisdiction to render judgment on the facts of the case.

There are, in effect, two grounds on which an English court will consider that a foreign court has exercised its jurisdiction in personam in a competent manner: (1) a period of residence by the defendant; and (2) submission by the defendant to the jurisdiction of the court.

- Residence – the principle that courts have competent jurisdiction over persons resident within their territory is internationally recognised and is possibly the most fundamental principle in establishing a jurisdictional nexus between an individual and a particular court: see *Schibsby* v *Westenholtz* (1870) LR 6 QB 155.

- Submission to the jurisdiction – if a defendant has voluntarily submitted to the jurisdiction of a foreign court, any judgment rendered by that court will be recognised and enforced in England: *Emanuel* v *Symon* [1908] KB 302.

In addition to the need to demonstrate that the judgment has been pronounced by a court of competent jurisdiction, the judgment must also satisfy the following additional requirements.

- The foreign judgment must be final and conclusive. All the points of law must be settled by the judgment. However, a judgment may be final and conclusive, notwithstanding the possibility of an appeal to a higher court, if no appeal is made: *Colt Industries Inc* v *Sarlie (No 2)* [1966] 1 WLR 1287.

- The judgment must for a specific sum of money in order to be enforceable. An English court will not implement a foreign judgment for an injunction, specific implement or for delivery of goods.

ii) Judgments rendered inside the European Union

The Civil Jurisdiction and Judgments Act 1982 is designed to ensure that defendants are sued in the legal system in which they are domiciled for the purposes of the Act and the 1968 Brussels Convention. Hence, Article 26 of the Convention provides that a judgment given in a European Union state 'shall be recognised' in the other Member States without any special procedure being required.

As regards enforcement actions, Article 31 of the Convention states that a judgment given in one Member State and enforceable in that state shall be enforceable in another European Union state when, 'on the application of any interested party', it has been declared enforceable in the other Union state.

Judgment is broadly defined in the Convention. Any judgment given by a court or tribunal of a European Union state including a decree, order, decision or writ of execution, as well as the determination of costs or expenses, shall be deemed to be a judgment for this purpose. It should also be noted that proceedings for enforcement under the Convention are not limited to monetary judgments.

There are a number of limited exceptions to the general rule that a judgment from a European Union court must be recognised and enforced in the English courts. These are contained in Article 27 and are as follows:

- Where such recognition would be contrary to the public policy in the state in which recognition is sought.

- Where the foreign judgment was given in default of appearance, if the defendant was not duly served with the document instituting the proceedings in sufficient time to enable an adequate defence to be arranged: *Thierry Noirhomme* v *David Walklate* [1992] 1 Lloyd's Rep 427.

- Where the judgment is irreconcilable with a judgment in a dispute between the same parties in the state where the recognition is being sought. In other words, the recognising court does not have to give preference to the foreign judgment over its own judgment: *Hoffmann* v *Krieg* [1988] ECR 645.

- Where there is a judgment from a non-Union state that has been given earlier and is irreconcilable with a European Union judgment, that judgment may be recognised.

- Where the judgment-granting state has decided a preliminary question concerning the status or legal capacity of natural persons, rights in property arising out of a matrimonial relationship, or will, in a manner which conflicts with the rules of private international law of the judgment-recognising state.

i) *Mareva injunctions*

A Mareva injunction is a special form of interlocutory relief designed to prevent a defendant to an existing action from avoiding the enforcement of a final decree by transferring assets within the jurisdiction to a foreign country or by concealing them within this country.

The remedy was first recognised in *Mareva Compania Naviera SA* v *International Bulk Carriers* [1980] 1 All ER 213 where the Court of Appeal approved the making of an injunction restraining the defendants from removing or disposing out of the jurisdiction money standing to the credit of the defendants at a London bank until trial.

The procedure is now enshrined in s37 of the Supreme Court Act 1981 which provides:

'1) The High Court may by order (whether interlocutory or final) grant an injunction or a receiver in all cases in which it appears to the court to be just and convenient to do so.

2) Any such order may be made either unconditionally or on such terms as the court thinks just.

3) The power of the High Court under subsection (1) to grant an interlocutory injunction restraining a party to any proceedings from removing from the jurisdiction of the High Court, or otherwise dealing with the assets located within the jurisdiction, shall be exercisable in cases where that party is, as well as in cases where he is not, domiciled, resident or present within the jurisdiction.'

The injunction takes effect immediately on its pronouncement and affects all the assets it is expressed to cover.

12.3 Recent cases and statutes

Seaconsar Far East Limited v *Bank Markazi Iran* [1993] 1 Lloyd's Rep 236: a case concerning the applicable standards for the court to grant leave to serve a defendant out of the jurisdiction under RSC Ord 11.

Union Transport Group plc v *Continental Lines SA* [1992] 1 All ER 161: application of Article 5(1) of the Brussels Convention to a case concerning breach of a charterparty contract where the principal and subsidiary obligations were to be performed in different countries.

Hamed El Chiaty & Co v *The Thomas Cook Group, The Nile Rhapsody* [1992] 2 Lloyd's Rep 399: the parties had agreed Egyptian law as the proper law of the contract in writing but the selection of jurisdiction was not stated. In the circumstances, the English court held that the parties had agreed to the exclusive jurisdiction of the Egyptian courts because of oral representations made.

Polly Peck International plc v *Asil Nadir* [1992] 2 Lloyd's Rep 238: one of the few cases in which a Mareva injunction was sought, and successfully obtained, against a bank. Lord Donaldson MR rendered a detailed dictum reviewing the principles underlying the Mareva jurisdiction.

12.4 Relevant materials

Dicey & Morris, *Conflict of Laws* (12th edition, 1993).

P Kaye, *Civil Jurisdiction and the Enforcement of Foreign Judgments* (1987).

P Kaye, *The New Private International Law of Contract of the European Community* (1993).

R Plender, *The European Contracts Convention* (1991).

R N Ough & W Flenley, *The Mareva Injunction and Anton Pillar Order* (second edition, 1993).

12.5 Analysis of questions

Questions involving conflict of laws are almost invariably difficult quite simply because there is always an underlying related legal question such as the rights of parties in the sale of goods or the construction of contracts.

The most common themes in this area of the syllabus are the jurisdiction of the English courts, the proper law of a contract and the recognition and enforcement of foreign decisiions and decrees. The following questions take this fact into consideration.

12.6 Questions

Question 1

Marconi, a British electronics company agrees to sell to Carey, an American national, who is resident and carrying on business in Haiti, a consignment of computer spare parts. The contract was negotiated and signed in London and was in the standard form used by the British Computer Parts Association.

The price payable was US$ 200,000 and was due on the delivery of the goods to Haiti. The contract provided that any dispute arising from the performance of the contract was to be submitted to arbitration in Haiti.

When the goods were delivered to Haiti, Carey refused to pay the full price insisting that several of the parts had been damaged in transit. Marconi is reluctant to submit the dispute to arbitration in Haiti because arbitrators in that country have a reputation of being corruptible and inefficient. There is also some doubt as to whether Marconi's negotiators and lawyers would be granted visas to attend the hearing.

What courses of action are open to Marconi and would your answer be different if Haiti was a member of the European Union?

Question prepared by the Editor
April 1994

General comment

The first point is to decide the matter of jurisdiction; since the defendant is in a non-EU country, this is a matter for the common law to decide. However, the question also asks for an alternative solution if Haiti was a member of the European Union.

Skeleton solution

Common law rules: Order 11, rule 1.

Plea of forum non conveniens.

Convention Rules: Article 2.

Suggested solution

Clearly, Marconi wishes to bring an action on the contract of sale against the buyer, Carey, for wrongful refusal to pay the price. The nature of the contract of sale has not been indicated. It seems however that the contract was an ex ship sale. Carey seems not to have been under an obligation to pay the price until the goods were delivered at the port of destination. There would otherwise have been no way of him knowing that some of the radios were damaged if such is the case.

The first obstacle which Marconi faces is serving a writ on Carey. There is no possibility of an action in rem against the vessel carrying the goods. The ship is to carry Carey's goods, but there is no suggestion that the ship is the property of Carey, and therefore amenable to the Admiralty jurisdiction of the English High Court.

Marconi would therefore have to seek the leave of the court to serve the writ out of the jurisdiction under Ord 11, r1 of the Rules of the Supreme Court ('RSC').

The decision whether to grant such leave is a two – stage process. First the applicant must fall within one of the heads in Ord 11, r1. He must 'make it sufficiently to appear' (Ord 11, r4(2)) to the court that he had a prima facie case against the defendant. Secondly he must convince the court that the case is a proper one for service abroad.

The most obvious head is Ord 11, r1 (d) that the contract was made in the jurisdiction. We are told that the contract was negotiated in London.

The application would be ex parte. Marconi must give full and frank disclosure. However provided that he can adduce evidence that the goods were shipped in good condition, he would have a prima facie case sufficient for the purposes of r1.

The second stage is answered by an application of the principle of 'forum non conveniens': see *The Spiliada* (1987).

The court however is exceedingly careful before allowing a writ to be served abroad. The court will lean against Marconi's application since he has agreed to submit to the jurisdiction of the Haitian courts. Leave was refused in such a case in *Mackender* v *Feldia AG* (1967). Nevertheless this is not an insuperable obstacle. In *The Fehmarn* (1958) the Court of Appeal held in a case where the defendant was seeking the stay of English proceedings on the basis of a foreign jurisdiction clause that the parties cannot by their bargain oust the jurisdiction of the English courts. The stay was refused since the English element of the case was stronger than the Russian.

The court will be sympathetic to an argument that the applicant is likely to be denied justice in the foreign tribunal should leave to serve abroad be refused.

The court will look at the reason for the arbitration clause. If it were incorporated merely to seek procedural advantages there or in the knowledge that Marconi would be prejudiced thereby, then the court is likely to give it little weight in its final consideration: see *The Eleftheria* (1970).

The evidence material to the case seems, however, to be in Haiti. If the contract were ex ship, the condition in which the goods were shipped is strictly irrelevant. What matters is their condition on arrival.

Also the court would be interested in assessing whether Haitian law differed from English law in any material respect. If not this would be a point in favour of granting leave to serve out of the jurisdiction.

On the balance of probabilities it would seem that leave would be granted, though this would principally be a question of weighing the convenience of the trial in Haiti against the risk of injustice and prejudice to Marconi.

The advice would be considerably different if Haiti were a member of the European Union and a party to the Brussels Convention 1968.

The general rule under the Convention and the Civil Jurisdiction and Judgments Act 1982 is that a defendant domiciled in a contracting state is to sued in the country of his domicile: Article 2. This rule is displaced if another country has exclusive jurisdiction within Article 16. This is not the case here. There is also concurrent jurisdiction if the defendant has submitted to the jurisdiction of another country, and the courts of his domicile should decline jurisdiction in favour of that other state should proceedings be commenced in both.

It seems that Carey is a domicile of Haiti. Also the state with prorogative jurisdiction under Article 17 of the Convention is Haiti. The English courts would therefore be bound to decline jurisdiction of their own motion. They could not grant leave to serve abroad. Marconi would have to sue in Haiti.

This would not prevent Marconi from applying to the English courts for a Mareva injunction over the cargo of computers within the jurisdiction.

In *X v Y and Y Establishment* (1990), it was held that by reason of Article 24 of the Convention and s25 of the Civil Jurisdiction and Judgments Act 1982 the English courts could grant interlocutory injunctions on the basis of actions brought in another Convention Territory.

Question 2

Alesandro, an Italian importer contracted with Aristotle for the carriage of Greek feta cheese from Athens to Bari (Italy). The contract contained no provision incorporating a choice of law.

However, the contract was written in English and one of its clauses provided that 'All disputes are to be referred to the British courts'. Another clause limited the carrier's liability and this limitation was expressed in amounts in £ sterling. On the other hand, throughout the contract there were references to United States dollars and German Deutsche Marks.

During carriage, the cheese was not stored in a sufficiently cool manner and was ruined. Alesandro has commenced an action for breach of contract in the English courts.

What would your advice be to Aristotle on whether or not the jurisdiction of the English courts may be challenged, whether the limitation clause may be relied on and the factors which the English courts will select when deciding the applicable law of the contract.

Question prepared by the Editor
April 1994

General comment

A complex question requiring the student to apply the relevant conflicts of law provisions to the facts presented in the question. The major difficulties are caused by the need to consider the 1982 statute on jurisdiction and the 1990 statute on applicable contractual law. Both statutes present difficulties in their application, but since the

1990 statute only came into effect in April 1991, there is a dearth of relevant case law and principles.

Skeleton solution

i) Jurisdiction of the English courts.

Applicable provisions of the 1982 Act.

Grounds for challenge.

ii) Distinction between substantive rules and procedural rules.

Effect of the distinction after the 1990 Act.

iii) Rules of the 1990 Act.

Concept of characteristic performance.

Suggested solution

The contract of carriage was made between Alesandro, an Italian importer, and Aristotle, a Greek shipowner. While many of the terms were in English, a number of others were not. The question asks: (i) whether the jurisdiction of the English courts is valid; (ii) whether the limitation clause can be relied upon; and (iii) the factors that the English courts take into consideration in ascertaining the proper law of the contract.

i) Since the parties are nationals of the European Union seeking jurisdiction in another Member State, the relevant principles for deciding the issue of jurisdiction are contained in the Civil Jurisdiction and Judgments Act 1982 which gives effect to the 1968 Convention on Jurisdiction and the Enforcement of Judgments.

While the main ground for jurisdiction under the Convention is the domicile of the defender, Article 17 of the Convention envisages the situation in which the parties to a contract agree to submit disputes to a particular jurisdiction. According to Article 17, if the parties to an agreement, one or more of whom is domiciled in a EC state, have agreed that the English courts are to settle any disputes arising between them, those courts shall have exclusive jurisdiction to resolve the dispute.

However, in order to found jurisdiction, the agreement must be 'in writing or evidenced in writing, or in international trade or commerce, in a form which accords with practices in that trade or commerce'. The carriage contract contains an express reference to the jurisdiction of the British courts and is sufficient to allow the English courts to exercise jurisdiction.

The jurisdiction of the courts is exclusive unless the courts themselves decline to exercise jurisdiction over the parties. This may be for a number of reasons.

Firstly, where proceedings that involve the same cause of action between the same parties have been brought in another court prior to litigation in the English courts, jurisdiction may be declined on the basis of the principle of lis pendens. This principle means that the courts not seized first of jurisdiction should decline jurisdiction on the basis that an action has already been raised in another forum.

Second, the courts may decline to exercise jurisdiction on the basis of the principle of forum non conveniens. This simply means that, in the circumstances of the case, the exercise of jurisdiction would be inappropriate and that another forum is more suitable.

However, from the facts of the case presented before us, there appears to be no reason why the English courts should apply either of these principles, and therefore it is unlikely that a valid challenge may be made to the jurisdiction of the English courts.

ii) In common law, the choice of applicable principles depends on whether the courts of the lex fori decide that the applicable rules of law are procedural or substantive. Procedural matters are regulated by the rules of law of the local court, while substantive issues are decided in accordance with the applicable law.

The common law position has been altered by the Contracts (Applicable Law) Act 1990, which gives effect to the Convention on the Law Applicable to Contractual Obligations 1980. Article 10 of that Convention provides that the law applicable to a particular contract will govern, inter alia, the consequences of a breach of a contract, including the assessment of damages. This represents a dramatic reversal of the common law position which treated the nature of the remedy as a procedural matter to be determined by the lex fori.

This being the case, it is necessary to ascertain the proper law of the contract by applying the principles in the 1990 statute. This is, in fact, the process that is required to answer the last part of this question.

iii) The parties, while making an express choice of jurisdiction clause, did not include a choice of law provision in their contract. While the contract is written in English and the parties prorogate to the exclusive jurisdiction of the English courts, elsewhere there is reference to payment in various foreign currencies.

The proper law of the contract falls to be determined under the Contracts (Applicable Law) Act 1990, which came into force on 1 April 1991 and applies to all disputes arising out of facts occurring after that date. It applies in this case because the facts of the dispute happened in 1992.

This statute implements the Convention on the Law Applicable to Contractual Obligations 1980 which applies to all situations in which a choice of law question arises in a contractual dispute in the forum of a Member State. There is no need for the parties to be nationals or domiciled in a particular Community state for the terms of the statute to apply.

Under the act, the parties to an agreement remain free to determine the law that will apply to their contractual relationship: see Article 3 of the Convention. This choice may be express or implied. In the event that a particular law is to be implied, the parties must have demonstrated with reasonable certainty, in either the terms of the contract or in the circumstances of the case, that such laws are to apply.

In the circumstances of this particular case, the parties have made no express choice and none of the various factors cited in the question could be deemed to amount to an implied choice of law that is beyond reasonable certainty. While the contract is in English, payment is specified in three different currencies and neither of the parties is British. In the absence of an express or implied choice, the applicable legal rules are determined in accordance with Article 4 of the Convention.

Article 4 provides that where the parties to a contract make no express or implied choice of law, the applicable law is the law of the country in which the obligations that are 'characteristic of the contract' are to be performed.

In a contract of carriage, the place that is presumed to be characteristic of the performance is the country in which the carrier has his principal place of business, if this is also the place of either the loading or discharge of the goods: Article 4(4) of the Convention.

However, this is merely a presumption and, if this does not definitively determine the place of characteristic performance, another country that is more closely connected with the contract may be chosen by the courts. It is not stated in the question where Aristotle has a place of business, although it is more likely that his place of business will be Athens since he is a Greek carrier.

The case law on this point is not settled, but from the facts of the question it is clear that there are sufficient reasons for the courts to rebut this presumption which would act in favour of Greek law as the applicable law. There are few factors to indicate that the place that is characteristic of performance is Greece. In contrast, there are elements to suggest that Italy is the country where the contract is to be performed, ie the delivery of the goods.

The fact that the goods are to be delivered in Italy is an important element in deciding the place of characteristic performance. Also payment for freight is to be made in Italian lire and one of the parties is Italian. Each of these factors would be taken into consideration by the courts in deciding the law to be applied.

The reference to United States and German currencies can be disregarded because a reference to a currency is rarely deemed to be decisive by itself.

Question 3

Commercial Suicide, an English company, agreed to sell goods to Alter Ego Ltd, an Estonian company, but failed to deliver. Alter Ego sued Commercial Suicide in an Estonian court and obtained leave to serve the writ on Commercial Suicide in England. Commercial Suicide entered appearance before the Estonian court and argued (a) that leave to serve the writ should be refused since the breach of contract had not occurred in Estonia, and (b) the court should stay the proceedings as the English courts were a more suitable forum for the action.

After the Estonian court dismissed these arguments, Commercial Suicide refused to take further part in the action and judgment was awarded against them for £100,000. The award consisted of £50,000 compensatory damages, £40,000 exemplary damages (although this was based on an error in Estonian law) and £10,000 in legal expenses. Commercial Suicide was allowed six months to appeal against the decision but failed to do so. The company has since learned that the Estonian judge hearing the case owns a large number of shares in Alter Ego Ltd.

Alter Ego has started proceedings in England to enforce the judgment. Advise Commercial Suicide on the best course of action to prevent enforcement.

Question prepared by the Editor
April 1994

General comment

The fact that the country issuing the judgment is not a member of the European Union should provide a significant hint that the common law rules on the enforcement of foreign judgments will apply and not the 1968 Convention. Thereafter it is a matter of remembering the relevant common law rules and applying them to the facts.

Skeleton solution

Enforcement of foreign judgment – competence of foreign court in eyes of English court – submission – CJJA 82 s33.

Defences – natural justice – exemplary damages – error of foreign law – payment to state, whether fine or for services – finality of judgment.

Suggested solution

It is first necessary to decide whether, in the eyes of the English court which is being asked to enforce the Estonian judgment, the Estonian court had jurisdiction, ie whether it had 'international competence' (as it is sometimes called). Notice that this is (a) an issue of English conflicts law, (b) quite separate from any question as to whether the Estonian court had jurisdiction by Estonian law. To be thus competent, Estonian jurisdiction must have been founded on either (i) the presence of Commercial Suicide Limited within Estonia (*Adams* v *Cape Industries plc* (1990)) at the time of commencement of the action in Estonia (*Sirdar Gurdyal Singh* v *Raja of Faridkote* (1894)); or (ii) the submission of Commercial Suicide Limited to the Estonian court. English courts, while they claim for themselves 'long arm' jurisdiction by service of an English writ abroad by leave of the court under RSC Ord 11, do not recognise this as a basis for the jurisdiction of foreign courts, thus the fact that the Estonian court gave leave to serve the writ on Commercial Suicide Limited in England will not serve as a ground of Estonian jurisdiction for the purposes of recognising and enforcing the judgment in England, even though the ground on which the Estonian court allowed itself to be seized of the case is a ground on which English courts are prepared to take jurisdiction (RSC Ord 11, r1(1)(d)).

On the facts there is no suggestion that Commercial Suicide Limited was present or resident in Estonia, thus jurisdiction must be founded if at all on submission; the law here is now to be found in the Civil Jurisdiction and Judgments Act 1982, s33. Commercial Suicide Limited did enter an appearance in Estonia; the question is whether either of the two arguments which it presented to the Estonian court amounts to a submission.

Argument (b), that the English courts are more suitable, clearly falls within CJJA 82 s33(1)(b) and so does not amount to submission. Argument (a) is more doubtful. If it is in substance a denial of the jurisdiction of the Estonian court, then it falls within s33(1)(a) and is not a submission; if it is an argument on the merits as to Estonian law it is a submission.

Assuming now that the Estonian court had jurisdiction, the Estonian judgment to be entitled to recognition in England must be final and conclusive and for a fixed sum of money. It is for a fixed sum of £100,000, and it is 'final and conclusive' as regards the court which pronounced it. The fact that Commercial Suicide Limited has time to appeal is not as such a defence to recognition, though an English court would probably stay enforcement of the Estonian judgment here if Commercial Suicide Limited shows that it intends to exercise its right of appeal in Estonia.

However, Commercial Suicide Limited has a defence in the fact that the Estonian judge was financially interested in the outcome of the case; it matters not whether he was in fact prejudiced. In these circumstances the Estonian judgment should be refused enforcement here on the ground of fraud, or on grounds of breach of natural justice.

Apart from the foregoing points relative to the recognition of the Estonian judgment, there are also points to consider on the enforcement of its various elements. Clearly the £50,000 compensatory damages are recoverable by Alter Ego Ltd under the judgment if the judgment were to be entitled to recognition here, and the same probably holds for the exemplary damages, cf *SA Consortium General Textiles* v *Sun & Sand Agencies Ltd* (1978), though it would be necessary to enquire further as to the nature of this award in Estonian law. While exemplary damages are not irrecoverable as such, penal damages would be. Similarly Commercial Suicide Limited should enquire further as to the rationale behind the award in favour of the Estonian legal aid fund. If this is an award as against Commercial Suicide Limited of costs actually incurred in the provision of services to Alter Ego Ltd which had been initially funded by legal aid, it should in principle be enforceable; aliter if it is in the nature of a penalty.

Question 4

a) In what circumstances will an English court restrain foreign proceedings?

b) In what circumstances may an English court refuse to recognise a judgment of a French court?

University of London LLB Examination
(for External Students) Conflict of Laws June 1993 Q3

General comment

A good question in that it strikes a fair balance between common law and Brussels Convention provisions. It certainly discourages attempts at question spotting – which is to be welcomed.

Skeleton solution

a) Review of law pre and post *Spiliada*.

Significance of *SNIA* case and later developments.

b) Article 27 Brussels Convention and recent case law.

Suggested solution

a) Two points arise from s37 Supreme Court Act 1981 which empowers the High Court to grant an injunction restraining a party 'who has sufficient connection with this country' from commencing or continuing as plaintiff with foreign proceedings. First, the injunction is not to the [foreign] court but to the party engaged in the proceedings; ie the injunction acts in *personam* and a disobedient party may be liable for contempt of court. Secondly, the implicit interference with the jurisdiction of the foreign court whenever the English court grants an injunction restraining foreign proceedings means that it is necessary for the English court to exercise its discretion 'with great caution'.

Within these parameters, Lord Scarman, in the pre-*Spiliada* case of *Casthano* v *Brown and Root (UK) Ltd* (1981), said that in relation to the 'criteria [which] should govern the exercise of the court's discretion to impose a stay or grant an injunction [restraining foreign proceedings] ... the principle is the same,' and that the *MacShannon* test should apply *mutatis mutandis*. In effect, this meant that a defendant had to show both that the English court was a forum to which he was amenable and in which justice could be done at less expense and inconvenience than in the foreign court, and that the grant of an injunction to restrain the plaintiff from suing in the foreign court would not deprive him of a legitimate personal or juridical advantage. Lord Scarman did not categorise instances in which the court would exercise its discretion and grant an injunction since 'the width and flexibility of equity are not to be undermined by categorisation'. Accordingly, an injunction would be granted whenever justice so demands.

Whereas two House of Lords decisions, *British Airways Board* v *Laker Airways* (1985) and *South Carolina Insurance Co* v *Assurantie NV* (1987), affirmed that the *MacShannon test* should apply mutatis mutandis, the majority opinion in the *South Carolina* case was that the earlier House of Lords cases had decided that the power of the High Court to grant an injunction was, in fact, limited to three categories, viz;

  i) when there is a choice of forum (of which England is one);

  ii) where one party, by bringing, or threatening to bring, proceedings abroad, has invaded, or threatens to invade, a legal or equitable right of the other party not to be sued abroad;

iii)   where the bringing of the proceedings abroad would be unconscionable.

No injunction was granted in the *South Carolina* case because (a) the case did not come within one of the three categories specified and (b) there was no choice of forum. On the facts of the case there was no need to grant an injunction in order to preserve the English jurisdiction.

Furthermore, one result of the decision in *Spiliada Maritime Corporation* v *Cansulex* (1987) is that the role of 'legitimate personal or juridical advantage' – a significant factor in *MacShannon* – is much reduced: it has become a factor which 'clearly ... cannot be decisive', per Lord Goff. It could have led to undue emphasis on England being regarded as the natural forum for trial. This would have been the result of injunction being granted too readily.

Although Lord Goff's opinion in *Spiliada* did not make any reference to injunctions restraining foreign proceedings, his view was clarified in the Privy Council case of *SNIA* v *Lee Kui Jak* (1987) where he said:

'Where a remedy for a particular wrong is available both in the English court and in a foreign court, the English court will, generally speaking, only restrain the plaintiff from pursuing proceedings in the foreign court if such pursuit would be *vexatious or oppressive.*'

Clearly, then, there is a distinction between what, in *Casthano*, Lord Scarman had seen as an assimilation of the same principle 'whether the remedy sought is a stay of English proceedings or a restraint or for foreign proceedings'. The decision whether to restrain foreign proceedings is now based on a resurrection of the old ideas of vexation or oppression being combined with the modern idea of the natural or appropriate forum.

In the *SNIA* case, the plaintiff, who wished to pursue claims resulting from a fatal helicopter crash, commenced proceedings for damages against two defendants, D1 and D2, in Brunei and Texas. However, it was decided that, since the Texan courts probably had jurisdiction over D1, but not over D2, if D1 were found liable they would have to seek a contribution from D2 in some other country. On that basis the Privy Council granted an injunction restraining the Texan proceedings, holding that Brunei was the natural forum for trial.

Whereas the *SNIA* decision is incompatible with the House of Lords decision in the *Casthano* and *South Carolina* cases, it was followed in the Court of Appeal case of *Du Pont* v *Agnew* (1987). Furthermore, although the *SNIA* decision was in respect of a case in which there was a choice of forum, and proceedings had been commenced in both of them, the same principles would appear to apply to cases in which there is no choice of forum: *Du Pont* v *Agnew (No 2)* (1988); *British Airways Board* v *Laker Airways*.

In conclusion, then, it is to be noted that, apart from the incompatibility of the *SNIA* case with the two House of Lords cases, the difficulty of specifying the circumstances in which an English court may restrain foreign proceedings is compounded by the uncertainty of the meanings of 'vexation' and 'oppression'. Old case law, decided in a different context, will not elucidate the meaning of these words. This will be a matter for future cases to decide.

b) A brief explanation of 'judgment' in Article 25 of the Brussels Convention is followed by Article 26 providing that a 'judgment given in a contracting state shall be recognised in the other contracting states without any special procedure being required'. However, this is qualified by Article 34 which provides that an application for recognition may be refused as long as it is only for one of the reasons specified in Article 27, which provides six reasons why a foreign judgment may be refused, ie it provides for six potential defences.

First, Article 27(1) provides that recognition may be refused where 'such recognition is contrary to public policy in the state in which recognition is sought'. As Article 27 does not have a specific provision relating to fraud, such a defence may be based on Article 27(1) but only if the plaintiff has no means of redress in France. If he has, then it has been held that there is no breach of public policy in recognising and registering in England a judgment alleged to have been obtained by fraud: *Interdesco* v *Nullifire* (1992); *Sisro* v *Ampersand* (1993).

Article 27(2) provides for non-recognition where the French judgment was given in default of appearance if the defendant was 'not duly served' with the document instituting the proceedings in a French court 'in sufficient time to enable him to arrange for his defence'. Under this provision, the concept of 'due service' must comply with the law of the judgment-granting (French) court, but that of 'sufficient time' is for the judgment-recognising (English) court: *Klomps* v *Michel* (1982); *Pendy Plastic Products* v *Pluspunkt* (1983).

A third situation in which an English court may refuse to recognise a judgment of the French court arises where that judgment is irreconcilable with one given in a dispute between the same parties in England, ie the English court does not need to give preference to the French judgment over one of its own.

A fourth reason for non-recognition arises where the French judgment is irreconcilable with one given in a non-contracting state on the same cause of action between the same parties, provided that the earlier judgment is entitled to recognition by English law.

A fifth situation in which an English court may refuse to recognise a judgment of the French court is where the French court has decided a preliminary question concerning the status or legal capacity of natural persons, and/or rights in property arising out of a matrimonial relationship, wills or succession, in a way that conflicts with a rule of private international law of England unless the same result would have been reached by the application of the rules of private international law of England.

Finally, recognition of a French judgment may be refused if, and only if, the jurisdiction assumed by that court conflicts with the provisions regarding insurance and consumer contracts or regarding exclusive jurisdiction.

Question 5

a) What measures can an English plaintiff take against a foreign defendant to ensure that the latter does not dissipate his assets, remove them from the jurisdiction or otherwise deal with them so as to prevent the plaintiff executing against them?

Does it make any difference whether or not the defendant is domiciled in a Contracting State to the Brussels Convention?

b) Discuss the requirement in Article 17 of the Brussels Convention that jurisdiction agreements must be in writing or evidenced in writing. What is the purpose of the requirement and how has it been interpreted?-

University of London LLB Examination
(for External Students) Conflict of Laws June 1993 Q8

General comment

a) Straightforward contrast of the application of principles to defendants who are and who are not domiciled in Contracting States, and a review of 'a remarkable series of Court of Appeal decisions'.

b) Focus on a relatively narrow aspect of an article of the Brussels Convention.

Skeleton solution

a) As defined by the question: Mareva injunctions.

How they originate and how they are served.

Contrasts between situations where the defendant is and is not domiciled in a contracting state.

b) What Article 17 permits.

Case law which has addressed aspects of formality under review.

Suggested solution

a) A plaintiff with a good arguable case, who fears that the defendant may dissipate his assets, remove them from the jurisdiction or otherwise deal with them so as to prevent the plaintiff executing against them, may seek, ex parte, an interlocutory injunction under s37(3) Supreme Court Act 1981 to prevent the defendant from so acting.

Where the defendant is not domiciled within a contracting state to the Brussels Convention the traditional rules may apply, so for leave to serve a writ out of the jurisdiction the plaintiff would need to bring his case within one of the sub-heads of RSC Ord 11, r(1)(1) excluding (1)(1)(b) which provides for 'an injunction [being] sought ordering the defendant to do or refrain from doing anything within the jurisdiction ... '. There is no power under this sub-head to order the issue of a writ out of the jurisdiction merely because an interlocutory (Mareva) injunction is sought: *The Siskina* (1979). *The Siskina* was also authority for a Mareva injunction only being granted where the English court had jurisdiction over the main action between the parties; the grant of the interlocutory (Mareva) injunction had to be founded on a pre-existing cause of action against the defendant arising out of an invasion, actual or threatened, by him of a legal or equitable right of the plaintiff for the enforcement of which the defendant is amenable to the jurisdiction of the court. An interlocutory injunction did not stand on its own.

In contrast, in proceedings which have been or are to be commenced in another contracting state to the Brussels Convention, s25 Civil Jurisdiction and Judgments Act 1982 (CJJA) provides for an English court to grant 'interim relief', such as a Mareva injunction, if the proceedings are or will be proceedings whose subject matter is within the scope of the Convention. In effect, this is a statutory reversal of *The Siskina*.

Section 25 CJJA 1982 does not apply in a non-contracting state unless it has been extended to that state by an Order in Council, but neither does it require the defendant to be domiciled in a contracting state: *X* v *Y & Y* (1990). However, whereas leave is not required to serve a writ on a defendant who is domiciled in a contracting state, the general rule is that a plaintiff must seek leave to serve a writ on a defendant who is not so domiciled: RSC Ord 11, r(1)(1). One exception to this is provided for under Ord 11, r(1)(2), which provides that 'service of a writ out of the jurisdiction is permissible without the leave of the court' in cases which are within the Convention (ie they are, under Article 2, civil and commercial matters) but in which the defendant is outside the jurisdiction: *Republic of Haiti* v *Duvalier* (1990).

There is no requirement that a Mareva injunction should be confined to the assets of the defendant which are within the jurisdiction of the court. In 1989 the extent to which an injunction may issue to restrain the defendant from dealing with assets which are already outside the jurisdiction was clarified in 'a remarkable series of Court of Appeal decisions' (per JD McClean in Morris, *The Conflict of Laws*, 4th edn 1993, at p398). In the first, and leading, case, *Babanaft International Co SA* v *Bassatne* (1990), when a past-judgment Mareva injunction was granted, it was said that it would be 'improper for the court to grant, after judgment, an unqualified Mareva injunction extending to the defendant's assets outside the jurisdiction because such an injunction would amount to an exorbitant assertion of extraterritorial jurisdiction over third parties; [accordingly] such post-judgment injunctions should be restricted so as to bind on the defendant personally and should contain a limiting provision to ensure that they did not purport to have an unintended extraterritorial operation and to make it clear that they did not affect third parties'.

In this case, Kerr LJ expressly held that, in appropriate cases, there was nothing to prevent the grant of injunctions from extending to assets outside this jurisdiction.

In *Republic of Haiti* v *Duvalier* it was decided that a pre-judgment Mareva injunction could extend to assets outside the jurisdiction. Finally, McClean notes that 'in *Derby* v *Weldon (No 1)* (1989) the power to grant a Mareva injunction in respect of assets outside England and Wales, both before and after judgments, was declared to be established law'.

b) Prorogation of jurisdiction, as provided for in Article 17 of the Brussels Convention, refers to the ability of the parties to a contract to confer exclusive jurisdiction on the courts of a particular contracting state in the event of any legal disputes 'which have arisen or which may arise' between them. However, one of three requirements as to form has to be complied with in order to satisfy this agreement. The one that is a focal point of this question is that the jurisdiction agreement must be in writing or evidenced in writing.

In essence the purpose of Article 17 in relation to form is that it contains specific requirements which have to be met in order to prove the consensus of the parties. However, the strictness of a specified formality may need to be tempered by standard commercial practice, if different. If such a situation arises this becomes a 'balancing act' on which the ECJ has to formulate appropriate principles.

In the case of a written contract containing a choice of jurisdiction clause, it was decided by the ECJ in Case 24/76, *Colzani* v *Ruwa* (1976) that where the clause is contained in general conditions on the back of a signed contract there must also be express reference to the general conditions within the text of that contract. A further measure of the ECJ which reinforces its determination not to have a contracting party overlook this requirement of form is to provide that if only one party has signed the contract then the other must signify its consent in a separate document. The intention of these measures is to ensure that the choice of jurisdiction clause does not go unnoticed.

In the case of an oral contract being confirmed in writing, initially the ECJ decided that the party receiving the written contract containing the choice of jurisdiction clause had to have it accepted in writing by the other party. This was deemed necessary as, otherwise, there was no contract evidenced in writing. However, a relaxation of emphasis on form and a more practical approach towards balancing form with standard commercial practice was the outcome of later decisions. Here the ECJ held that a written choice of jurisdiction clause in a bill of lading could be regarded as written confirmation of an initial orally-communicated agreement between the parties in which there was express reference to that clause. Similarly, the recipient of a written contract, a term of which confirmed an earlier oral contract and which expressly agreed to a jurisdiction clause, was held to have satisfied the evidential requirements of Article 17 when he raised no objection to the clause: *Berghoefer* v *ASA SA* (1986).

13 ARBITRATION

13.1   Introduction

13.2   Key points

13.3   Recent cases and statutes

13.4   Relevant materials

13.5   Analysis of questions

13.6   Questions

13.1   Introduction

Arbitration plays an extremely important role in the settlement of international commercial disputes. Its popularity as an alternative form of dispute resolution procedure stems largely from the fact that it is an extremely flexible procedure. Arbitration offers the prospect of a relatively expedient and often cheaper means of settling disputes because the parties can choose the country in which the arbitration will take place, as well as the forum. These qualities give the process a more neutral appearance in contrast to litigation in the courts of a particular country.

Most jurisdictions recognise the authority of properly conducted and formulated arbitration decisions. Nevertheless, the fact that some courts are increasingly willing to grant judicial review of arbitration decisions, and effectively unravel the original findings of an arbitrator, has contributed to undermining many of the benefits of the process.

Notwithstanding these drawbacks, arbitration remains a popular means of resolving disputes, and the process will undoubtedly continue to remain an important aspect of international commercial transactions.

13.2   Key points

a) *Domestic and non-domestic arbitration*

The distinction between domestic and non-domestic arbitration has been created by statute, namely the Arbitration Act 1979, which defines a domestic arbitration as one created by an arbitration agreement:

'... which does not provide expressly or by implication for arbitration in a State other than the United Kingdom and to which neither:

   a)   an individual who is a national of or habitually resident in any State other than the United Kingdom; nor

248

b)   a body corporate which is incorporated in or whose central management and control is exercised in any State other than the United Kingdom;

is a party at the time the arbitration agreement is entered into.'

All other arbitrations falling outside this definition are non-domestic.

The distinction between domestic and non-domestic arbitration is important for two reasons. First, the power of an English court to break an arbitration clause is wider in the case of a domestic arbitration. Second, the possibility for the parties to exclude judicial review of the arbitration is more substantial in non-domestic arbitrations in contrast to their domestic counterparts.

b) *The form of arbitration*

There are two main forms of arbitration:

i)   Ad hoc arbitration – this is where the parties themselves prescribe the mode of the appointment of the arbitrator and the arbitrator has control over the proceedings himself subject only to the limits of his powers imposed by law.

ii) Institutional arbitration – in this form of arbitration the mode of the appointment of the arbitrator and the procedure to be followed will be governed by a series of codified rules normally laid down by a trade association, chamber of commerce or similar institution.

The international organisations most commonly associated with commercial arbitration are the International Chamber of Commerce, the London Court of Arbitration, the International Centre for Settlement of Investment Disputes and the United Nations Commission on International Trade.

c) *The law governing the arbitration*

Obviously some body of rules must be agreed by the parties in advance before an arbitrator can render an effective and proper decision on the merits of the case. English law requires that the arbitration is conducted, and the arbitrator makes his or her decision in terms of the law of the forum and/or the place where the final decision is to be enforced.

The law applicable will govern all those matters not covered by the express and implied terms of the arbitration agreement.

The applicable law not only regulates the relationship between the parties but also the legal relations between the parties and other parties outside the arbitration. For example, whether or not an arbitration decision will be recognised by the courts will be decided in terms of the applicable law as will any judicial review of the decision.

d) *The jurisdiction of the arbitrator*

The general principle that the jurisdiction of the courts cannot be circumscribed by private agreement continues to apply in arbitration and so an arbitrator must confine his inquiry and decision to the terms of reference conferred by the parties. In the event that an arbitrator exceeds his terms of reference, his or her decision may be set aside on application to the courts.

e) *The arbitration agreement*

An arbitration agreement is simply a special type of contract between two or more parties whereby they agree to apply particular rules to any dispute which may arise between them. Alternatively, agreement to arbitrate may be contained in a clause within a contract dealing with much broader issues between the parties.

While the parties are generally free to decide the terms of the arbitration, there are several statutes which provide the framework within which such agreements operate. These are:

    i)   the Arbitration Act 1950;

    ii)   the Arbitration Act 1975;

    iii)   the Arbitration Act 1979.

The 1950 Act contains the principal provisions regulating arbitration under English law. The 1975 Act gives effect in the United Kingdom to the New York Convention on the Recognition and Enforcement of Foreign Arbitral Awards 1958. The 1979 Act extends the principle of the finality of the arbitral award by limiting the scope for judicial review.

These statutes apply to all written agreements submitting a dispute to arbitration and to actual submissions after the dispute has been referred provided these are evidenced by written memoranda.

From a procedural point of view, the statutes imply a number of requirements into arbitration agreements including the following:

    i)   the parties should submit themselves to examination on oath by the arbitrator;

    ii)   witnesses called should give their testimony on oath;

    iii)   any award made by the arbitrator should be binding and final;

    iv)   the arbitrator should have discretion as to the award of costs;

    v)   the arbitrator should have the same power as the courts to award specific performance of the contract; and

    vi)   the arbitrator should have power to make an interim award.

f) *Powers of the arbitrator*

The powers of an arbitrator are prescribed by the law applicable under the arbitration agreement. In English law, these powers extend to ordering pleadings from the parties at any time, fixing dates for hearings, granting postponements, ordering discovery of documents and inspecting property and premises as required.

g) *The decisions of an arbitrator*

None of the Arbitration Acts require an arbitrator to give the reasons for his or her decision. Nevertheless, the parties may request such reasons and the arbitrator is bound to comply. If the reasons given for the decision are insufficient for a court to make a ruling in law, a court may order an arbitrator to supply sufficient reasons.

The content of a reasoned award should include the following points:

    i)   the evidence on which the decision was based;

    ii) the method and reasoning for reaching the final decision;

    iii) a clear exposition of the decision rendered.

An arbitrator is not required to present a detailed analysis of the law or the authority supporting his or her decision: *Antaios Compania Naviera* v *Salen Rederierna AB* [1984] 3 WLR 592.

h) *Judicial review and appeal*

Judicial review of arbitration decisions is regulated by the 1979 Act. Sections 1(3) and 1(4) provide that the parties are free to submit a decision to judicial review if there is unanimous agreement among all the parties concerned. In the absence of unanimity, a court may grant leave for judicial review but only if it considers that the determination of the question of law involved could substantially affect the rights of one or more of the parties to the agreement.

In the case of domestic arbitration, the parties may exclude judicial review by an exclusion agreement but only if entered into after the commencement of the arbitration. In non-domestic arbitration, the parties may make a valid exclusion agreement both before and after the commencement of the arbitration.

The grounds for judicial review are essentially two-fold:

    i)   error on a point of fact or law; and

    ii) misconduct by the arbitrator when conducting the investigation or making the award.

Misconduct includes errors in procedure as well as moral turpitude. Errors in fact or law must appear on the face of the award.

i) *Enforcment of arbitration decisions*

Under the 1950 Act, and by the leave of the court, an award under an arbitration agreement may be enforced in the same manner as a judgement or order of a court.

In the event that the arbitration agreement falls outside the Act it is incapable of being made a judgement or order of the court. Therefore, for example, if the agreement is not in writing or evidenced by writing, it cannot be enforced by an order of the court.

13.3   Recent cases and statutes

Harbour Assurance Co (UK) Ltd v *Kansa General International Insurance Co Ltd*
[1992] 1 Lloyd's Rep 81: the plaintiffs brought an action seeking declarations that they
were not liable under certain contracts because these agreements were illegal, null and
void. The agreements contained arbitration clauses and the defendants sought a stay of
the arbitration proceedings on the grounds that proceedings could not be brought to
enforce illegal contractual terms. The court dismissed the application for the stay
because the issue of initial illegality of the agreements was beyond the jurisdiction of
the arbitrator.

International Petroleum Refining & Supply Sdad Ltd v *Elpis Finance SA, The Faith*
[1993] 2 Lloyd's Rep 408: a dispute was referred to arbitration in October 1983 but the
award was not published until November 1991 and the award not taken up until
November 1992. Held that if an arbitration decision was not brought before the court
within 21 days of the award, it is effective and final for all purposes.

13.4   Relevant materials

A Bevan, *Alternative Dispute Resolution* (1992).

H Brown & A Marriott, *Alternative Dispute Resolution: Principles and Practice*
(1993).

Russell on Arbitration (20th edition, 1982).

A Redfern & M Hunter, *Law and Practice of International Commercial Arbitration* (2nd
edition, 1992)

13.5   Analysis of questions

Questions requiring the student to answer detailed points on the substantive or
procedural law of arbitration are generally rare. More commonly, an examiner will
wish the student to demonstrate an understanding of the general principles of the
process especially when compared to formal proceedings through the courts. This
tends to make questions in this area of the syllabus more easy to answer.

13.6   Questions

Question 1

Discuss the advantages and disadvantages of inserting a clause referring disputes to
arbitration rather than litigation in the English courts.

Question prepared by the Editor
April 1994

General comment

This is an essay-type question requiring a straightforward narrative answer. Its general
nature allows ample scope for addressing the primary issue of comparison between the
procedures.

Skeleton solution

Advantages of arbitration: selection of forum and arbitrator; benefits of informality; relative savings in legal costs; expedited procedure; enforcement of the award abroad.

Disadvantages of arbitration: limited powers of the arbitrator in comparison to those of a judge; lack of legal experience or qualifications; third party proceedings; references to the ECJ.

Suggested solution

In deciding whether or not arbitration is to be preferred to litigation in a contractual provision it is necessary to consider at the outset what the needs of the parties will be and their expectations. The advantages and disadvantages of both types of proceedings must be weighed against each other in order to resolve this question.

The primary advantages of arbitration may be listed as follows.

First, arbitration proceedings allow the parties considerable latitude in selecting the forum and persons which will be seized of the dispute. Certain centres of commercial arbitration have a sizeable reputation for resolving particular types of disputes. Similarly, professional organisations and arbitration centres have developed specific expertise in many areas of commercial law which will facilitate the appointment of an expert in the field being disputed. Discretion in selecting the forum for arbitration, as well as the arbitrator himself, may give the parties a greater degree of confidence than might otherwise be the case if a matter is referred to the courts where the parties have no influence over the appointment of a judge.

Second, arbitration proceedings tend to be more informal and flexible than strict legal proceedings. While disputes referred to arbitration may be equally as contentious as those referred to the courts, proceeding by way of arbitration is generally considered to be less hostile and confrontational than litigation. The parties will be able to air their differences in a less formal venue than the courts and the procedure itself will generally be more relaxed.

Third, the arbitration hearing can be held in private and the award need not be published. This provides a greater degree of confidentiality, not only as to the existence of a dispute between the parties but also as regards the outcome. A lack of publicity may be a significant consideration for the parties and more beneficial to their business relationships.

Fourth, as a general rule, the cost of arbitration is less expensive than formal legal proceedings. This depends of course on the nature of the dispute, but one of the more attractive aspects of arbitration is the significant savings in legal costs. Legal briefs and submissions are limited, as are the oral presentations made on behalf of the parties. On the other hand, with arbitration, the parties are required to meet the arbitrator's fees as well as paying for the venue.

Fifth, arbitration is a more expedient manner of proceeding particularly when compared to a High Court hearing. Arbitrators often fix the date for hearing at an earlier stage and deliver their opinions within a relatively short period of time.

Finally, arbitration awards are enforceable in England by virtue of s26 of the Arbitration Act 1950. Although the leave of the court is required for enforcement, this has become an increasingly automatic process subject to the rights of the parties to appeal decisions. In addition, final awards may also be enforceable abroad if the country where enforcement is anticipated is a party to the New York Convention on the Enforcement of Foreign Arbitral Awards 1958. Enforcing a judgement of a court abroad is a difficult, if not impossible, task. An arbitration award is a more flexible instrument to enforce.

On the other hand, arbitration does have drawbacks over formal litigation. Briefly, these may be summarised as follows.

First, the powers of an arbitrator are considerably more limited than those available to High Court judges. This is a significant disadvantage. An arbitrator's powers are prescribed by the Arbitration Act 1979 but these are less extensive than the equivalent interlocutory powers exercised by a High Court judge. For example, where a party has a strong case, it may apply to the court under Order 14 of the Rules of the Supreme Court for summary judgment. This allows an immediate judgement to be given where a party is unable to prove that there is a stateable defence to the claim.

Similarly, injunctions, Mareva injunctions and Anton Pillar orders may only be issued by a High Court judge. Also, subject of course to rights of appeal, a court's judgment is definitive of the dispute whereas judicial review of an arbitration order, at least on the face of it, deprives such awards of this quality.

Second, arbitrators may have commercial experience in particular matters but lack legal experience or qualifications. Resolution of a dispute will invariably involve the application of legal principles and an arbitrator's inability to make a structured judgement may be considered a deficiency in the procedure. A lack of legal experience may also result in the arbitrator paying insufficient attention to the legal principles and instead he may rely too heavily on the weight of the evidence. Such an approach will render the final award open to appeal.

Third, the utility of arbitration is limited when there are more than two parties to the dispute. An arbitration clause is a creature of the consensus between the parties to the agreement. Where a third party is involved which is not a party to the agreement, an arbitrator will be unable to exercise jurisdiction. Litigation, on the other hand, allows for joining any number of defendants to the action and offers the prospect of commencing third party proceedings.

Finally, as a matter of procedure, High Court litigation allows a reference to be made to the European Court of Justice where the court is seized of a question of European Union law. This procedure is not automatically available in arbitration. Instead an arbitrator would have to make an application under s2(1) of the Arbitration Act 1979. This would considerably delay the arbitrator in reaching a final decision.

Which of these factors are important in selecting between arbitration and litigation is a matter for the parties to decide. Unfortunately, these considerations will vary for each of the parties to the contract. For example, one party may consider the enforceability of an arbitration award abroad to be a decisive point, whereas another party may be wary of depriving itself of the possibility of interim injunctions in the event of a dispute. Like all matters in commercial agreements, the final determination will be a blend of the relative strengths of the parties in the negotiation process.

Question 2

Outline the principal clauses contained in an arbitration agreement which govern the procedural aspects of the process.

Question prepared by the Editor
April 1994

General comment

This is another essay-type question again with considerable latitude. Attention should be paid in particular to the structuring of the answer as well as the legal points raised for consideration.

Skeleton solution

Appointment of the arbitrator.

Notice of initiation.

Hearings and pleadings.

Powers of the arbitrator and the award

Judicial review and appeal

Suggested solution

Agreements to submit a dispute to arbitration must contains provisions to regulate the procedural aspects of the process in order to be effective. This is achieved in one of two ways. First, the arbitration agreement will expressly identify the procedure to be followed by the arbitrator in reaching a decision. Alternatively, and more commonly, the reference in the agreement to a particular forum or type of arbitration will imply that the procedural rules of that forum or type will regulate the arbitrators deliberations. In both cases procedural guidelines are established to govern the process.

The first procedural matter is the appointment of the arbitrator himself. There are two separate methods whereby an arbitrator is appointed. Either the arbitration agreement will identify an particular individual as arbitrator, or a named individual will be given authority to appoint the arbitrator. In the former case, the individual need not be specifically identified; the parties may be allowed to select a particular individual. Where the parties are given discretion to appoint arbitrators, all the parties to the arbitration must be notified of the appointment as soon as it has been made.

An agreement to arbitrate need not confine the process to arbitration by a single individual. Two or more arbitrators may be appointed. However, where an even number of arbitrators is used, by s8 of the Arbitration Act 1950 a provision is implied into every arbitration agreement that the arbitrators can nominate an additional arbitrator to act as an umpire in the event of deadlock.

An arbitrator can usually be removed only by the mutual agreement of the parties to the agreement. The exception to this rule is that a single party may apply to the court to have an arbitrator removed. In such circumstances, the court will only exercise its discretion to remove where the arbitrator has an interest in the case, is biased or has been guilty of misconduct.

After the arbitrator has been appointed, the party invoking the arbitration must serve notice on the defendants of the initiation of the process. Failure to serve notice within the contractually agreed period may render the proceedings time barred. In the absence of an express time period, arbitration proceedings become time barred after the expiry of the six year statutory time limit set out in the Limitation Act 1980. The time period starts to run from the moment that a claim is made by a party.

Once an arbitrator has accepted his or her appointment, he or she is required to ensure that he or she is properly qualified to act. Once this has been confirmed a preliminary meeting is held at an early stage in the proceedings. A date is then agreed for the formal hearing.

The parties cannot be compelled to attend the hearing, but obviously it is in their interests to do so. Similarly, legal representation is not compulsory, but is advisable.

Prior to the hearing, pleadings are submitted on behalf of the parties. Pleadings usually comprise: (a) a statement of the points of claim; (b) a reply in defence to the statement of points; and (c) counter replies. The arbitrator has discretion to order the pleadings deemed appropriate. Copies of all the pleadings must be made available to the other side.

Both discovery and inspection take place after the close of pleadings. Discovery is, of course, not compulsory as would be the case in litigation. It usually takes place by an exchange of documents between the parties. Each party provides the other with a list of all documents relevant to their pleadings which are under the control or in the possession of the other party. Privileged documents cannot be compelled. Inspection occurs immediately after discovery.

The parties may make interlocutory applications to the arbitrator. Such applications usually deal with the following points: (a) obtaining further directions; (b) amending pleadings; (c) extensions of time for the production of documents; (d) the granting of interrogatories; (e) granting supplementary discovery; and (f) ordering and preparing expert reports. In addition, the lodging of security for costs can be required through an interlocutory application.

At the hearing the parties are given an opportunity to present oral arguments in favour of their case. This may be dispensed with if the parties mutually agree to such a dispensation. The hearing is usually convened in private with the arbitrators, the parties, their legal representatives, experts and witnesses being the only parties present.

The actual proceedings at the oral hearing are generally similar to those in the High Court. The claimant's counsel will usually open the discussion followed by the defendant's counsel. Witnesses can be called at the request of the parties. Cross-examination will also occur. Once the parties have been heard at the hearing, the arbitrator will normally retire to consider his decision. He is legally required to consider both the evidence and the arguments of the parties before arriving at his decision. Both parties will be notified once the arbitrator has reached his final decision.

As regards the form of the award, there are no specific requirements. Under s16 of the Arbitration Act 1950, every arbitration agreement is deemed to contain a provision that the award shall be 'final and binding on the parties and the persons claiming under them respectively'. The arbitrator must therefore ensure that the award covers all aspects of the dispute, including interest and costs. As a general principle, once the award has been made it cannot be altered even at the instance of the arbitrator himself.

Again in general terms, any arbitration award should cover the following: (a) the identity of the parties to the dispute; (b) the background to the dispute; (c) the arbitration clause and the appointment; (d) the various stages in the arbitration; (e) the issues in dispute; (f) the findings in law and fact; and (g) the award itself. It is an additional requirement that the award is a reasoned one in order to avoid challenge under the High Court's powers of judicial review.

In most cases, arbitrators issued reasoned awards and if they do not the courts have authority under s1(5) of the Arbitration Act 1979 to order the arbitrator to do so. This power is to enable the court to analyse the reasoning of the arbitrator for the purposes of proper review.

Section 26 of the 1950 Act as amended enables parties to an arbitration to enforce an award by registering the award with the courts. This procedure allows the award to be enforced in a similar manner as would be the case with a judicial decision.

The Arbitration Act 1979 regulates the judicial review of arbitration awards. Any appeal under this section must be made either with the consent of the arbitrator or the unanimous consent of the parties. The alternative is for a single party to seek leave of the court to appeal in the event that the necessary consents are not forthcoming. Only in these circumstances will a court consider the judicial review of an arbitrator's decision.